The Crime World
of Michael Connelly

ALSO BY DAVID GEHERIN
AND FROM MCFARLAND

Carl Hiaasen: Sunshine State Satirist (2019)

*Funny Thing About Murder: Modes of Humor
in Crime Fiction and Films* (2017)

Small Towns in Recent American Crime Fiction (2015)

*The Dragon Tattoo and Its Long Tail: The New Wave
of European Crime Fiction in America* (2012)

*Scene of the Crime: The Importance of Place
in Crime and Mystery Fiction* (2008)

The Crime World of Michael Connelly

A Study of His Works and Their Adaptations

DAVID GEHERIN

McFarland & Company, Inc., Publishers
Jefferson, North Carolina

LIBRARY OF CONGRESS CATALOGUING-IN-PUBLICATION DATA

Names: Geherin, David, 1943– author.
Title: The crime world of Michael Connelly : a study of his works and their adaptations / David Geherin.
Description: Jefferson, North Carolina : McFarland & Company, Inc., Publishers, 2022 | Includes bibliographical references and index.
Identifiers: LCCN 2022044325 | ISBN 9781476687018 (paperback : acid free paper) ∞
ISBN 9781476647791 (ebook)
Subjects: LCSH: Connelly, Michael, 1956—Criticism and interpretation. | Connelly, Michael, 1956—Film adaptations. | Connelly, Michael, 1956—Television adaptations. | Detective and mystery stories, American—History and criticsm. | LCGFT: Literary criticism.
Classification: LCC PS3553.O51165 Z65 2022 | DDC 813/.54—dc23/eng/20220926
LC record available at https://lccn.loc.gov/2022044325

BRITISH LIBRARY CATALOGUING DATA ARE AVAILABLE

ISBN (print) 978-1-4766-8701-8
ISBN (ebook) 978-1-4766-4779-1

© 2022 David Geherin. All rights reserved

No part of this book may be reproduced or transmitted in any form or by any means, electronic or mechanical, including photocopying or recording, or by any information storage and retrieval system, without permission in writing from the publisher.

Front cover image of LA lights against the night sky © Vianores/Shutterstock

Printed in the United States of America

McFarland & Company, Inc., Publishers
Box 611, Jefferson, North Carolina 28640
www.mcfarlandpub.com

For Chris and Cristina,
Pete and Kathleen, Dan and Lisa

Contents

Preface	1
Introduction: Biography	3
1—Harry Bosch and the Bosch Megaseries	9
2—The Novels	17
3—Standalone Novels, Short Stories, and Journalism	161
4—Movies, Television, and Podcasts	173
5—Artistry: Turning Fact into Fiction	184
6—The Portrait of L.A. and the LAPD	189
Conclusion: Connelly's Recipe for Success	197
Bibliography	201
Index	207

Preface

The two most obvious facts about crime novelist Michael Connelly are that he is prolific—thirty-six novels since 1992—and wildly popular—his books have sold over eighty million copies worldwide and are translated into forty-five languages. But even more impressive than those numbers is how he has maintained a consistently high level of excellence throughout his entire career. This book takes a close look at all his work and examines the various factors that have made him, in the view of many, America's greatest living author of crime fiction.

In addition to his acclaimed series of novels featuring L.A. homicide detective Harry Bosch, Connelly has also created four other series characters: Jack McEvoy, a newspaper reporter; Terry McCaleb, an FBI profiler; Mickey Haller, a criminal defense attorney; and Renée Ballard, a policewoman on the night shift. By integrating each of these characters into the Bosch series, he has created something unique in crime fiction—a megaseries in which characters move freely from one series to another, constantly expanding the Bosch series.

This book examines all of Connelly's work, beginning with a brief biography of Connelly in the introduction. Chapter 1 introduces Harry Bosch and describes the creation of the Bosch megaseries. Chapter 2 includes detailed commentaries in chronological order of each of the thirty-four novels that compose the megaseries. Chapter 3 looks at Connelly's standalone novels, short stories, and journalism. Chapter 4 features the movies and television shows based on Connelly's novels as well as his podcasts. Chapters 5 and 6 discuss the artistry of his novels and his portrait of Los Angeles and the LAPD. The book concludes with an overall assessment of Connelly's accomplishments.

Spoiler Alert: The analyses of the individual novels necessarily reveal plot developments. Readers who do not want to know how the novels end may wish to read the books before reading the commentaries.

Introduction: Biography

Michael Joseph Connelly was born in Philadelphia, Pennsylvania, on July 21, 1956, to W. Michael Connelly, a property developer, and Mary McEvoy Connelly, a homemaker. The second oldest of six children, three boys and three girls, he grew up in a house designed and built by his father in Devon, a Philadelphia suburb. When he was twelve, the family relocated to Fort Lauderdale, Florida.

Connelly became an avid reader at an early age. His mother was a big Agatha Christie and P.D. James fan so he read those authors along with the Hardy Boys mysteries. Early on he discovered John D. MacDonald, whose character Travis McGee docked his boat, *The Busted Flush*, at the Bahia Mar Marina in Fort Lauderdale, where Connelly worked while in high school. His boss was even mentioned in a couple of the novels. He would later follow MacDonald's practice and use the names of real people, especially detectives, in his own novels.

An incident that happened when he was sixteen further sparked his interest in cops and crime. As he was driving home around midnight from his late-night job as a dishwasher at a beachside resort in Fort Lauderdale, he was stopped at a traffic light. The streets were deserted and he considered running the red light when he happened to look out the window and spotted a man dressed in street clothes with shoulder-length hair and a big beard running down the street. He saw him stop, take his shirt off and wrap it around an object, which he then stuffed into a hedge. Curious, when the light changed, he did a U-turn and got out of the car to pull the shirt from the hedge. Inside was a gun. He put the gun back, returned to his car and began following the runner until he saw him duck into a biker bar.

He drove to a nearby gas station to call his father to ask him what to do. His father advised him to tell the police who were gathered a few blocks away about the gun. They informed him that someone had just shot a man in the head during an attempted car-jacking, likely with the gun he found, and they hoped he could help them identify the running man he saw hide the gun in the hedge.

He spent the next four hours answering the detectives' questions. When they brought in several suspects from the bar who matched his description to stand in a lineup, Connelly was unable to identify any of them as the man he saw. The detectives thought he was just too intimidated to tell the truth and he couldn't convince them that they didn't have the right guy. "They just thought I was this white kid from the suburbs who wouldn't stand up and do the right thing. It left me feeling very poorly about myself. I was telling the truth. But I was found guilty by those cops and it really bothered me" (Heilpern). The shooting victim survived, but Connelly never heard from the police again and never found out if the shooter was ever caught. But his first exposure to detectives and police stations prompted him to begin reading true crime stories, both in books and in the daily newspaper.

A self-described mediocre student, Connelly attended four Catholic schools in four years, but never fit in, citing their strictness. After graduating from St. Thomas Aquinas High School in Fort Lauderdale in 1974, he headed to the University of Florida. He had little motivation for going to college other than pleasing his parents and securing a draft deferment to avoid being sent to Vietnam. Nor was he overly excited about his choice of major, building construction sciences, with an eye to becoming a builder like his father and grandfather.

But the teacher of his freshman literature course, famed novelist Harry Crews, would change everything. A colorful figure who often held court in a Gainesville bar, usually seated in a barber's chair, Crews was the first author Connelly had ever seen in the flesh, and his course was the only one he attended regularly. After being asked to leave the university after his freshman year because of poor grades, he spent the next eighteen months working as a dishwasher and reading books by writers like Hunter S. Thompson, Ken Kesey, and Kurt Vonnegut, Jr.

(Connelly wasn't the only University of Florida student who was inspired by Harry Crews to become a novelist. Carl Hiaasen, who graduated just a few months before Connelly arrived on campus, said it was Crews's 1992 novel *Car*, about a man who declares he will eat an entire car from bumper to bumper on live television, that taught him that anything is possible when you sit down to write a novel.)

It was a chance viewing of Robert Altman's 1973 film version of Raymond Chandler's *The Long Goodbye* at the student union on dollar-movie night that dramatically changed Connelly's life at age nineteen. He had become an avid reader of contemporary crime novels but deliberately avoided older books in the genre. But he was fascinated by the character of Philip Marlowe, an outsider with a tough-guy exterior but who was soft inside, a mixture of the cynical and the hopeful. He was so blown away by the film that he stopped going to class and spent the next two weeks reading everything Chandler wrote.

> It was his prose and his marvelous way of evoking Los Angeles—a place I had never been—that drew me to his work. Also, his depiction of a man alone against the odds and the system. Maybe because I was at the right age but I found it intoxicating and inspiring. I read the books over and over and whereas before when I read mysteries I fantasized that I was the detective on the case, winning the day and vanquishing evil, with Chandler I fantasized that I was the writer behind that wonderful prose [Anderson, *Triumph* 181].

When he returned home to inform his parents that he wanted to be a writer, he expected to encounter resistance. But he learned that his father once had to shelve his own dreams of attending the prestigious Art Institute of Philadelphia and becoming a visual artist in order to provide for a growing family. He encouraged his son to pursue his dream but reminded him that there were few successful novelists his age and that he needed to experience more of life first. He suggested that he should consider becoming a cop, or a lawyer, or maybe even a reporter, where he could earn a steady salary, and then think about becoming a novelist. The idea of becoming a reporter appealed to Connelly so he returned to the university, this time to major in journalism and minor in creative writing.

Following graduation in 1980 with a journalism degree, he was hired as a police reporter for the *Daytona Beach News-Journal*. Two years later he joined the police beat at Fort Lauderdale's *South Florida Sun-Sentinel*. Here he happened to encounter the same gruff detective who didn't believe him when he was sixteen and insisted that none of the suspects the police had rounded up was the man he saw hide the gun in the hedge. Though he was often in the police department, he still couldn't convince that detective he was telling the truth.

Connelly's first attempts at writing fiction began while he was still working at the Daytona Beach newspaper. His girlfriend and later his wife Linda McCaleb, whom he had first met in a journalism course in college, lived two and a half hours away, limiting their time together to weekends. So he took advantage of his down time to use his nights writing fiction. (They married in 1984.) He would eventually write two crime novels set in Florida, but he realized he didn't yet have all the skills necessary to make them good enough. He might have started with a promising setup or an interesting character but then didn't really know what to do with them. "The thing I learned is that you have got to have a lot of things ready before you should start. The one thing I didn't have in either of those attempts was I did not know where the story was going. Now, I'm not a person who likes to outline, so I don't mean you have to know everything, but I did not have the goal of the horizon in sight where I was heading the story" (Silet 43). So he put the fiction aside and concentrated on his journalism.

In 1987, he got an assignment with the Fort Lauderdale Police Department that would help shape his future as a crime novelist: after lengthy negotiations, he was granted full access to the homicide squad for an entire week. It turned into a great story for him but not so great for the three people who were murdered during his time with the detectives. "The irony of crime beat journalism," he says, "is that the best stories are really the worst stories. The stories of calamity and tragedy are the stories that journalists live for. It gets the adrenaline churning in their blood and can burn them out young, but nevertheless it is a hard fact of the business. Their best day is your worst day" (*Crime* 8).

Connelly noticed that Sgt. George Hurt, the head of the homicide squad who was investigating the 38th, 39th, and 40th murders in Fort Lauderdale that year, would crouch down like a baseball catcher beside each of the murder victims, remove his eyeglasses, hook the earpiece in his mouth, and close his eyes. When Connelly asked him what he was thinking, Hurt wouldn't tell him. At the end of the week, he got a closer look at the glasses when Hurt took them off and placed them on his desk. He noticed that the earpiece had a deep groove cut into the plastic from being gripped so tightly by Hurt's teeth.

"It was a telling detail that opened up a window into this man's life," he said. "It said all that needed to be said about his dedication, motivation and relationship to his job. It was the most important thing I had seen in a week of seeing things I knew were important and vital to me" (*Crime* 10). He realized he had to look for the telling detail in everything he would write about. If he was going to be successful as a writer, "I had to find Sergeant Hurt's glasses over and over again in my stories" (10).

What comes through in the story Connelly wrote, and would later become the foundation of his Harry Bosch novels, was his respect and admiration for the dedication and hard work of those given the responsibility of finding the killers in our communities. The words of Sgt. Hurt that conclude the article serve as a fitting tribute to what they do: "I could say that old saying about it being a dirty job but somebody has to do it, but I don't look at it that way. I see it as being a dirty job but somebody has to know how to do it. We know how. We do good work here" (*Crime* 36).

Introduction: Biography

A feature article Connelly wrote with fellow *Sun-Sentinel* reporters Robert McClure and Malinda Reinke would end up changing his life. On August 2, 1985, Delta Flight 191, a Lockheed jumbo jet flying from Fort Lauderdale to Los Angeles, hit a microburst and crashed as it was making a scheduled stop at the Dallas/Fort Worth airport, killing 136 passengers. The trio of reporters spent six months interviewing many of the twenty-seven survivors. The story, which appeared in the paper's Sunday magazine one year after the crash, was a tribute to those who perished as well as a portrait of the challenges faced by the survivors.

The article, which Connelly has said was his favorite in his fourteen-year career as a journalist, was a finalist for the 1987 Pulitzer Prize for Feature Writing, which brought the trio of writers to the attention of larger newspapers. It also resulted in Connelly's first trip to Los Angeles, Flight 191's intended destination, for a job interview with the *Los Angeles Times*. During the interview, an editor handed him a copy of that day's paper, which featured a story about a daring bank heist in which the thieves had entered the city's underground storm-water system and then tunneled beneath the bank's safe-deposit vault. He was given fifteen minutes to read it and tell the editor how he would write a follow-up story.

He passed the interview and he and his wife moved to Los Angeles in 1987. His assignment at the *L.A. Times* was as a front-line police reporter, meaning he wrote about the daily occurrence of crime, which in L.A. usually meant a murder. Soon after starting on the police beat, he had an opportunity to sit in on a detective squad briefing about the tunnel caper, which remained unsolved. That night he went into his office at home and began writing what would become *The Black Echo*. He put a lot of pressure on himself. His first two attempts at novel writing were unsuccessful. If he was ever going to realize the dream he had since the age of nineteen of becoming a crime novelist, he felt this was his last chance.

His earliest influences were Raymond Chandler, Ross Macdonald, and Joseph Wambaugh, but he was now also reading Lawrence Block's Matt Scudder novels and James Lee Burke's Dave Robicheaux series. So when he completed the manuscript in 1990 he decided to send it to their agents as well as to those of several other writers whose work he admired. Eight months later, he received a phone call from Philip Spitzer, James Lee Burke's literary editor, who agreed to seek a publisher for it. *The Black Echo* was published in 1992 by Little, Brown. At age thirty-two, Connelly had achieved his dream: he was a crime novelist.

Connelly's fledgling career got a pair of big boosts when *The Black Echo* won the Edgar Award for Best First Mystery Novel and from this enthusiastic (and prophetic) endorsement by James Lee Burke that accompanied the novel: "One of the most authentic pieces of crime writing I've ever read. It is an extraordinary story, one that engages the reader on the first page and never lets go.... It's hard to believe that this is Connelly's first novel. I'm convinced that his career will be a major one."

Connelly intended to devote his second novel to the story of Bosch's investigation into his mother's murder, but his publishers advised holding off on that. Instead he wrote what was a nod to Raymond Chandler's *The Long Goodbye.* His original title for this novel was *The Art of the Cape,* a reference to a bullfight that is described in the book, but his publishers wisely changed it to *The Black Ice,* hoping readers would see it as the second book in a series.

Connelly got another big boost when President Bill Clinton was reportedly spotted coming out of a Washington bookstore with a copy of the third Bosch novel, *The Concrete Blonde,* under his arm. Connelly had now reached a point where he felt he was going to have to choose between being a journalist and a novelist. The sale of the film rights to his first three Bosch novels to Paramount Studios allowed him to take a six-month sabbatical from his newspaper job in 1994 to write *The Last Coyote.* He returned to the *Times* for two more months, but he was miserable because he decided he wanted to be a full-time novelist. Whenever asked to pick his favorite among his books, he cites *The Last Coyote*, not because it's necessarily his best (it's certainly among his best) but because it was the first novel he wrote as a full-time author. He also felt it represented a big advance in quality because he now had greater confidence in what he was trying to do and it confirmed his belief that he could have a career as a writer of a successful crime series.

And what a career it turned out to be, which we examine in the following pages.

1

Harry Bosch and the Bosch Megaseries

Introducing Harry Bosch

Philip Kerr, author of an acclaimed series of novels about Bernie Gunther, a private eye in Berlin during the Nazi years, said he was inspired by asking himself what Raymond Chandler might have written if he had moved from England to Berlin instead of Los Angeles in 1912. Michael Connelly said he started out by asking himself what would have happened "if Raymond Chandler and Joseph Wambaugh had got together and created a character" (Willets). Given his years on the crime beat, he wanted to create a police hero like some of Wambaugh's cops but he also wanted some of the features of a brooding outsider like Chandler's private eye Philip Marlowe.

The result was LAPD homicide detective Harry Bosch, who would have a badge and carry a gun as a duly-sworn representative of the state, but wouldn't be comfortable about it—he'd be suspicious about his place in his own department. A cop with a private eye's outsider attitudes. He's what Darren Brooks describes as a noir cop: "a contemporary urban policeman—with all the responsibilities such a position entails—yet characterized by the internal darkness that inhabits the traditional noir antihero" (57).

One of the most unusual things about Harry Bosch is his name. He was originally called Pierce, a name Connelly said was inspired by Raymond Chandler, who once described the fictional detective as someone who must be willing and able to pierce all veils and layers of society. But while working on the second draft of his first novel, *The Black Echo*, he was suddenly reminded of the fifteenth-century Dutch painter Hieronymus Bosch, whose most famous work, *The Garden of Earthly Delights*, he had studied in an art history class in college. The three panels of that painting, filled with richly detailed nightmarish images, tell the history of evil from its source in the story of Adam and Eve in the Garden of Eden, through the chaos it unleashed upon the world, to the depiction in the third panel of the horrifying punishments awaiting evildoers in hell.

Suddenly, Connelly saw a connection to the crime novel he was writing. "After all," he noted, "what was a murder scene but a world gone wrong? What was a homicide investigation about but chaos and its consequences?" ("Hieronymus" 57). He hoped that readers who were familiar with Hieronymus Bosch's art would see Harry Bosch as a person whose job took him through a similarly hellish landscape.

Hieronymus is the Latin source of the name Jerome, so Bosch's detective should rightly be called Jerry for short. But Connelly decided to go with the name Harry as a nod to a pair of favorite film detectives—Dirty Harry Callahan, a tough cop played in several movies by Clint Eastwood, and Harry Caul, a surveillance expert played by Gene Hackman in Francis Ford Coppola's *The Conversation* (1974)—and novelist Harry Crews, his first creative writing teacher at the University of Florida.

Connelly gave Bosch a full back story. The idea for the plot of what would become *The Black Echo* came to him on his first day in Los Angeles when he read a newspaper account of a tunnel robbery that had just occurred in the city. The tunnel aspect triggered a childhood memory of growing up in Devon, a suburb of Philadelphia. From his second-floor bedroom window he could look out and see the mouth of a storm-water tunnel that ran under the street near the front of his house. It was a rite of passage for all young boys in the neighborhood to crawl through the dark and muddy tunnel alone or be taunted for being a sissy. The thought of someday having to go through the tunnel gave the ten-year-old boy nightmares: "It was always the same scene: I entered the tunnel, ready for the challenge, but a few steps in, the brick walls suddenly started to contract. Then, rippling violently in front of me, up out of the mud, a giant tongue lashed about at me" ("Hieronymus" 50). And then he would wake up. But once he finally made the journey through the tunnel, the nightmares went away.

After moving to Florida, Connelly said his father worked with a man who had been a tunnel rat in Vietnam. He said the man wore a full beard to cover facial scarring from wounds he had received during his service, but he refused to talk about his experiences ("Hieronymus" 50). His curiosity sparked, Connelly later read *The Tunnels of Cu Chi* (1985), a non-fiction account of the tunnel rats by Tom Mangold and John Penycate, that he said "scared the crap out of me" (Lutz). This gave him a detailed picture he could use to describe Bosch's experiences as a tunnel rat in Vietnam.

1. Harry Bosch and the Bosch Megaseries   11

Connelly borrowed another element of Bosch's back story from fellow crime novelist James Ellroy, whose mother was murdered when he was ten, a trauma that played a role in his decision to be a crime writer. Bosch's mother was a prostitute who lost custody of her son at age ten, when he was placed in a youth shelter that felt like a prison for kids. One year later she was found strangled to death in an alley off Hollywood Boulevard. The young boy spent the next several years in a series of foster homes, where he wasn't always welcomed. Before writing *The Last Coyote*, which is about Bosch's search for his mother's killer, Connelly wrote Ellroy to ask if he had any objections. Ellroy replied, "Unfortunately I don't have a franchise on murdered mothers, so good luck with your work" (McDonald).

When we first meet Harry Bosch in *The Black Echo*, he's a forty-year-old detective assigned to the Los Angeles Police Department's Hollywood Division. He's described as being a few inches short of six feet tall, lean and wiry with curly hair flecked with gray. He sports a mustache and his eyes "seldom betrayed emotion or intention" (*Echo* 9). He has a tattoo he got in Vietnam of a rat with a gun emerging from a tunnel, but over time it has blurred into what now looks more like a painful bruise.

When he was old enough, Bosch joined the Army and served fifteen months with the First Infantry in Vietnam, where he volunteered to become one of those intrepid soldiers who, armed only with a gun and a flashlight, descend into the complex labyrinth of tunnels that lie deep beneath the surface of the land to search for enemy soldiers and bombs. Upon his return, like many Vietnam vets, he joined the LAPD. Some were simply looking for another job that required carrying a gun. Others, like Bosch, were attracted by the thrill of the job. Descending into the darkness of a tunnel, which he did more than one hundred times, always gave him an adrenaline jolt. Looking to recapture it, he became a cop.

Over a period of eight years he advanced his way upwards from patrolman to detective in the Robbery-Homicide division. Along the way, he worked some famous cases. As a patrolman in 1974, he was assigned guard duty and crowd control at the scene of the famous firefight with the Symbionese Liberation Army that left a house burned to the ground with five bodies dead inside. He and his partner were given the task of digging through the rubble to see if the body of missing heiress Patty Hearst was among them.

He later became something of a celebrity thanks to his role in solving what became known as the Beauty Shop Slasher case. It was turned into a bestselling book by a local crime reporter and a TV movie, for which Bosch and his partner were paid $50,000 each for the use of their names and for technical assistance. Bosch used the money to buy a one-bedroom stilt house on Woodrow Wilson Drive in the hills above Studio City that boasts a breathtaking view of the city below.

A second case brought him into the limelight again, but this time the results were not so positive. In the Dollmaker case, he shot and killed the suspect while he was lying in bed. Bosch claimed he saw the man reaching under the pillow for a gun; it turns out he was simply reaching for his toupee. His superiors wanted to fire him, but because of favorable publicity for solving both cases, the best the department could do was issue a short suspension and demote him to the Hollywood Division.

Bosch is an outsider in the LAPD, which is signified by several small details: he's left-handed in a right-handed world and a heavy smoker who must leave the building to light up, usually by himself, emphasizing his separation from a workplace that values conformity. He's always assigned a regular partner, but he manages to find a way to go it alone whenever it suits him. It's also important to him that he find a way to make each case personal, even if he doesn't know the victim. "The key for him as a detective is to get angry about cases," says Connelly, "and that gives him the juice he needs to be relentless to carry out the mission." He needs to find the little thing that gets under his skin, that makes it personal. "And he does this knowingly. It's not subconscious. He knows he's got to start a fire somehow and he looks for it in each case" (McDermott).

Bosch has few interests outside of his job—"The only things he spent money on were food, booze and jazz" (*Echo* 60)—but jazz is especially important to him. Connelly didn't grow up loving jazz; it was his father's music and its appearance in his novels was initially intended to be a tribute to his late father, who had passed away shortly before the publication of his first novel. However, he quickly realized he could use Bosch's love of jazz as a way of revealing important insights into his character.

The sound of the jazz saxophone is "the only music that had ever been able to truly light him up" and "the goddam light at the end of all his tunnels" ("Christmas"). Connelly drew a connection between Bosch and his favorite saxophone players, Art Pepper and Frank Morgan, both of whom were sidelined by drugs and imprisonment for much of their careers. But both were able to overcome their pasts and resume playing their music. The story of their lives gives Bosch hope by reminding him of the possibility of redemption. (The title of a 2014 documentary film about Frank Morgan that Connelly produced bears the title *Sound of Redemption*.) A solo performance of "Somewhere Over the Rainbow" that Bosch listens to by a young jazz saxophone artist named Grace Kelly also deeply resonates with his own experience: "It was plaintive and sad but it came with an undeniable wave of underlying hope. It made Bosch think that there was still a chance for him, that he could still find whatever it was he was looking for, no matter how short his time was" (*Burning* 75).

Working as a homicide detective is more than a job for Bosch: "It was a mission. As surely as murder was an art for some who committed it, homicide investigation was an art for those on the mission. And it chose you, you didn't choose it" (*Concrete* 44). He always finds a way to get the job done, never gives up, and is able to pick himself up again whenever he's derailed in the completion of his mission. Though often difficult to complete, that mission can be summed up in a few simple words: "Everybody counts or nobody counts." And his dedication to it is equally straightforward: "My job in this world, badge or no badge, was to stand for the dead" (*Lost* 23).

The Bosch Megaseries: "It's All One Story"

Creating a long-running crime series can be a mixed blessing. A series relieves the burden of having to create a new protagonist for each book, and it can also be the path to fame and fortune. Readers enjoy returning again and again to a familiar character and those who discover an author's work in mid-series often purchase the earlier books to catch up. But because a long-running series can become a cash cow, publishers want the assembly line moving without interruption, even if the author loses interest and/or inspiration. Even death won't bring a long-running series to an end; other writers will simply be hired to continue producing more books. There are far too many examples of series that limp on well past their prime.

For those writers who commit to a series, there are two important factors to keep in mind: (1) create a character you like well enough to want to keep writing about over and over again and (2) find ways of keeping yourself and your series as fresh as possible. To ensure he would like the character of Travis McGee enough to want to continue writing about him, John D. MacDonald completed five novels before he would allow the first to be published. Agatha Christie, on the other hand, eventually found Hercule Poirot to be such an insufferable character that she once confessed, "Why did I ever invent this detestable, bombastic, tiresome little creature? Eternally straightening things, eternally boasting, eternally twirling his moustache and tilting his egg-shaped head," yet continued the series out of a sense of duty to her readers (Flood). Arthur Conan Doyle became so weary of writing about Sherlock Holmes, about whom he once said, "I have had such an overdose of him that I feel towards him as I do towards *pâté-de-foie-gras*, of which I once ate too much, so that the name of it gives me a sickly feeling to this day" (James 42), that he killed him off, only to be forced to resurrect him a decade later after the negative public response from his readers.

In their book *Serial Crime Fiction*, the editors note that though the repetition of a formula is an integral part of a series, "it is not simply repetition, but the tension between repetition and development, between initiation and transformation, that builds the narrative chain, making reiteration an essential part of change, and change an essential part of reiteration" (Anderson et al. 1). Connelly knew from the beginning that his character couldn't remain the same from book to book or the series would quickly turn stale. One way he found of keeping him fresh was to have him age in real time, so he naturally evolves as he ages from forty to seventy over the course of the series. Although he regrets he didn't make Bosch a younger man when he started the series because he now has to find realistic ways to keep him on the job, he says it was the best decision he ever made for it kept his interest alive. Now he looks forward to seeing what his character has been up to in each book he writes.

In Harry Bosch, Connelly has created a character with the perfect combination of background, personality, and dedication to his job that is built for the long haul. As his relationship with his hero developed over time, he happily found that sitting down to write a new Bosch book was like putting on a comfortable old coat. Each time he would reach into the pockets of that old coat, he would "find something you didn't know was in there" that he could "pull out and write about" (Kellogg).

He also discovered the importance of taking regular breaks from his series in order to recharge his creative batteries. After writing his first four Bosch books, he felt it was time to try something new. The result was *The Poet* (1996), which introduced a new character, journalist Jack McEvoy, who becomes involved in a nationwide hunt for a serial killer. He returned to the Bosch series for one more novel, then wrote another non-series novel, *Blood Work* (1998), featuring an FBI profiler named Terry McCaleb.

And then he did something that has energized and enlarged the Bosch series even more. Beginning with *A Darkness More Than Night* (2001), his tenth novel, he began integrating characters from two of his standalone novels into the Bosch series, creating what he has described as "one big mosaic of time and place" (Tierney). He isn't the first crime writer to do this. Though he never wrote a series, Elmore Leonard would sometimes feature a protagonist in more than one novel and on occasion brought characters from different novels together in a single novel. But no one has achieved what Connelly has by integrating characters from five separate series into a single megaseries.

This wasn't part of any longtime plan but grew organically, like his novels, which he never outlines in advance. The resultant megaseries has become crime fiction's version of the Marvel Cinematic Universe. Because all his characters exist in the same world, each series cross-pollinates with the others and readers get the sense that all of them continue living their lives between appearances in the novels. Having multiple series allows Connelly to return to Bosch only when he feels he has something new to say about him, not simply to grind another book out. This has kept the series both fresh and timely as Bosch's experiences reflect both the many changes in his life as well as those in the city and country he lives in.

The Bosch series invites a comparison to another one set in L.A. by Walter Mosley, whose novels feature a reluctant Black private eye named Ezekiel "Easy" Rawlins, who made his debut in 1990 in *Devil in a Blue Dress*. Like Connelly's, Mosley's series spans a lengthy period of time (1948–1969) in order to tell an important story about the often-difficult experiences of southern Blacks who moved to South Central Los Angeles after World War II in search of a better life. Like Bosch, Rawlins ages in real time, though Mosley's series is set in the past rather than being a year-by-year chronicle of the passing years like Connelly's. And his picture of Los Angeles isn't intended to fill the large-scale canvas Connelly has been painting.

Cop-turned-crime-novelist Joseph Wambaugh is one of the trio of L.A. crime writers (along with Raymond Chandler and Ross Macdonald) Connelly has singled out as being the most influential on his own writing. One lesson he learned from Wambaugh was the importance of showing not just how cops act on the job but how the job acts on them. Cops see things on a daily basis that could turn anybody's life upside down. What Connelly sought to show in his books is a cop who doesn't get pulled down into it. "Harry Bosch goes into darkness every day of his life," he notes. "Some of that darkness has gotten into him and his struggle not to succumb to it underlines the nobility of the job. That's what I write about. I have known real cops who have fallen, become addicted, killed themselves, but to me the ones that don't fall and beat the darkness are much more interesting to write about" (Filippi).

The Bosch megaseries keeps expanding beyond the novels. Terry McCaleb and Mickey Haller have both been featured in movies (*Blood

Work and *The Lincoln Lawyer*). Harry Bosch appeared in a streaming series on Amazon Prime that ran for seven years and led to a spinoff about his post–LAPD career that is about to launch. Titus Welliver, the actor who portrays Harry Bosch in both series, is now the voice of the audiobook versions of Connelly's novels. And a new series featuring Mickey Haller is also about to begin streaming on Netflix.

In this book we take a close look at all of Michael Connelly's work, although the primary focus remains on Harry Bosch. Readers and now TV viewers have been given the rare opportunity of following a character whose life has been filled with joy and heartbreak, hope and disappointment, success and failure. He has his ups and downs but never stops looking for the light that keeps him going amidst the darkness. All of this has earned him a prominent place in the pantheon of crime fiction heroes.

2

The Novels

The Black Echo (1992)

As the novel begins, Bosch is summoned to a tunnel alongside the Mulholland Dam in the Hollywood Hills where the body of a man has been found, the likely victim of a drug overdose. But details at the scene—the body had been dragged thirty feet inside the tunnel—lead Bosch to conclude he was murdered. More importantly, Bosch recognizes the victim as Billy Meadows, a fellow tunnel rat he served with twenty years earlier in Vietnam.

Bosch uncovers an important clue to the reason behind Meadows's murder after finding a pawn ticket during a search of his apartment. At the pawn shop, he learns that the item Meadows pawned—an antique gold bracelet inlaid with jade dolphin figures—was recently stolen from the shop. It turns out it was previously stolen from a safety deposit box during a daring robbery at a bank that involved gaining access to the vault by tunneling underground. Bosch, a firm believer that there are no coincidences, now sees a connection between the two crimes. But who killed Meadows and why?

The real tunnel heist the novel was based on gave Connelly the inspiration for a traumatic episode in Bosch's life. At the age of twenty, Bosch became a tunnel rat, one of those soldiers brave enough to climb into a hole in the ground, a "blurred, forbidding darkness, like the ghastly mouth in Edvard Munch's painting *The Scream*" (65), and armed only with a pistol and a flashlight, enter into the elaborate system of tunnels underneath many of the villages in Vietnam: "Out of the blue and into the black is what they called going into a tunnel. Each one was a black echo. Nothing but death in there. But, still, they went" (65).

His final tunnel experience was hellish. After only two of the three soldiers on a previous mission into a tunnel returned, Bosch and Billy Meadows were given the task of finding the missing comrade. The two men become separated and Bosch, now alone in the darkness, finds the dead soldier sitting upright with a bloody crotch and his testicles in one hand. Suddenly, Bosch feels the walls of the tunnel closing in on him and he curls into a fetal position, sobs racking his entire body. When he finally returns home, like many Vietnam vets he joins the L.A. Police Department, but that traumatic tunnel experience has left him with a chronic case of insomnia and claustrophobia.

Billy Meadows's return from Vietnam was far more troubling. Although he was fearless about entering the tunnels, he too was left severely damaged when he didn't return from another mission with Bosch in which a tunnel was demolished in an explosion. Meadows wasn't located until two days later when a search crew found him sitting on the ground, spouting gibberish and sporting a necklace. When they pulled him out, he was wearing a necklace adorned with thirty-three ears he had removed from the enemy soldiers he had killed.

Meadows remained in Vietnam until Saigon fell in 1975. Shortly after returning home he was arrested on heroin charges and later spent six and a half years in prison on a conviction for armed robbery. More recently, he had been living in a halfway house for addicted Vietnam vets and seemed to have been on the road to recovery when he was murdered. Bosch hadn't seen him in twenty years, though after receiving a phone call from him a year earlier, he helped get him into a drug-treatment program. The search for Meadows's killer becomes a mission more than a job for Bosch, for the code of the tunnel rats promised that no one, even if you died in a tunnel, would be forgotten. That still applies, even if the tunnel you died in was located in L.A.

Bosch learns that Meadows was a member of the gang that carried out the bank heist and that all three of them were friends in Vietnam. Meadows was killed after he pawned the bracelet because it brought unwelcome new attention to the bank heist that could possibly endanger the success of a second one being planned. The primary object of the robbery was an eighteen-million-dollar cache of diamonds that had been smuggled out of Vietnam by high-ranking Vietnamese generals.

Early in his investigation, Bosch teams up with a beautiful blonde FBI agent named Eleanor Wish who also has a Vietnam connection: her brother died there just a week before he was to return home. Their professional relationship starts out prickly but soon turns into a romantic one, and thanks to the questions she asks Bosch, we gain additional insight into his private life.

After finding a listening device hidden in his telephone, Bosch suspects he and Eleanor are being followed, either by his own department or by someone in the FBI trying to sabotage their investigation. Bosch is correct in his suspicions about the department as we learn that Deputy

Chief Irvin Irving, head of the department's Internal Affairs Division, has assigned a pair of his officers to secretly follow Bosch. While he is forced to admit that Bosch is a good detective, he considers him too much of an outsider and not loyal enough as a member of the LAPD family. Frustrated at not having been able to fire him after he shot the killer reaching for his toupee thinking it was a gun, he hopes his agents can turn up a reason that will allow him to get rid of Bosch this time.

Bosch's suspicions about a possible insider in the FBI also turn out to be correct, when he discovers that Wish's FBI partner John Rourke also knew Meadows in Vietnam and helped smuggle the diamonds into the U.S. He was the one who came up with the plan to steal them. It was he who killed Meadows and is now about to pull off another tunnel heist. After spending much of the novel up to this point sitting at a desk poring over files or in his car driving all over the city, Bosch is roused into action and the novel switches from a procedural to a thriller. Unfortunately for him, it requires him to enter another tunnel in pursuit of a pair of robbers, one of them wounded, who have escaped there after an explosion in the vault room.

As Bosch begins to crawl through the narrow space, he begins perspiring from the heat and the fear. He eventually comes upon the first man, who has succumbed to his injuries, but then is shot in the shoulder by the second man, who runs away. Then he hears two men talking, followed by a shot. When the shooter comes close enough, it confirms his suspicions: it is Rourke. As Rourke prepares to finish off Bosch, Eleanor Wish, like a convenient *deus ex machina* figure in Greek classical drama, miraculously arrives in the nick of time to save him.

There is one more surprise waiting and once again it has its roots in Vietnam. After Eleanor Wish announces she's quitting her FBI job and moving out of L.A., Bosch is emotionally hurt by the news. But something else bothers him. At the veterans' cemetery in Westwood, Bosch visits a replica currently on display there of the original Vietnam Veterans Memorial Wall in Washington to search through all 58,132 names of the dead looking for the name of Eleanor's brother, whom she claimed had been killed in combat one week before he was to return home. His name is missing. Why?

It turns out Eleanor was the mastermind behind the entire crime. Only recently did she learn that her brother didn't die in Vietnam, as she had been told, but in Hollywood, where he, too, was murdered by Rourke after he tried to keep the package of diamonds Rourke had him smuggle into the U.S. for himself. She plotted to get revenge against him and his partners by planting the idea of the tunnel robbery in Rourke's mind. Once she learned that Bosch knew Meadows, she set things up so that he would become involved in the search for his killer. Her plan was to let the gang steal all the diamonds and then take them for herself. Though she never intended for anyone to get hurt, all four members of the gang were killed in one way or another. But at least she saved Bosch's life.

This presents Bosch with the same kind of difficult decision Sam Spade faced at the end of *The Maltese Falcon* when he was forced to choose between love and duty after learning that his lover Brigid O'Shaughnessy is the murderer of his partner he has been searching for. Like Spade, Bosch chooses justice over love by forcing Eleanor to give herself up to the authorities. But before she goes off to jail, she sends him a final gift: the framed copy of Edward Hopper's famous painting *Nighthawks* that Bosch saw hanging over the couch in her apartment. That was the painting he spent an hour looking at when he first saw it at the Art Institute in Chicago. It now hangs near his front door as a reminder of Eleanor. It also makes him realize something else: "The stark loneliness. The man sitting alone, his face turned to the shadows. I am that man" (412).

The Black Ice (1993)

"Sophomore slump" is the dreaded term familiar to college sophomores, professional athletes, recording artists, and even writers that describes a follow-up effort that fails to live up the high standards set in the first outing. *The Black Echo* is a hard act to follow and whether or not *The Black Ice* can be deemed a slump, it's not as surefooted in its execution as Connelly's first novel.

The initial setup is promising. Calexico Moore, a member of the narcotics unit, is found dead in a motel room of a shotgun blast to the head, an apparent suicide. Bosch is angry because the incident happened on his watch and by rights he should have gotten the call to investigate. Instead, department higher-ups have taken over. After he complained to Deputy Chief Irving about being shut out, Irving gives him the unpleasant assignment of breaking the news to Moore's estranged wife.

The usually dreaded task surprisingly turns into something more meaningful as Bosch finds himself attracted to the woman, whose name is Sylvia. He wonders why and concludes that he has always seen something of himself in the women who attracted him: "Like himself, he knew, she carried her scars on the inside, buried deep, each one a mystery. She was like him" (39). Just as he's about to leave, she begins to cry and he walks over and comforts her with a hug.

He later gets another special assignment, this one from Lt. Pounds, his immediate boss. One of the department cops, Lucius Porter, is quitting to deal with a serious problem with alcohol. Pounds is unhappy with the number of unsolved homicides in the department and wants Bosch to look through the files on eight unsolved homicides that Porter was working on. If he finds one he can solve by New Year's Eve, it would up the department's yearly rate of success to the halfway mark. Unlike most detectives in the department, Bosch doesn't mind working alone, and chooses to focus on the most recent unsolved murder, that of an unidentified Mexican known only as Juan Doe #67, whose body was found dumped behind a restaurant. An autopsy reveals a pair of fruit flies in his stomach, the kind that could have only come from a facility in Mexicali, Mexico, where they are radiated to render them sterile, then sent to L.A. to be used to help halt the damage caused by the invasive species.

A third death, that of a known drug dealer that Calexico Moore had mentioned in the one meeting he and Bosch ever had, also interests him. An autopsy revealed that his stomach contained forty-two condoms filled with black ice, a combination of cocaine, heroin, and PCP in rock form that is currently being smuggled into the state from Mexico. At that same meeting, Moore had mentioned in passing that he was named after the California town of Calexico, where he was born and raised and which is located just across the Mexican border from the city of Mexicali. The three deaths look to Bosch "like different spokes on the same wheel" (111), and its hub is in Mexicali.

The final third of the novel is set in Mexico, which emphasizes Bosch's go-his-own-way approach to investigation, especially when he ignores an order to return to L.A. Bosch proudly considers himself an outsider within the department, but that's doubly true when he is in Mexico, where he is hampered by the fact that he isn't fluent in Spanish and lacks any legal jurisdiction. Writers of long-running series sometimes try to shake things up a bit by transporting their detectives to an unfamiliar location, but after only one appearance in L.A., it's much too soon for a fish-out-of-water Bosch novel. Nor does it allow Connelly to continue building upon the portrait of Los Angeles he began in his first novel. It does, however, allow him to pay tribute to Raymond Chandler's *The Long Goodbye*, the film version of which was his first introduction to Philip Marlowe. In Chandler's novel, Marlowe makes a brief visit to Mexico, which is also the site of a faked death, in order to assume a new identity, key plot elements in *The Black Ice*.

In *The Black Echo*, Bosch spent much of his time driving to a variety of interesting locations all over L.A. Here he spends much of the time in his car sitting in traffic while slowly driving back and forth across the border. And for much of the time in Mexico his role is limited to that of an observer rather than an active participant in the action. We sit with him for several hours at a bullfight, where he hopes to get a look at Humberto Zorillo, the notorious "pope of Mexicali" behind the smuggling of black ice into L.A. as well as the person behind all the murders whom Bosch has been looking for. But after sitting through several fights, he leaves without ever seeing Zorillo, who fails to show up. Later, he gets to ride along in one of the helicopters engaged in a top-secret DEA-Mexican militia operation aimed at capturing Zorillo at his ranch, but we watch most of the action below from a safe distance in the air.

Bosch does get a couple of opportunities to strut his stuff as an action hero. There is a tunnel running underground between Zorillo's hacienda and the factory from which he smuggles the black ice, which presents Bosch with another opportunity to confront his fears and crawl into it, but the episode passes without consequence. He gets a better chance to demonstrate his coolness under pressure when the helicopter he's riding in is bowled over by a raging bull when it lands. After crawling out of the wreckage he finds himself squarely in the path of Zorillo's champion bull, known as El Trembla. It turns out that the time he spent at the bullfight wasn't a complete waste, as thanks to watching the matadors, he has learned how to maneuver the bull's horns safely away from his body as it charges past him.

In the end, it is Bosch's usual close attention to detail that solves the crime. This time it's a footprint made by Zorillo as he eluded Bosch that reveals a distinctive mark on the heel that is an exact duplicate of the one he saw on the floor at the scene of Moore's suicide. Suddenly, everything comes together in a shocking conclusion. The dead man in Moore's tub wasn't Moore, it was Zorillo, an old friend of his. The Zorillo he's chasing is really Calexico Moore, who killed Zorillo in order to gain control of his wealth. Bosch eventually tracks him down to his childhood home, where Bosch is forced to kill him in a gunfight.

Despite Bosch's rule of thumb that there are no coincidences in an investigation, *The Black Ice* contains several plot contrivances. For example, in order to arrange a second meeting between Bosch and Sylvia Moore, the novel relies on the implausible coincidence of her arrival at her late husband's apartment at 10:45 at night to retrieve his dress uniform for his burial when Bosch is conveniently there after breaking in to search for clues. While there he asks her to take a look at an empty picture frame on the bedroom wall to see if she remembers what it contained. She doesn't recall, but the nearby bed is soon happily occupied by the two of them.

The novel includes several scenes aimed at further illuminating

Bosch's character, both as a cop and as a person. When Lt. Pounds, head of the homicide division, asks him to take over Porter's unsolved cases, he accepts the assignment not to please Pounds but because solving murders is what he does. To his way of thinking, Pounds, who had never worked a homicide, wasn't even a cop anymore: "He was a bureaucrat. He was nothing. He saw crime, the spilling of blood, the suffering of humans, as statistical entries in a log. And at the end of the year the log told him how well he did. Not people. Not the voice from within. It was the kind of impersonal arrogance that poisoned much of the department and isolated it from the city, its people" (55).

Another incident in the novel reveals a softer side of Bosch, one that others seldom get to see. He pairs up with a cop on the drug beat to arrest a young kid named Kerwin who is selling drugs outside a club. They offer to let him go if he provides the name of another drug dealer Bosch is trying to locate. Kerwin refuses, so they arrest him and transport him to be locked up overnight, hoping the experience will change his mind. But what Bosch witnesses the next day turns his stomach: Kerwin looks like he's aged ten years and the distance in his eyes reminds Bosch of soldiers he knew in Vietnam. He is reminded of the first night he spent in a juvenile facility, but at least he was surrounded by other kids like himself, not the wild animals this kid was forced to spend the last twelve hours with.

Bosch is both disgusted at how much the other cop seems to be enjoying the whole incident and ashamed at forgetting that "solving cases was simply getting people to talk to you. Not forcing them to talk" (180). Bosch demands that Kerwin be released, and then drives him to a seedy hotel, pays for a week's rent, and gives him all the money he has left in his pocket. He also warns him to get out of town before it's too late. He tells Kerwin he's not doing this for him but for himself, as he sees himself in the kid's situation. He wonders where Kerwin will be in a year, then reminds himself that despite spending much of his own youth in rundown motels, he has survived. There is always the chance this kid might be as lucky.

Bosch never knew his father, but after returning home from Vietnam, he decided it was time to try to find him. Like the good detective he will later prove to be, he succeeds in tracking him down. His name is J. Michael Haller, a prominent defense attorney whose clients included one of the Manson girls as well as Bosch's own mother. He meets the man for the first and only time two weeks before his death. At his funeral, he spots Haller's other son, his own half-brother, who is also a defense lawyer like his father. The two don't speak and Bosch figures they probably never will. That will change twelve years later when Connelly debuts a series of novels featuring that attorney, Mickey Haller, the Lincoln Lawyer.

Despite the many difficult challenges in his past, Bosch always clung to the belief "that he was struggling toward some kind of resolution and knowledge of purpose. That there was something good in him or about him. It was the waiting that was so hard. The waiting often left a hollow feeling in his soul. And he believed people could see this, that they knew when they looked at him that he was empty. He had learned to fill that hollowness with isolation and work" (235). Readers will be given an opportunity through the rest of the series to witness Bosch as he struggles to fill the emptiness in his life and find meaning in what he does.

The Concrete Blonde (1994)

The Concrete Blonde introduces a new feature—a courtroom drama—and then combines it with a search for a serial killer. In both instances, Bosch is at the center of the action.

In the Dollmaker case four years earlier, Bosch shot and killed a serial killer named Norman Church, who used makeup to paint the faces of his eleven female victims. He shot Church when he thought he saw him reaching for his gun, but it turned out what he was reaching for was his toupee. Bosch was exonerated in the shooting, but did face disciplinary charges for failing to call for backup before entering Church's apartment. The case eventually brought Bosch fame and a $50,000 check thanks to a bestselling book and a TV show based on the case.

Now four years later, Bosch is in the news again, this time as a defendant in a federal courtroom facing a civil rights suit brought by Church's widow accusing him of using excessive force in killing an innocent man. But on the very first day of the trial, a note is dropped off at the Hollywood station front desk claiming to be from the Dollmaker that taunts Bosch for killing the wrong man and reveals the location where another victim can be found.

Under the rubble of a burned-out building the police find the remains of a woman encased in concrete who bears all the telltale signs of the Dollmaker's work. But she has been dead for only two years, so she couldn't possibly have been one of Church's victims. Did Bosch really kill an innocent man? Could the Dollmaker still be at large? During the trial Honey Chandler (nicknamed "Money" for her success in cases involving police brutality) proves to be a tough antagonist as she makes the case that Bosch is a trigger-happy cop who killed an innocent man.

She also suggests that the department was under such pressure to find the person who killed eleven victims that he may have even fabricated evidence in order to tie an innocent man to the crimes.

Details begin to emerge, however, that raise the possibility that there might be two Dollmakers, one of them a copycat who is still at large. During the trial, a friend of Church's provided video evidence that he could not have killed one of the women he was suspected of killing. In addition, Becky Kaminski, the woman found in the concrete, as well as two other victims, were all buxom blonde porn actresses who did not resemble Church's victims. It becomes increasingly clear that there is another serial killer on the loose, this one they dub the Follower, whom they must stop before he can kill more victims.

Connelly's handling of the trial is effective and suspenseful as we observe the effect the proceedings have on Bosch, who is forced to sit there silently while Chandler paints a damning portrait of him. After obtaining a copy of the confidential psychological assessment done on Bosch following his shooting of Church, she asks him to read it aloud to the jury. The report concludes that he has become desensitized to violence: "He speaks in terms of violence or the aspect of violence being an accepted part of his day-to-day-life, for all of his life. Therefore, it is unlikely that what transpired previously will act as a psychological deterrent should he again be placed in circumstances where he must act with deadly force in order to protect himself or others" (195). As for his fitness to return to his job, the report says he will be able to act without delay. "He will be able to pull the trigger. In fact, his conversation reveals no ill effects at all from the shooting, unless his sense of satisfaction with the outcome of the incident—the suspect's death—should be deemed inappropriate" (195).

Chandler tightens the screws by asking him if the reason he became a policeman in the first place was because of the unsolved murder of his own mother when he was eleven. Bosch becomes increasingly unsettled by this very revealing line of questioning, and when he defends his actions by claiming that Church deserved to die because he was a monster who killed women, she asks, "Like the one who killed your mother?" (203). She goes on to paint a devastating portrait for the jury of a rogue cop "with a deep-seated motive for killing a man who he thought might be a serial killer of women, of women from the street ... like his own mother" (259).

Despite his discomfort at having been so publicly exposed, Bosch still has a job to do, so after sitting in court all day long, he spends his evenings searching for the Follower. The Dollmaker task force is reconvened and as bits and pieces of the puzzle emerge, the plot takes several surprising twists and turns. Initially, Bosch suspected that the Follower might be Ray Mora, the department's most experienced expert on the porn industry with whom he has been working the case. Unlike most cops, who transfer after one year, Mora has been a vice cop for seven years. During the trial, Honey Chandler had quoted Friedrich Nietzsche's famous words that "whoever fights monsters should see to it that in the process he does not become a monster. And when you look into the abyss, the abyss also looks into you" (36). She was referring to Bosch, but now Bosch wonders if it was Mora who has been sucked into the evil he was supposed to be fighting.

Bosch decides to break into Mora's home to search for incriminating evidence, but all he finds are some videos Mora made of having sex with underage girls, nothing connecting him to any of the Follower's murders. His suspicion then shifts to Dr. John Locke, the expert in psychosexual behavior who testified at his trial and with whom he has been consulting. When Bosch checks the index of a textbook he wrote, *The Private Sex Life of the Public Porn Princess*, he finds the names of all three porn actresses who were murdered by the Follower. It must be him.

Bosch is then jolted when he receives another note from the Follower, this one promising to take "your precious blonde" off his hands. Bosch becomes frantic when he is unable to locate his girlfriend Sylvia Moore to warn her of the danger she's in. But he's wrong again: the blonde the Follower kills is Honey Chandler. When Locke can't be located, he's convinced he must be her killer, but when Locke is able to present evidence that he was out of town when Chandler was killed, Bosch has to look elsewhere again. There is now only one other person who had enough inside information about the Dollmaker case to have been able to pull off the copycat murders—Joel Bremmer, a crime reporter for the *L.A. Times*, the author of the best-selling book about the case that made Bosch famous, and one of the few journalists he trusted.

Despite his ordeals, there are a few bright spots for Bosch. Even though the jury finds him guilty of depriving Church of his civil rights to protection against illegal search and seizure, it awards the plaintiff a mere two dollars for compensatory and punitive damages. His prickly relationship with Chief Irving also improves. Previously, Irving had been his nemesis, overly critical of his tendencies to act on his own, but during the trial Irving compliments him on his work in the Follower investigation. He also wants him to know he fully supports his actions in the Dollmaker shooting, reminding him that a jury has no idea what it's like to be out there on the edge. And then, after telling Bosch how sorry he is that Honey Chandler brought up the issue of his mother's death, he drops a bombshell: some thirty years earlier, he was the patrolman who found his mother's body in the alley where she had been murdered.

The biggest bright spot comes in Bosch's relationship with Sylvia Moore, with whom he has been spending several nights each week for the past year. Having experienced the failure of her previous marriage to a cop with a dangerous job who also kept secrets from her, she's wary of making the same mistake with Bosch. Despite his difficulty in opening up emotionally and determination to keep his past buried to everyone, his protective barriers gradually break down and for the first time in his life he is able to utter the words "I love you" to Sylvia. Although she tells him she needs to take a break to sort things out, the novel ends on a happy note when she returns and agrees to go off with him for a weekend together.

Connelly also introduces one other new feature into this novel, i.e., social commentary. The shadow of the Rodney King beating looms large over the proceedings, giving Connelly an opportunity to consider the role of the police in American society. On March 3, 1991, a Black man named Rodney King was pulled over by the LAPD on suspicion of drunk driving and subjected to a brutal beating by four cops, three of them white, who pummeled him at least fifty times while he was lying helpless on the ground. A video of the assault made by a bystander and broadcast around the country sparked nationwide outrage. One year later, the four officers involved in the incident were put on trial, but after three of them were acquitted and the jury was unable to reach a verdict on the fourth, the city erupted into five days of rioting. Over a thousand buildings were burned down, sixty-three people were killed, and over 2000 injured.

The King incident is first mentioned when Bosch arrives at the scene where the body of Becky Kaminski was dug up from under the remains of one of the many buildings that were torched during the riots. Honey Chandler loses little time in mentioning that detail in Bosch's trial, where she reminds the jury of the LAPD's long history of brutality. Bosch himself weighs in on the same subject after viewing a mural painted on the wall of a police station that depicted Black and white and brown children playing together and smiling at friendly police officers. At the bottom of the mural someone had spray-painted "This is a damnable lie!" (208). Bosch understands the dilemma. Citizens want their police to protect them, but "those same John Q.'s are the first to stare wide-eyed and point the finger of outrage when they see close up exactly what the job they've given the cops entails" (208). While he doesn't condone the actions of the police in the King beating, he understands where they came from.

Bosch also points to the political opportunism and ineptitude that allowed the department to "languish for years as an understaffed and underequipped paramilitary organization" (209). It has become top-heavy with managers and so understaffed that cops on the street only ventured out of their cars to deal with dirtbags rather than the people they served. Consequently, "it had created a police culture in which everybody not in blue was seen as a dirtbag and was treated as such" (209).

The risk that comes with commenting on topical issues is that as time goes by, the book can seem dated. Not so with *The Concrete Blonde*. Connelly had no way of knowing how prophetic Bosch's words would become when, referring to both the Watts riots in 1965 and those that followed the Rodney King beating in 1991, he observes that "every twenty-five years or so the city had its soul torched by the fires of reality. But then it drove on. Quickly, without looking back. Like a hit-and-run" (17). Twenty-six years after the publication of *The Concrete Blonde*, American cities once again erupted in violence as a rash of police shootings of unarmed Black men across the U.S. painfully reminded the country that it still has not come to terms with its history of racism.

The Last Coyote (1995)

Bosch is dealing with a trio of personal setbacks: after a year-long relationship, girlfriend Sylvia Moore has left him and moved to Italy; his house has been declared inhabitable due to structural damage from the devastating earthquake that hit L.A. on January 17, 1994; and he has been suspended from his job. The cause of being placed on what the department calls "involuntary stress leave" is a violent attack on his boss, Lt. Harvey Pounds.

A number-cruncher who has never worked the streets, Pounds is held in contempt by the homicide detectives under his command. They consider him to be nothing but a bureaucrat with a badge who doesn't understand the first thing about closing cases. The incident that results in Bosch's suspension occurs after he brings a suspect in the killing of a prostitute in for questioning. Experienced cops know that if they can get the suspect talking, it often leads to inconsistencies they can later use against the person, so they are careful not to arrest him so they don't have to read him his Miranda rights.

But when Bosch leaves the interrogation room briefly, Pounds notices the man sitting there and reads him his Miranda rights. When Bosch returns, the suspect clams up and demands a lawyer. Bosch is so angry at Pounds that he slams him through his office window. The glass is quickly replaced, the bureaucrat who let a murder suspect go free without ever being charged is back behind his desk, and Bosch, who is convinced he did the right thing, is suspended.

While on suspension, Bosch uses the phrase "everybody counts or nobody counts" for the first time when he asks himself whether the murder of a prostitute is as meaningful as the murder of the mayor's wife. Was it "merely a slogan like the one on the back of his shirt or was it something he lived by" (23)? He is bothered by the fact that Pounds's blunder allowed the killer of a prostitute to go free. But what about the unsolved murder of another prostitute, his own mother? He now realizes that after twenty years as a cop, that's the one crime he must solve. When Irving orders him to cease his investigation into his mother's death or risk losing his job, he replies, "This is all that matters to me and I don't care what I have to do, I'm doing it.... What does doing what I do for the department matter if I can't do this for her ... and for me" (280)?

Crime writers often use the past, either for the opportunity to illustrate their detective's skill in solving a cold case or, like Ross Macdonald, to show how events in the past often provide the key that unlocks mysteries in the present. Connelly combines both elements in that as Bosch relentlessly investigates a three-decades-old mystery, he finds answers that help him solve some of the mysteries of his own life. Some things he discovers are as unsettling as the earthquake that destroyed his house.

Bosch's investigation is a casebook study in how to go about investigating a thirty-three-year-old cold case. He begins by digging out the original files on the case, examining a box of his mother's clothing, and then trying to match fingerprints found on the buckle of the belt used to kill her. He befriends an *L.A. Times* reporter to get her to search the paper's obituaries to find out which of the names he comes up with are still alive. He tracks down one of them, a woman named Meredith Roman, a fellow prostitute who was a close friend of his mother and the last person to see her alive. He also flies to Florida at his own expense to interview one of the detectives on the case who has retired there.

His snooping leads to two important conclusions: (1) his mother's murder wasn't a sex crime; she was murdered somewhere else, likely by someone she knew, and her body then dumped into a trash bin in an alley; and (2) there was a police cover-up in order to protect some important and powerful political figures, especially a man named Arno Conklin who was running for District Attorney. His face appears in a photo with his mother, and Meredith Roman had previously identified him as the man she was going to meet the night she was murdered.

Bosch is then jolted by a pair of new developments. After returning from Florida, he is summoned to Irving's office, where he learns that his nemesis Harvey Pounds has been tortured and murdered and that the killer also took his badge. The main suspect is Bosch, who was heard threatening Pounds's life when he returned to his office to surrender the keys to the department car he was driving. Not only is he worried that the internal affairs cops will find out that he has been using Pounds's name and badge (which he had stolen) whenever he needed to prove he was a cop, he knows that pretending to be Pounds while he was snooping around was what likely got the man killed.

Bosch eventually comes face to face with his primary suspect, Arno Conklin, now a resident in a full-care retirement facility. Bosch intends to accuse the frail man of his mother's murder, but is taken aback when Conklin recognizes his name. He even knows his first name is Hieronymus. Bosch is stunned when Conklin confesses that he had fallen in love with his mother and that they were planning to get married. This was to be his mother's escape from the life she was leading and marriage to an upstanding man like Conklin would help her regain custody of her son and rescue him from the youth shelter.

Conklin tells Bosch that the last time he saw his mother was when she went home to change her clothes for the drive to Las Vegas, where they planned to get married the next day. Instead, she ended up dead in an alley. He tells Bosch that Gordon Mittel, his campaign manager, vehemently opposed the marriage, arguing that if it ever got out that he married a prostitute, it would ruin his political career. It is Conklin's belief that Mittel was responsible for Marjorie Lowe's death.

As he walks to his car after talking with Conklin, Bosch is hit on the head with a tire iron and knocked unconscious. When he awakens, he finds himself lying on the floor of Gordon Mittel's mansion in the hills above Hollywood. He learns that Mittel had Pounds killed and Conklin tossed to his death out of a window in his room right after he interviewed him. Using the only weapon he has—a billiard ball he had taken from the pool table—he disables Mittel's henchman before he can kill him and then chases Mittel across the lawn and down the hillside. The two of them begin wrestling until Mittel slips and falls to his death in the hot tub of the house below.

Despite seeming to have connected all the dots in the case, Bosch doesn't much feel like celebrating. He is still experiencing headaches and vertigo from the concussion he received when he was attacked and feels guilty over the knowledge that two innocent people—Pounds and Conklin—are both dead as a result of his snooping. He also feels bad after learning that it was his mother's effort to regain custody of him by marrying a respectable man like Conklin that cost her life. Something else keeps nagging at him. As he thinks back to his final conversation with Mittel, he realizes that the man never actually confessed to the murder of his mother. He now recalls him saying only that he used her death to his advantage. When he compares Mittel's fingerprints with those found on the belt used to kill his mother, they don't match. If Marjorie Lowe wasn't murdered for political reasons, who else could have had a reason for killing her?

The answer comes thanks to Dr. Carmen Hinojos, the police psychiatrist he has been seeing since his suspension. He has never been able to look at the photographs of his dead mother, so he asks her if she would examine them. Perhaps it took a woman's eye to notice that the silver in the belt used to strangle her did not match the gold jewelry she was wearing. Nor did the dress she was wearing have any belt loops, suggesting to her that the belt might have belonged to the person who killed her. Bosch knows only one other person who also wore that belt— her mother's friend Meredith Roman, whom Bosch remembers helping him pick out that very belt to give to his mother as a birthday gift. A fingerprint match confirms that she was the killer. And the motive wasn't political; it was simple jealousy over the fact that Conklin chose Marjorie to rescue from a life of prostitution instead of her. In the end, it was nothing but "a cat fight between whores" (398) that ended his mother's life.

During his suspension, Bosch is required to meet three times each week with Dr. Hinojos, who will determine his fitness to return to work. Her probing questions reveal a much more intimate and sympathetic picture of Bosch than the one painted by Honey Chandler in *The Concrete Blonde*. These scenes are reminiscent of a similar strategy employed a few years later in *The Sopranos*, where Tony Soprano begins seeing a psychiatrist after suffering a panic attack. Over the course of that series, the viewer is also given an intimate look into the more vulnerable side of the tough gangster.

In their first session, Bosch is angry and uncooperative. He tells Dr. Hinojos that he considers their sessions to be "bullshit" and vows to himself that she'll have to pull every single word out of him. He's not mollified by her assurance that what he tells her will remain confidential and that all she is trying to do is to get him to take a closer look at himself in order to answer questions like "What are you doing? What are you about? Why do these problems happen to you?" (2). Her questions get under his skin because they hit close to home, but Hinojos reminds him that the more contentious he is, the longer he will be unable to return to his job.

Things begin to change in their second meeting. Bosch begins to admire the way she is able to cut him open and has to admit to himself that she was telling the truth when she promised she was there only to help him. As the sessions continue, we learn more about Bosch's relationship with his mother and how her death has profoundly affected him, from his feelings of abandonment when she was forced to surrender custody of him to his shame at having let her down for failing to look for her killer for the past thirty years. We also are given some loving memories he has, like sitting outside their apartment at night while listening to the music coming over the hill from the nearby Hollywood Bowl.

Bosch eventually feels enough trust in Dr. Hinojos that he even confides in her that he has been having dreams about a lone coyote he spotted near his home and shares his fears that it might be the last one still out there. She is able to explain to him what those dreams represent—that he identifies with the coyote and fears he too might be an endangered species, that there aren't many policemen like him still left. She also offers him some helpful advice: "The past is like a club and you can only hit yourself in the head with it so many times before there is serious and permanent damage," she warns him. "I think you're at your limit. For what it's worth, I think you are a good and clean and ultimately kind man. Don't do this to yourself. Don't ruin what you have, what you are with this kind of thinking" (404). Whether or not he follows her advice won't be answered until his next appearance.

The Poet (1996)

The Poet is Connelly's first standalone novel and in some ways his most autobiographical in that its protagonist, Jack McEvoy, is a newspaper reporter. The novel follows in the tradition of the great serial-killer novels perhaps best exemplified by Thomas Harris's *Red Dragon*, which Connelly once praised as "the most influential crime thriller in the last 40 years" (Connelly "Five"). However, it is the character of Francis Dolarhyde rather than Harris's more famous Hannibal Lecter that Connelly chooses as his favorite villain: "He remains in the shadow of Hannibal Lecter, but I find him more realistic and a reminder that these sorts of killers are more banal than genius. That makes them scarier" (Connelly "By").

Connelly distinguishes *The Poet* from the Bosch books in several significant ways: the main character is a journalist, not a cop; the majority of the settings—Denver, Chicago, Washington, Baltimore, Quantico, VA—are far from L.A.; for the first time, Connelly employs first-person narration, allowing us to see most of the events through the eyes of the main character. The novel also includes several chapters written in third-person narration that follow the activities of a serial killer, which allows Connelly to draw upon his own professional background: his very first murder story was about a notorious serial killer named Christopher Wilder. He also had several phone conversations with another killer, Jonathan Lundh, about whom he has said, "No person I have ever spoken to in my life was creepier" (*Crime* 13).

The novel begins with the death of Sean McEvoy, a Denver homicide cop who is found dead in his car of an apparent self-inflicted gunshot wound. Written on the car's fogged windshield is a final message: "Out of Space. Out of Time." McEvoy had become obsessed with the murder of a female college student whose body was found cut into two pieces in a local park. He had recently begun seeing a therapist to deal with the depression he began to experience over his failure to clear the case. It appears that he has become another in a long line of cops who reach their limit in having to deal with another dead body.

Jack McEvoy, a reporter for the *Rocky Mountain News*, is Sean McEvoy's twin brother. While Sean was dedicated to solving murders and seeing that the guilty party paid for his crime, Jack McEvoy is mainly concerned that the killing makes a good thirty-inch story. He's a disinterested outsider, as is clear from the opening words of the novel: "Death is my beat. I make my living from it." He likens his job to that of an undertaker: "somber and sympathetic about it when I'm with the bereaved, a skilled craftsman with it when I'm alone. I've always thought the secret of dealing with death was to keep it at arm's length. That's the rule. Don't let it breathe in your face" (3). Elsewhere he describes himself as "a tourist of the macabre" who can move from "murder to murder, horror to horror without blinking an eye" (133).

McEvoy has an enviable job at the newspaper in that he is free to roam the entire Rocky Mountain region looking for a good murder story. He decides to write about the death of his brother and gets the go-ahead from his editor for an article about the causal relationship between job stress and police suicides. He begins by searching for stories about police suicides in other newspapers around the country. He comes across one about the suicide of a Chicago homicide detective who, like his own brother, became depressed over his failure to solve a murder, this one of a twelve-year-old boy whose fingers were severed before he was killed.

Like his brother, this cop also shot himself in the head with his own gun and left an ambiguous suicide note: "Through the pale door." When the newspaper report mentions that the line is a quote from a poem in Edgar Allan Poe's famous story "The Fall of the House of Usher," McEvoy is stunned. He remembers seeing the name Rusher written down on the last page of his brother's chronology of the case: it was the name of a person who called him on the day he died. A search of Poe's works reveals that his brother's suicide note was also a quote from a Poe poem, "Dream-Life." This can't be a coincidence.

McEvoy's next stop is Washington, where he meets with members of the FBI's Behavioral Science Section (BSS). They conduct a computer search that identifies thirteen homicide detectives who had committed suicide within the past few years. (The majority of police suicides are of patrol cops.) Further digging reveals that six of these homicide detectives in different cities across the U.S. who appeared to have committed suicide all left behind quotes by Edgar Allan Poe. It now appears that their suicides were staged and all were victims of a serial killer they call the Poet. An all-out effort is launched by the FBI to catch him before he can kill more.

The officials at the FBI thank McEvoy for his efforts, but they don't want a reporter hanging around with them. But by threatening to publish a story about what he has already uncovered, which would compromise their search, McEvoy forces the FBI to agree to let him tag along as an observer. He is teamed up with an attractive agency profiler named Rachel Walling and the two of them head off to Denver to take a closer look into Sean McEvoy's death.

Connelly heightens the suspense by alternating the story of the search for the Poet with several chapters written in third-person that follow the activities of a man named William Gladden. The first seems innocent enough as it describes Gladden watching some young children riding on a carousel, but what do those references to Raiford (a notorious Florida prison), the closet where Gladden awaited visits by his Best Pal when he was a child, and the camera he carries with him mean? That becomes clear in his next appearance when he is arrested for taking photographs of naked children at the public bath.

In subsequent chapters, the picture becomes increasingly chilling. The photographs Gladden looks at on his laptop are described as "a macabre collection of the dead and the living" (117) and his mood switches from finding solace in what he calls his "little sacrifices" to "the self-loathing and disgust that always came" (118). And then we begin to witness his murders. He kills a motel housekeeper because he suspects she might have seen his pictures. After killing a former porn actress he has invited to his motel room, he continues to hide out there for several days while her body slowly decomposes, forcing him to constantly burn incense to hide the smell.

The FBI eventually zeroes in on Gladden as the Poet. They have determined that he is an ex-convict who had served time for molesting minors. He now supports himself by selling photographs of naked children to a network of pedophiles. They also know that the police confiscated his expensive camera when they questioned him about taking pictures of naked children, so he needs to buy a new one. They identify the store where he ordered a new one and plan to arrest him when he comes to pick it up. But it all goes haywire when he arrives disguised as a woman wearing the blonde wig and clothes of the woman whose body he has been living with. He surprises the FBI agent waiting for him by stabbing him in the neck. Then he grabs the agent's gun, which McEvoy tries to take away from him. During the struggle, the gun goes off, killing Gladden.

The Poet case appears to be solved, but McEvoy is puzzled when he remembers hearing Gladden mention that he killed his brother to save him from becoming someone like himself. He realizes that Gladden was referring to one of the young boys he killed, mistakenly assuming that was the brother McEvoy was talking about. Somebody else must have murdered Sean. There must be a second Poet, someone who followed in Gladden's footsteps and killed all six homicide detectives investigating the murders, and then used Gladden to cover his tracks. This second Poet is also a person with close knowledge of the FBI's investigations. McEvoy now suspects that Rachel Walling, the FBI agent he has fallen in love with, is the killer he's looking for.

Bob Backus, the head of the FBI task force searching for the Poet, asks McEvoy to meet him at an abandoned hillside house the FBI leases where he says he has set a surprise trap for Rachel. But the one who is trapped is McEvoy when Backus pulls a gun and admits that he, not Rachel, is the Poet. He forces McEvoy to swallow some codeine pills, immobilizing him the same way he did with his other victims. As he is about to kill him, Rachel, who had ignored Backus's order to go to Florida and had instead been following McEvoy, arrives with only moments to spare in time to save his life. A gunfight breaks out and she shoots Backus. The last time we see him he's tumbling down the hillside into the dark arroyo below. However, his body can't be found. It appears he has escaped, his whereabouts unknown.

Connelly didn't end the novel with the killer's escape simply to a set up a sequel, although he did end up writing one eight years later with *The Narrows*. Instead, he wanted to make a point that in the real world people get away with murder every day. "I was bothered by the contradiction of art not imitating life," he said. "All the crime novels seemed to end with the bad guy getting caught. In L.A., that happened about seventy percent of the time. This, and what was happening in the O. J. Simpson case, added up to me deciding to let the Poet slip away" (Anderson, *Triumph* 184).

Connelly has said that *The Poet* was the easiest of his novels to write because he was able to draw upon his own experience as a reporter. But he also acknowledged that he missed the enjoyment that comes with the challenge of figuring out how someone in a different profession like Bosch would handle a new case. Writing about his own profession did, however, give him an opportunity to include a number of observations about journalism. For example, the character of Michael Warren, a former reporter who quit to take a job with the FBI, illustrates one of the hazards of the reporter's job: burnout caused by the demands of the "always-on-deadline and always-need-to-produce life" (123). There are also examples that illustrate the negative opinion many in law enforcement have of reporters. When informed that the reason McEvoy is taking notes during an FBI meeting is to ensure he has the facts right, one agent scoffs, "That'll be the day one of them reports the facts" (184).

Even Jack McEvoy has become disillusioned about his job. To his cynical eyes, the real truth about journalism is that "there wasn't much that was altruistic about it anymore. It wasn't about public service and the people's right to know. It was about competition, kicking ass and taking names, what paper had the story and which one was left behind. And which one got the Pulitzer at the end of the year" (132). It's lucky that most people don't know what journalists' secret thoughts are, he says, or "we'd all be seen for the cunning, self-aggrandizing fools we are" (132).

In the end, McEvoy the reporter has every reason to be happy: a lucrative book deal; the sale of film rights to his story for a hefty fee; and appearances on *Nightline* and *Larry King Live*. But for McEvoy the person, it's a different story. He has to live with the fact that he destroyed his relationship with Rachel Walling by believing what her jealous ex-husband told him—that she was like the Painted Desert, beautiful on the outside but cold and desolate inside—rather than listening to his own heart.

He also has to wonder about his priorities. In return for being allowed to shadow the FBI he had agreed not to print anything about what he already knew about the Poet, with one exception: if another reporter broke the story, he would publish his, even if it compromised the FBI's search for the killer. He's stung by Walling's reaction—"If that's true, that you'd trade catching the guy who killed your brother for a story, then that makes me feel very sad for you"—for it reminds him of some lines from Poe he had read the previous night that he hasn't been able to forget: "I dwelt alone / In a world of moan / And my soul was a stagnant tide" (182).

Trunk Music (1997)

After a two-year absence we rejoin Bosch, whose life has begun to return to normal. His house, which had to be torn down because of earthquake damage, forcing him to live in a hotel for a year, has been rebuilt. And after a lengthy hiatus, including eight months on desk duty, he's happy to be back at his old job. He has a new boss, Lt. Grace Billets, an experienced administrator about whom Bosch has good feelings because "she wasn't always right and she was willing to admit it" (39). He also has new responsibilities after she has reorganized the homicide detectives into groups of three and appoints him head of one group. Along with regular partner Jerry Edgar he is joined by Kizmin Rider, a young Black female detective on the fast track up the departmental ladder.

He gets called to the Hollywood Hills where the body of a man has been found shot to death in the trunk of his Rolls-Royce. The victim is identified as Anthony Aliso, a small-time producer of cheap straight-to-video films. The murder gets Bosch's investigative juices flowing again and he realizes how much he has missed being on the job. Where *The Last Coyote* was an instruction manual on how to investigate a cold case, *Trunk Music* offers a detailed description of the steps taken in investigating a crime from the discovery of the body to the task of breaking the news to the dead man's wife.

Over the period of time between sundown and four a.m. we get to observe the meticulous process of investigation as crime scene technicians scour the site for clues that might help provide an initial understanding of how, where, and why the murder occurred. We learn that Aliso, who was shot twice in the back of the head, didn't appear to be the victim of a robbery (he was still wearing his Rolex watch). We also learn how a jacket dunked into a tank of water into which a Hard Evidence packet is dropped will emit cyanoacrylate fumes that attach to the amino acids and oils of fingerprints, making them visible enough to be photographed. This produces a fingerprint that will later play a key role in the case.

But what started out as a routine procedural heats up after Bosch heads to Las Vegas, where we learn Aliso had been on one of his frequent visits just before he returned home and was murdered. With the help of the local police there, he learns that Aliso was laundering money through his film production business for a Vegas crime boss named Joey Marks and that the IRS was about to audit his finances. The signs increasingly point to what the police call, when a guy is found dead in the trunk of his car after a mob hit, "trunk music."

While reviewing hours of videotapes of Aliso playing poker at the Mirage casino every night, Bosch is stunned to recognize a woman playing at the same table with him: it's Eleanor Wish, the former FBI agent he fell in love with five years earlier in *The Black Echo* and then sent to prison. He learns that she was released after serving three and a half years of her sentence and moved to Vegas where she now supports herself playing poker several nights a week. He has been unable to forget the woman who five years earlier had betrayed him and put his life in danger, but had also saved his life in the end. The fire that still smolders between them is quickly rekindled and they soon find themselves back in bed together.

Bosch's investigation in Vegas eventually zeroes in on Luke Goshen, manager of one of Joey Marks's strip clubs where Aliso was a regular. When he and the Vegas police enter Goshen's home to arrest him, Bosch finds a gun hidden behind the tank of the bathroom toilet. Goshen denies it's his, but when Bosch has it tested, it matches the murder weapon. And Goshen's fingerprints match the ones found on Aliso's jacket. Seems like a slam dunk, but then Eleanor Wish goes missing, which brings Bosch face to face with Joey Marks, who insists he had nothing to do with Aliso's murder. But he demands that Bosch release Goshen from custody; if he doesn't, he promises he will never see Eleanor Wish, whom he has kidnapped, alive again.

Bosch figures his only hope of solving this dilemma is to rescue Eleanor, which he manages to do by locating where she is being held captive and freeing her. He can now take Goshen to L.A. to face murder charges. But then he is summoned to a meeting with a trio of FBI agents from L.A., Las Vegas, and Chicago who drop a bombshell: Luke Goshen is an FBI agent who has been working undercover for eighteen months gathering crucial inside information about Marks's criminal activities. Bosch has compromised the entire operation. Even worse, he is accused of being the person who planted the gun to frame Goshen for Aliso's murder.

Who really did plant the gun in Goshen's bathroom? The obvious answer is Joey Marks, who must have discovered that Goshen was an undercover FBI agent and wanted him out of the picture. But Eleanor informs him that while she was a captive, she overheard a conversation during which Marks also wondered who planted the gun. Bosch is forced to conclude that the entire Vegas investigation was nothing but a big red herring, an elaborate misdirection orchestrated by the real killer or killers. Now what? It's back to the very beginning of the case and to the very first two people Bosch questioned: Ray Powers, the patrol officer who found Aliso's body, and Aliso's wife Victoria. Could there be a possible connection between the two of them?

After all the frantic back and forth travel between L.A. and Vegas, the action now switches to a tense scene in a small room when Bosch brings Powers in for questioning. One of them is an experienced interrogator, the other a cop who knows all the tricks Bosch will try to pull. It's like a championship fight, with each winning a round. Bosch has to figure out a way to convince Powers to talk before calling a lawyer, but Powers is smug enough to believe he can parry all of Bosch's punches. After four hours, Bosch leaves the room for a break, having gotten no admissions. Powers wins round one.

Round two begins with Bosch bringing some evidence into the room that his partners had just found during a search of Powers's house. He shows him a batch of photos taken by someone who was secretly shadowing Aliso in Vegas, proving a connection between the two men. And then he delivers the *coup de grâce*: he plays a tape of a conversation with Aliso's wife, who he says is in the next room, placing the blame for the killing on Powers. What Powers doesn't know is that what she said was actually some lines she spoke in one of her husband's movies Bosch had watched. This, of course, is completely illegal, but perhaps it can be excused because it solves a murder and exposes a crooked cop.

There are some noticeable changes in Bosch's behavior and mood in *Trunk Music*. He is less inclined to go it alone, regularly teaming up with his two partners. He even seeks approval from his new boss, with whom he has developed a positive working relationship. And he seems to have put all the emotional turmoil related to the search for his mother's killer in *The Last Coyote* behind him. Reuniting with Eleanor Wish is another emotionally stabilizing factor.

Their relationship, however, places him in a difficult situation. Deputy Chief Irving reminds him that if he wants to keep his job, he must abide by the department prohibition against keeping company with a convicted felon. Which will he choose? His job? Or Eleanor? Happily, he finds a way to keep both when he discovers a clause in the department policy that allows exceptions for family relationships through blood or marriage. The novel ends with Bosch enjoying a honeymoon in Hawaii with his new bride Eleanor Wish.

Blood Work (1998)

As a homicide detective, Harry Bosch is required to investigate whatever murder comes his way. Then he would try to find a personal reason that would ignite his passion. The protagonist of this novel, ex–FBI profiler Terry McCaleb, is different. A veteran of sixteen years with the FBI, many of them spent investigating serial-killer cases in L.A. including that of the Poet, he is now on disability retirement, living on a forty-two-foot fishing boat docked in a San Pedro marina. He was forced to retire when a virus triggered by the stress of his job weakened his heart. After waiting almost two years for a transplant, he's now in the second month of a lengthy period of recovery.

One day, a young woman named Graciela Rivers seeks him out on his boat and tries to persuade him to look for the killer of her sister Gloria Torres, a nurse who was gunned down during a robbery at the convenience store she stopped at after leaving work. Given his current medical condition, the last thing McCaleb feels able to do is investigative work, so he firmly declines. But then she tells him something that changes everything: "Your heart.... It was my sister's. She was the one who saved your life" (11). How can he refuse to find her killer?

He can't, but there are several hurdles in his way: his doctor has ordered him to rest quietly for months; the L.A. cops don't want a retired FBI agent, "a tin man amateur without a badge or his own heart" (244), snooping around their cases, second-guessing them; and he's not allowed to drive, so he's largely limited to being an armchair detective, restricted to doing unexciting desk work. When he needs to travel, Buddy Lockridge, his neighbor at the marina, has to drive him around.

The first half of the novel details the tedious process of searching for any small detail that might provide a clue to a solution. But McCaleb no longer has the full resources of the FBI at his disposal. Aside from some assistance from Jaye Winston, an L.A. County sheriff with whom he worked on a case several years earlier, he mainly has to rely on the help of friends. From a reporter at the *Los Angeles Times,* he obtains a list of all recent armed robberies in the area that fit the pattern of Gloria Torres's death. This reveals a similar shooting at an ATM that left a man dead. By poring over surveillance videos and crime scene photographs of both murders, he discovers a link between the two killings when he notices that a personal item was taken from each victim. He suggests to Winston that she request a search of DRUGFIRE, the FBI's computer program with a nationwide database of bullet profiles, which reveals that both victims, as well as a third victim he finds, were all shot with

2. The Novels 41

the same gun. All of this leads to a troubling conclusion: the shootings were not random. All three victims were targeted by the same killer. But why?

Thanks to Graciela Rivers, an ER nurse, and Bonnie Fox, his transplant surgeon, both of whom are able to gain access to BOPRA (the Blood and Organ Procurement and Request Agency), McCaleb learns that all three victims also had the same rare blood type he has, one found in less than 1 percent of the population. Gradually he begins to formulate a theory. Someone was looking for a person with that rare blood type in order to obtain an organ needed for a transplant. It took three killings before the third victim—Gloria Torres—made it to the hospital in time for her organs to be used.

At this point, the reasonable thing for McCaleb to do would be to alert the police, but since he was the one who received Gloria's heart, he would be at the top of the list of suspects who would have benefited by killing her. When the FBI later searches his boat and finds each of the personal items that were stolen from the victims, he realizes they were planted there by the killer to frame him. The action now heats up as he must race the clock to find the killer before he himself is arrested.

McCaleb concludes that the killer knows too much about him to be a stranger. He's shocked when it turns out that person is the serial killer known as the Code Killer he was tracking down when he was forced to retire from the FBI. Now the Code Killer, whose real name is Daniel Crimmins, has returned with a new purpose in mind: he killed all three victims until he was able to get the heart that would save McCaleb's life. He wanted McCaleb to live so he could be a witness to how clever he really is. As he put it in a note to him: "What I wanted was a place in your heart, Agent McCaleb. I wanted always to be with you. Cain and Abel, Kennedy and Oswald, darkness and light" (350). He calls Gloria Torres "my Valentine to you," and boasts, "You are mine forever, Agent McCaleb. Every breath you take belongs to me. Every beat of that stolen heart is the echo of my voice in your head. Always. Every day" (350).

Clint Eastwood had purchased film rights to the novel even before its final draft was completed. In his film, the identity of the killer was changed to a different character in the novel and Eastwood encouraged Connelly to do the same thing. Connelly declined, but he did heed Eastwood's suggestion that his ending needed higher stakes, which in its final published version it certainly has.

On a hunch, McCaleb, now driving himself, heads to Mexico in search of the deserted beach area where he suspects Crimmins has fled to, which is exactly what Crimmins hoped he would do. When McCaleb arrives, Crimmins is waiting for him. But there's a twist. He has kidnapped Graciela Rivers and Gloria's son Raymond and brought them to Mexico with him. They will perish if McCaleb dies. Luckily, he survives the shootout with Crimmins and after a frantic search eventually locates where Graciela and Raymond are imprisoned in a buried septic tank in time to save their lives.

McCaleb is a less complicated and consequently a less interesting character than Harry Bosch. The most interesting aspect is how he must deal with the physical and emotional aftereffects of his heart transplant. *Blood Work* is dedicated to Terry Hansen, who inspired the character of McCaleb. An engineer turned rare book dealer, Hansen met Connelly in 1992 at a book signing for his first novel, *The Black Echo*. A year later, he underwent a successful heart-transplant operation and shared his experiences with Connelly.

Like many transplant patients, McCaleb faces several challenges. One is medical as he has to constantly monitor his temperature, take thirty-four pills a day, and avoid any activity that might put stress on his new heart. There is also the disorienting sensation that "the man he had once been was gone now forever" (22). Sometimes when he looked at himself in the mirror, it felt like he was looking at a stranger. Like those who survived the plane crash Connelly wrote about in his Pulitzer-nominated newspaper story, he also suffers from survivor's guilt. Inside himself he carries not just a stranger's heart but also "the secret belief that he had been the wrong one saved. It should have been someone else" (174). His feelings of guilt are intensified even more after learning that he received the gift of life only because of the murder of an innocent person.

After Graciela and Gloria's young son Raymond, who is now in Graciela's care, started visiting McCaleb on his boat, Graciela and McCaleb begin a romantic relationship and he credits her with helping to bring him back to life after his near-brush with death. But that relationship is threatened when he learns that while Gloria's heart may have saved his life, he must now break Graciela's heart by confessing that he was the cause of her sister's death. This results in a pause in their relationship to give Graciela time to think about whether or not she wants to continue seeing him.

Although Bosch doesn't appear in the novel, McCaleb's profiling skills enable him to offer his professional opinion about what the demanding job of being a homicide detective really involves. He has worked with enough of them to conclude there wasn't a single one who didn't have a healthy ego: "It was an absolute job requirement. To do the job, you had to know in your heart that you were up to the task and that you were better, smarter, stronger, meaner, more skilled and more patient than your adversary. You had to flat-out know that you were going to win. And if you had any doubts about that, then you had to back off and work burglaries or take a patrol shift or do something else" (30). That pretty much sums up Harry Bosch.

Angels Flight (1999)

Angels Flight is Connelly's most ambitious and darkest novel to date. It features one of his most convoluted plots involving a pair of murders, one of a twelve-year-old blonde girl, the other a well-known Black attorney. He uses the investigations into both cases to address a number of serious issues including racial tensions that threaten to engulf the city in violence once again, bad policing methods, departmental politics, and pedophilia. In the end, everything comes together but in a hurried way that may leave only the police brass completely satisfied.

As the novel begins, Bosch is awakened in the middle of the night and told to report to Angels Flight, a 300-foot inclined railroad that carries passengers up and down Bunker Hill in downtown L.A., far from his normal jurisdiction. Two people have just been shot to death on the train's final run of the night: a Mexican woman named Catalina Perez and a well-dressed Black man named Howard Elias. This spells trouble for the police for Howard Elias is among the most famous Black lawyers in L.A., a media-savvy attorney with a successful record of winning over half of the one hundred suits he has brought against the LAPD and its patrol officers, detectives, even its chief of police. Among his mainly Black supporters he has earned a reputation as "a lone voice crying out against the abuses of a fascist and racist paramilitary organization known as the LAPD" (17). The police, on the other hand, despise him.

LAPD officials, who note that Elias's wallet and watch have been taken, hope this is a simple matter of robbery, for that will protect the department's reputation. Bosch, however, thinks otherwise. He notes that one of the bullets was fired at close range into his anus, suggesting a vindictive act by someone who hated him. He also finds evidence that the robbery was staged by the cops at the crime scene. It increasingly appears that the primary suspect is a cop, the last thing the department wants to hear, for news of Elias's murder will "blow through the city like the hottest Santa Ana wind, setting nerves on edge and possibly turning silent frustrations into loud and malevolent actions" (153).

There are several factors that make this an extremely difficult case for the LAPD. The Rodney King case and the O.J. Simpson trial have put the department under a microscope for its own crimes, including brutality against Blacks and planting evidence. It also turns out that in two days Elias was scheduled to represent an ex-convict named Michael Harris, who is suing fifteen members of the Robbery-Homicide Division on charges of planting evidence in the case of the kidnapping and murder of twelve-year-old Stacey Kincaid, the daughter of a multimillion-dollar car dealer. Harris also charges that the cops tried to force him to confess by placing a plastic bag over his head and shoving a pencil into his ear, puncturing his ear drum. Despite evidence linking him to the victim—a notebook with his fingerprints was found in her bedroom and her body was located two blocks from his apartment—he was acquitted on all charges. Now with the help of Elias, he wants the police to pay.

Bosch knows that every one of those fifteen cops had good reason for killing Elias and isn't happy that Deputy Chief Irving assigned him and his team to the case. As a person who insists, "I don't like politics.... I just like putting cases together" (118), he knows he's facing a political minefield created by higher-ups whose priority isn't the truth but protecting the department's reputation. His investigation is also hampered by a number of restrictions: Irving has placed several additional detectives under his command on this case; one is his nemesis John Chastain, the Internal Affairs investigator who has twice investigated him, and another is Carla Entrenkin, the department's new inspector general, a civilian watchdog with the authority to oversee all police investigations.

He must also deal with some personal challenges. He is struggling to quit smoking after who knows how many years and worries that since he always did his best analytical thinking while puffing on a cigarette, stopping might affect his ability to put the pieces of a case together again. And after only one year of marriage, which gave him a "feeling of contentment and peace that he had never experienced before" (71), his wife Eleanor decided that marriage wasn't for her and moved back to Las Vegas.

Midway through his investigation, Bosch takes a closer look at a series of anonymous notes Elias had received that suggest that Michael Harris may in fact be innocent in the murder of Stacey Kincaid. One of the notes contained the mysterious message: *dot the i in Humbert.* Bosch recognizes the reference to Vladimir Nabokov's *Lolita*, a novel about a man named Humbert Humbert who is sexually attracted to a fourteen-year-old girl. But that's as far as he can go. He may be an expert in interrogations and in sensing when someone is lying, but when it comes to computers, he's useless. Fortunately, Kiz Rider, the newest member of his team, is a computer whiz. She uses that note to track down a website for pedophiles, where they find graphic photos of young Stacey Kincaid being forced to engage in various sex acts with older men, one of them perhaps her own stepfather.

Presented with this information, Stacey's mother confesses that she recently found out what her husband had been doing to her daughter. When she confronted him, he admitted to accidentally killing Stacey when she threatened to make public what he and his friend had been doing to her. The mother also admits that she was the one who sent the anonymous notes to Elias in the hope that he would prove Harris's innocence by identifying her daughter's real killer. Connelly then hastily wraps up this subplot by having Stacey's mother commit suicide a few hours after she guns down her husband and his pedophile friend.

Guilt also plays an important role in the life of Frankie Sheehan, Bosch's former partner when he was a member of the Robbery-Homicide Division. A twenty-five-year veteran of the LAPD, Sheehan speaks for many of his fellow cops who are finding police work in the post O.J. world a difficult challenge. "Ever since the Juice, nothing is solid anymore. No evidence, no cop, nothing. You can take anything you want into a courtroom and there will still be somebody who can tear it to shreds, drop it on the floor and piss on it. Everybody questions everything. Even cops. Even partners" (215).

Sheehan is one of the fifteen cops about to go on trial for brutally assaulting Harris. Though he certainly would have a powerful motive for killing Elias, he assures his old partner that he didn't kill him, though he would shake the hand of any cop who did. But then he confesses that after seventy-two hours of questioning Harris, who wouldn't admit to killing Stacey Kincaid, he lost control. He was the one who put the plastic bag over his head in an effort to kill him. As tears streak down his face, he is forced to admit, "I became the very thing that I spent all these years hunting" (218).

Things then take a dramatic turn when Sheehan is arrested for Elias's murder after it is learned that he had once publicly threatened to kill him. Bosch believed Sheehan when he denied killing Elias, but the angry public is clamoring for the arrest of a white cop and Sheehan fits the bill as a sacrificial lamb. He also is forced to admit that by proving that Harris wasn't Stacey's killer, it only made Sheehan feel even worse about his attack on him. Bosch later finds Sheehan dead of a gunshot wound to the head, an obvious suicide victim. Now he must carry the added guilt of being responsible for his death. "I knocked down the one thing he believed in all these months, the one thing that kept him safe. I told him we had cleared Michael Harris. I told him he was wrong about Harris and that we could prove it. I didn't think about what it would do to him" (311).

Even though he later learns that the bullet from the gun that Sheehan used to kill himself matched the bullets that killed Elias, Bosch is still bothered. So he begins looking for what he calls a boomerang, an overlooked detail that would change his interpretation of everything and send it in a new direction. What he finds jolts him: the high-level department snitch, the person who killed Elias, who faked the bullet evidence that tied Sheehan to Elias's murder, and who killed Sheehan and made it look like a suicide, is none other than Bosch's nemesis John Chastain. He killed Elias because he feared he was going to expose him in the upcoming trial. The man whose mission was weeding out bad cops has turned into the very monster he was supposed to root out.

Earlier in the novel, Bosch had complained about the decision to replace unmarked police cars with ones painted black and white, clearly identifying them as cop cars. A scam designed to convince the public that there were more police cars patrolling the streets, all it did was make those cars easy targets, especially now when the anti-police anger is boiling up over Elias's murder. Bosch gets firsthand experience of this anger when a sniper's bullet crashes through the back window of his car as it speeds along the freeway. A second attack is even worse, for as he is bringing Chastain into the station, a chunk of concrete is tossed into his car, followed by a firebomb. He manages to speed to safety, but somehow a large group of rioters had managed to drag Chastain from the car and beat him to death in the street. In an ironic ending, the man who provoked the riots by killing Elias is now being used as the one who ends the riots before they get out of hand by being hailed as a martyr who gave his life in the line of duty.

While the investigations into the killers of Stacey Kincaid and Howard Elias are handled with Connelly's usual skill in maximizing suspense with unexpected twists, there is a hurried quality to the way each is resolved. With the deaths of the two murderers and the department's coverup of the truth, we are denied satisfaction in seeing the holier-than-thou Chastain publicly exposed to his fellow officers as being a worse cop than any of those he investigated. Thanks to Sam Kincaid's powerful father, who knows how to pull the right strings, the truth about what his son did will never be revealed and Michael Harris's innocence will never be affirmed. And though we learn that the Harris trial will begin as scheduled, we are left in doubt as to whether the department will be held accountable for the brutal attack on Harris.

The effects of racism on the Black community and the role the LAPD have played in fueling widespread distrust and anger over some of its practices is a central focus of the novel. Connelly also pays attention to how racism affects even Harry Bosch. Unlike many of his fellow cops, he's no racist. He works comfortably with his two Black partners and cringes when they are subjected to racist comments. But a conversation Bosch has with the department's new civilian watchdog Carla Entrenkin highlights how individuals with different perspectives can view people and events differently. After watching TV coverage of a fire in South L.A., Bosch accuses the media of overreacting. People will see that one fire, he says, and their anger will grow and the result will be a manufactured riot.

Entrenkin sees things differently. "Civil unrest occurs when the feelings of overwhelming powerlessness hit critical mass," she reminds Bosch. "It has nothing to do with television. It has to do with society not addressing the essential needs of overlooked people" (187). In a similar manner, from Bosch's perspective Elias is nothing but "a suckerfish—making his life off bullshit cases against cops just trying to do their jobs" (170). Entrenkin points out that to people with no money and no power, Elias was a "symbol of hope for a day when things will be equal, when their voice will be heard. Of a day when they need not fear the police officers in their community" (187). Bosch nods. And then he replies, "I understand."

But he still can't understand the looting. He recalls a photo of a man in the 1992 riots leading his young child out of a store with each of them carrying a ThighMaster. "They saw it on TV and so they thought it was valuable," he says (188). Entrenkin once again sees it differently. "It didn't matter what they took," she explains. "They were acting out frustration.... The important thing was that they took something, that in some way they made a statement. They had no use for those things but by taking them they were showing The Man" (190).

Shortly afterwards, Bosch has a conversation with his Black partner Jerry Edgar about Harris that further illuminates the implications of the previous conversation. When Edgar says that like Michael Harris, he too would trade three days in an interview room and a pencil in his ear to be a millionaire, Bosch asks if he believes Harris's story. When he says he does, Bosch has to ask himself how the privilege of his white perspective could have blinded him to such a degree that he never considered that the torturing of a Black suspect like Harris could be true. He is forced to acknowledge that Edgar's own experience of racism gave him a perspective on the situation that he lacked and "an edge he could never have" (238).

Poor Eleanor Wish. In this novel she is less a character than an impediment that needs to be removed. Connelly has described Bosch as the kind of protagonist who would always be faced with conflict, both external and internal. He knew that giving him a life of domestic bliss while he's out trying to solve murders just wouldn't work. "If he's fulfilled by life," he said, "he's not going to be as interesting" (McDermott). So after throwing Bosch a bone for putting up with him by allowing him to get married at the end of *Trunk Music*, the first thing he does in *Angels Flight* is to prepare him for her departure.

In the end, Bosch is forced to accept the fact that the truths he exposed about the two killers will be buried. He'll have to live with the heartbreak over the departure of his wife and the murder of his old friend and former partner. If he has any consolation, it's that because Irving knows that Bosch knows about the cover-up, he will be allowed to keep his job in return for his silence. And the fortune he sees printed in the book of matches he uses to light his first cigarette in the book—"Happy is the man who finds refuge in himself" (391)—offers him a glimmer of hope.

A Darkness More Than Night (2001)

The title of this novel was inspired by Raymond Chandler, who once wrote that in the pulp detective stories of the '30s and '40s, "the streets were dark with something more than night" ("Introduction" 1016). Darkness permeates the novel, which is Connelly's fullest investigation to date of what darkness means to a homicide detective like Bosch, and a warning that "you don't go into the darkness without the darkness going into you" (415). It's also the first Bosch novel that brings characters from Connelly's previous standalone novels—Terry McCaleb from *Blood Work* and Jack McEvoy from *The Poet*—into it, thus expanding the boundaries of the Bosch universe.

In the three years since he was introduced in *Blood Work*, FBI profiler Terry McCaleb has relocated to Catalina Island with his wife Graciela Rivers, stepson Raymond, and their four-month-old baby daughter he named Cielo Azul. He's now in the charter-fishing business with marina neighbor Buddy Lockridge, though he has to conceal his ownership, for if he earns any income, he'll lose his eligibility for the state medical assistance that pays for the fifty-four expensive pills he now must take each day to ward off rejection of his transplanted heart.

One day Jaye Winston, the L.A. County deputy sheriff he worked with in *Blood Work*, comes to him with another request for help in a murder case. A man named Edward Gunn was found dead in his apartment, a plastic mop pail over his head. He had been found in a reverse fetal position, with a length of baling wire tied behind his back between his ankles and his neck. Once his muscles became too fatigued to keep slack in the wire, it tightened and strangled him to death. Written inside the tape covering his mouth was a phrase in medieval Latin that translates to "Beware, Beware, God Sees," suggesting a possible religious motive for the murder.

Meanwhile, there is a second narrative in the novel, this one featuring Harry Bosch. He is testifying in a sensational murder trial against David Storey, a famous Hollywood director whose previous films were all box office hits. He's charged with the strangulation murder of a young actress named Judy Krementz, who was found dead in her bed at home. His defense is that after having consensual sex in his home, he drove her to her place, where she later died during an episode of autoerotic asphyxiation that went terribly wrong.

Edward Gunn turns out to be the link between the two narratives. He was the suspect in *The Last Coyote* that Bosch brought in for questioning in the murder of a prostitute six years earlier. Readers of that novel might remember that what followed was the incident that resulted in Bosch's suspension. While he had stepped out of the interrogation room, Lt. Pounds, his boss at the time, saw Gunn sitting alone and took it upon himself to read him his Miranda rights. When Bosch returned, Gunn clammed up, refusing to answer any questions. Bosch became so incensed at Pounds that he shoved him through his office window.

Gunn was eventually released and never charged with murder. Since then Bosch has had a standing request with the night officer on duty to be called whenever Gunn was arrested for drunkenness. It's his hope that Gunn might say something that would incriminate him in the murder. It turns out he was one of the last people to see Gunn alive when he visited him in jail after his most recent arrest. Shortly after he was released on bail, he was murdered.

As Terry McCaleb examines the videotape of the murder scene, he notices a two-foot-high, hand-painted plastic statue of an owl perched on a cabinet looking down upon the murder scene. Could the owl, like the quote on the tape, also have a religious meaning? McCaleb pays a visit to the J. Paul Getty Museum where he is treated to an informative lecture by an art expert on owls in the paintings of Hieronymus Bosch. As he views reproductions of several of Bosch's famous paintings, he notices other significant details: the phrase "Beware, Beware, God Sees" appears in Bosch's *The Garden of Earthly Delights*; a nude man in *The Last Judgment* is depicted with his arms and legs bound behind his back the same way Dunn's were; in *The Stone Operation*, a group of men are depicted removing a stone from the head of a man in the belief that this was a way to remove stupidity and deceit from one suffering from the maladies. The location of the wound is precisely where Gunn was shot in his head.

McCaleb is forced to the unsettling conclusion that there is a connection between Hieronymus Bosch the detective and the murder of Dunn. In McCaleb's experience, homicide detectives fall into two categories: those who see their job as a craft or skill and those who see it as a mission in life. The latter he classified as avenging angels: "It had been his experience that these cops/angels were the best investigators he ever worked with. He also came to believe that they traveled closest to that unseen edge beneath which lies the abyss" (124). Has Bosch become one of those angels who stepped too close to that edge and fell over?

At this point, the appearance of a third non-series character, Jack McEvoy, the *Rocky Mountain News* reporter first introduced in *The Poet*, complicates things for Bosch even more. Now living in L.A, he's covering the trial for the *New Times*, an alternative weekly. Someone had leaked to him McCaleb's suspicion that Bosch was Dunn's killer and he's preparing to write a story about it. If that story appears, Bosch's testimony in the Storey trial will be totally discredited and another killer will walk away free. Bosch must now find the killer in order to prove his own innocence.

McCaleb arrives unannounced at Bosch's home one night, ostensibly to ask him some questions about the Gunn case, but what he really wants to do is to see if he can gain an insight into Bosch's thinking about the murder that might confirm his suspicion that he has crossed over and become a killer. As the two begin talking and drinking beer, McCaleb shows Bosch a photograph of his wife and new daughter and tells Bosch that he found what was missing in his life when he saw the hand of God in his daughter's eyes. He advises Bosch not to give up if he hasn't yet found what might be missing in his life.

Then he asks Bosch if he hates having to "ride down into the plague every morning," to which Bosch replies, "Not as long as I get a shot at the carriers every now and then" (194). What about the ones like Gunn who walk away, McCaleb asks. "Nobody walks away," says Bosch. "Sure we might not get every one of them, but I believe in the circle. The big wheel. What goes around comes around. Eventually. I might not see the hand of God too often like you do but I do believe in that" (194). When McCaleb spots the reproduction of Bosch's *Garden of Earthly Delights* hanging on the wall as he's leaving, he becomes even more convinced than ever that it was Bosch who set that big wheel spinning in order to get justice himself.

Bosch later visits McCaleb on his boat to ask him why he would suspect someone he has known and worked with for a dozen years.

People change, McCaleb replies. "Any one of us is capable of anything, given the right circumstances, the right pressures, the right motives, the right moment" (290). Remembering what McCaleb had told him about finding the hand of God in his daughter's eyes, Bosch insists that even in the total darkness in the tunnels in Vietnam, he was always able to find enough light to see his way to safety. He and his buddies called it "lost light. It was lost but we found it" (291). Some people may be able to find God in a new baby's eyes and in a new heart, but others like him "find their salvation in truth, in justice, in that which is righteous" (295). He tries to convince McCaleb that he has overlooked some important detail and urges him to go back and find it in order to clear him. If he doesn't, he tells him he'll be allowing the real monster to go free and that will haunt him the rest of his life.

Bosch convinces McCaleb to take a second look. Even at the risk of endangering his own marriage, McCaleb assumes the role of a white knight in pursuit of the truth. He comes to the conclusion that it wasn't Bosch who had gone over to the dark side; it was a former LAPD colleague of his named Rudy Tafero. After leaving the department, Tafero became a bail bondsman and private eye who ended up working for David Storey. He followed an elaborate plan cooked up by Storey to kill Dunn in such a way as to create a link to Bosch. Then in the middle of the trial, the link could be leaked, destroying Bosch's credibility and securing Storey's acquittal.

Bosch then returns the favor by rescuing McCaleb after Tafero had followed him to his boat and trussed him up the same way he did Dunn. As McCaleb's leg muscles become increasingly fatigued and he is about to die of strangulation, Bosch arrives in time to save him. Then he extracts a confession from Tafero in Dunn's murder and obtains evidence from him that forces Storey to confess not only to the murder of Judy Krementz but also to that of a second woman Bosch suspected him of killing. Everything is neatly tied up.

But Connelly always has something up his sleeve to add one final twist to his story. McCaleb makes a final visit to Bosch's house to tell him he no longer wants to be friends with him. He accuses Bosch of being the real mastermind behind the murder of Edward Gunn. Rudy Tafero was a friend of Harvey Pounds and held Bosch responsible for his death. Bosch used Tafero's animosity towards him and the knowledge that he was now working for Storey to set him up to kill Dunn. He was the one who phoned Tafero to tell him that Dunn was in the drunk tank and then made no attempt to stop him from killing Dunn when he got out. Bosch denies making the phone call, but as he gazes down into the darkness below his deck, he makes this admission: "We do what we have to do.... Sometimes there is no choice, only necessity. You see things happening and you know they're wrong but somehow they're also right" (411). After a pause, he adds, "Three people—three monsters—are gone."

Employing a dual narrative allows Connelly to use McCaleb and other characters in the novel to offer their own perspectives on Bosch. The main one comes from McCaleb, who first worked with Bosch a decade earlier on what became known as the Little Girl Lost case. It involved the murder of a beautiful young girl, probably Mexican, whose identity they never learned. Bosch nicknamed her Cielo Azul, blue sky, which was the name McCaleb gave to his own daughter. (Connelly later expanded the incident into a short story titled "Cielo Azul," published in 2005.)

McCaleb remembers Bosch as being "abrasive and secretive at times, but still a good cop with excellent investigative skills, intuition and instincts" (37). On their first face-to-face meeting since then, he notes that Bosch still has the mustache and the eyes, which he says were always moving and observing. He also observes that "there had always been a spring-loaded feel to Bosch. He felt as though at any moment or for any reason Bosch could put the needle into the red zone" (79). McCaleb's neighbor Buddy Lockridge has a similar impression based on seeing Bosch testifying on *Court TV*: "He kind of looks like he's wound a little too tight" (163).

But we get a different impression from Jaye Winston, who recalls working on a case with Bosch four years earlier. They were on the trail of a killer who had kidnapped two young girls and kept them alive for several days before killing them. On a hunch, she and Bosch paid a visit to the main suspect's home, where as soon as Bosch spotted a baby monitor, he knew he had their killer. While Winston handled the arrest, Bosch never stopped talking with the girl on the other end of the baby monitor, comforting her until she could be found in an unplugged freezer in the garage. When Winston asked if he had kids because he talked to the frightened young girl as if she were one of his own, he said no, "I just know what it's like to be alone and in the dark" (162).

Darkness is almost a character in the novel. The title phrase is first used by the art expert who describes the paintings of Hieronymus Bosch as being infused with "a darkness more than night" (97). The profile McCaleb prepares on Bosch ends with the same phrase, this time with the word "darkness" underlined. The novel also contains lines like "it was time to go back to the darkness" (23) and "the darkness moved in and took him" (376). Even lyrics from the songs heard playing on a jukebox in a bar—Bruce Springsteen's "There's a darkness on the edge of town" (359); Van Morrison's "The wild night is coming" (370); John Fogerty's "There's a bad moon on the rise" (371)—hammer home the theme.

But all is not dark, as the final picture of the two men emphasizes. Following his conversation with McCaleb during which he acknowledged his role in Dunn's death, Bosch whispers to himself, "What did I do?... What did I do?" (413). Back home, he looks out his window and sees the lights of Hollywood glimmering below. He recognizes that the world out there was a place where "the earth could open beneath you and suck you into the blackness," but he also knows that his city was a city "of the second chance," a place to begin again. He then reaches his hands under the faucet and brings them to his face. "The water was cold and bracing, as he thought any baptism, the start of any second chance, should be" (414).

The novel closes with McCaleb about to set out on his boat in the dark of night to his home and family on Catalina Island. Before leaving, he phones his wife to tell her not to worry—"I'll be all right. I can see in the dark" (417)—and reminds her to put the deck light on so he can look for it when he gets close. Then he heads out to sea with the moon above laying down "a shimmering path of liquid silver for him to follow home" (418).

Novelist Joyce Carol Oates praised *A Darkness More Than Night* for being not so much concerned with the pursuit of evil "as it is about the cultivation of conscience: How can one live, amid evil, a decent life? How, policing violence, can one avoid committing violence?" (89). Grappling with questions like these is what gives Connelly's novels a depth and resonance lacking in most crime thrillers.

City of Bones (2002)

Connelly has set very high standards for himself when it comes to constructing complicated yet fast-moving plots so it shouldn't come as a surprise that in rare instances his plots sometimes let him down. *City of Bones* is a case in point. It's a watershed novel that focuses on a critical juncture in the life of Harry Bosch, but despite a promising beginning, some plot missteps and unconvincing actions threaten to draw attention away from the serious human drama that is at the heart of the novel.

In *A Darkness More Than Night*, we learned that Bosch had finally gotten too close to the darkness and had stepped over the line. The novel ended with his hope for a second chance to redeem himself. In *City of*

Bones, he is now a "plus-twenty-five," meaning that after more than twenty-five years of service in the LAPD, he is eligible to retire at the top of the pension scale. Working any longer won't raise his pension benefits. But then he gets a case that fires him up and offers the possibility of redemption.

A dog out for a run in the woods in Laurel Canyon returns home with a bone in its mouth. The dog's owner, a doctor, believes the bone is human. Bosch is asked to check it out. At the scene, he climbs up a hill to the spot where the dog dug up the bone and finds several more bones, including a human skull. What he learns next is truly sickening.

A forensic anthropologist determines that the body is that of a twelve-year-old boy who has been dead for some twenty years. During his short life the boy, later identified as Arthur Delacroix, was subject to chronic abuse. Forty-four different locations of trauma, including two dozen fractures, are found on the boy's body, some dating back to when he was only a few weeks old. After documenting all the subperiosteal lesions and latitudinal fractures, the anthropologist sums up the boy's plight in blunt terms: "Somebody beat the shit out of this boy on a regular basis" (57). After hearing this, Bosch excuses himself and goes to the bathroom where he is almost physically ill. As he bends over the sink to splash cold water on his face, he "thought about baptisms and second chances. Of renewal" (55), which echoes those thoughts he had at the end of *A Darkness More Than Night*. Then he vows to himself, "I'm going to get this guy."

Bosch and partner Jerry Edgar begin looking at residents in the neighborhood for possible suspects. They quickly find one in Nicholas Trent, a film set decorator whose home is located less than a hundred yards from the hillside where the boy's body was found. Bosch has learned that some thirty-five years earlier, Trent was charged with molesting a nine-year-old boy. Despite the fact that Arthur was not sexually molested and that Trent did not move into the neighborhood until four years after his murder, he's a likely suspect. Trent vehemently denies killing the boy and insists he has buried his past. He was punished for his crime and has been a model citizen ever since. "If I was a drug dealer or a bank robber, my debt would be cleared and you people would leave me alone. But because I touched a boy almost forty years ago I am guilty for life" (99). When reporters get the story about Trent's past and learn that Bosch had questioned him about the murder, he becomes front-page news. An innocent victim of the bones' discovery, he becomes so distraught over the revelations about his past that he commits suicide.

Then there's the bizarre death of Julia Brasher. A rookie patrol officer, she first met Bosch the night he was called to the scene where the dog found the bone and asked to borrow her flashlight to investigate. A romantic involvement soon developed. The two seem ideally matched. She's thirty-four, an ex-lawyer who worked at her father's firm before quitting to travel the world seeking adventures for four years before returning home and joining the LAPD. They share the same taste in music and own some of the same jazz CDs. She even explored one of the tunnels in Vietnam where Bosch served as a tunnel rat. There is one problem: she's a rookie and he is at a supervisory level, meaning their relationship violates department policy.

She is called in as backup to Bosch, who wants to question a man named Johnny Stokes, a schoolmate of Arthur Delacroix, about what he knows about what happened to his friend. As Bosch approaches, Stokes bolts, but is then run down by Brasher, who has him up against a wall, his arms and legs spread. From a distance, Bosch sees her take a step back from Stokes and look to both sides. Then he hears a gunshot. At first it appears that while Brasher was reaching for her gun, it fired accidentally. The bullet hit a bone in her shoulder, then ricocheted and pierced her heart, killing her. But as he mulls over what he just witnessed, Bosch concludes that Brasher shot herself in the shoulder intentionally so she could then have a reason to shoot Stokes, in the hope of earning recognition for heroism. Tragically, she died needlessly, for Bosch believes that Stokes had nothing to do with Arthur's murder.

The combination of Trent's suicide after being questioned by Bosch and Brasher's senseless death, not to mention Bosch's romantic involvement with her, prompts a meeting with Deputy Chief Irving. Irving has finally run out of patience with someone he calls a "shit magnet" and advises Bosch that he needs to think about retirement, and real soon. Not surprisingly, Bosch vows to continue his mission to find Arthur Delacroix's killer.

At this point, *City of Bones* begins to resemble a Lew Archer novel by Ross Macdonald. Macdonald, whose recurring theme was the influence of the past on the present, is another of the L.A. crime writers Connelly has cited as a major influence on him. In a typical Archer novel, a family secret buried deep in the past is exposed, leading to dire consequences for those responsible for past transgressions. Like Archer, Bosch now looks to Arthur's family for answers in his search for the truth about the boy's murder.

Bosch learns that Arthur disappeared after leaving home one day in 1980. His mother had abandoned the family when he was only two years old, leaving his father Samuel to raise the family on his own. It becomes clear to Bosch that a history of parental abuse finally led to the boy's death. When Samuel Delacroix is confronted, he readily confesses to the murder. But the man's eagerness to confess bothers Bosch. After he finds some naked photographs of Delacroix's daughter Sheila during a search of his trailer, he turns to her for answers to what was happening in the family home.

After Bosch shows Sheila the photographs of her being sexually abused by her father, she confesses that she, not her father, was the one who physically abused her brother. She was taking her anger out at being sexually abused by physically abusing her brother. Her father confessed to Arthur's murder because he thought she had killed him because of what he was doing to her and hoped that by taking blame for the murder he could atone for his sexual abuse. Sheila denies killing her brother but does plead guilty to not trying to stop him from running away from home the afternoon he was murdered. But if neither of them killed Arthur, who did? It turns out Bosch already had the murderer in custody—Johnny Stokes, Arthur's friend, who killed him with the skateboard he was trying to steal from him.

It isn't only Arthur's bones that give the novel its title. Dr. Golliher, the forensic anthropologist, is also examining another bone that was unearthed two days earlier in the La Brea Tar Pits. It's the skull of a woman who was killed by a fatal blow to the head some 9000 years earlier. The wound matches the one on the skull of another woman from the same period that was found in there in 1914, making her the earliest known murder victim in what is now L.A. All these buried bones emphasize the theme that the past is never entirely buried. Those ancient bones also remind Bosch about the reality of what he does: "True evil could never be taken out of the world. At best he was wading into the dark waters of the abyss with two leaking buckets in his hands" (181).

Bosch has never been what one would call a happy-go-lucky fellow, but he's even more downbeat than usual in this novel. There are plenty of good reasons for this: he knows that the case of a child's murder hollows you out and scars you for it leaves you "knowing the world was full of lost light" (24); an innocent man killed himself after he singled him out as a suspect on flimsy evidence; his latest girlfriend died senselessly; he's in hot water with his bosses; he was mistaken when he dismissed Stokes as having nothing to do with Arthur's murder; his longtime partner Jerry Edgar is mad at him for repeatedly keeping him out of the loop throughout the investigation; and at the end of the case he is ordered to report to the LAPD Office of Operations where he is convinced he'll be demoted.

But in a surprising twist, Bosch finds out he isn't being demoted;

he's being promoted to the Robbery-Homicide Division, a position he was demoted from ten years earlier. He's happy to learn that he will be joining Kiz Rider, a former member of his team who was promoted to RHD a year earlier. But why would Irving promote Bosch when just three days earlier he had all but ordered him to resign? The explanation Irving gives—that this would allow him to monitor Bosch more closely—doesn't entirely ring true.

The novel ends abruptly. Despite feeling elated about the promotion, when Bosch goes to his office late one night to clear out his desk before moving to his new job, he stops to think that he "had always known that he would be lost without his job and his badge and his mission. In that moment he came to realize that he could be just as lost with it all. In fact, he could be lost *because* of it" (392). Then he places his badge, gun, and ID card into his desk drawer, locks it, and puts the key on Lt. Billets's desk. He has just quit his job. And then he goes outside to wait in the rain for a cab to take him home.

While *City of Bones* focuses on Bosch's search for redemption, he's not the only one in the book trying to do that. After Nicholas Trent's suicide, Bosch finds a box filled with photos and cancelled checks that reveal that for many years he had been sending small monthly checks to charitable agencies around the world that fed and clothed children in an attempt to amend for his past behavior with a young boy. However, once this lone misdeed became public, it seemed to cancel out all his efforts at redemption and he killed himself. Samuel Delacroix jumped at the chance to save his daughter, whom he assumed had killed his son, by falsely confessing to his murder. But that turned out to be a meaningless gesture when it became known that she wasn't his killer after all.

After Arthur's funeral, Bosch gives Nicholas Trent's box of photos and charity envelopes to Arthur's mother, telling her that "someone once told me that life was the pursuit of one thing. Redemption. The search for redemption" (389). Perhaps she will find what seems to have eluded Bosch, for while he solves Arthur's murder and ends up getting promoted for his efforts, his impulsive decision to quit his job, the one thing that gave his life meaning, undermines any sense that he feels redeemed.

It's important to Connelly that his novels reflect what's happening in the real world at the time of their composition. *City of Bones* was written at an important point in his personal life, i.e., his decision to leave L.A. and move back to Florida. This seemed to him to be a good time to make a similar break in Bosch's life, which led to his decision to have him resign from the LAPD and make a new start the way his creator was doing.

Connelly was also profoundly shaken by the terrorist attack on the World Trade Center in New York on September 11, 2001. In an extended interview with Christopher Davies about the effect of 9/11 on him and his work, Connelly said: "It changed me and therefore it had to change the characters I was writing about. And it came down to relevancy. People, no matter what they do in life, want to feel that what they do matters. But when 3,000 innocent people are wiped out in a matter of minutes and on live television it really leaves you with the sense of what does it matter. I felt that and the way I worked through it was to put it into my characters, especially Harry Bosch" (161).

Although he had already completed the final draft of the novel shortly before September 11, he was able to include several revisions that refer to the event. The first comes in a conversation Bosch has with Dr. Golliher, the forensic anthropologist who has been examining the bones of Arthur Delacroix. Having been a consultant at other places where innocent people were killed—like Kosovo and more recently the World Trade Center—he agrees that such suffering is hard to comprehend. Maybe Arthur was better off leaving the world, he says, "that is, if you believe in a God and a better place than this" (55).

"And what if you don't?" Bosch asks. "Well, you see, this is why you must believe," Golliher insists. "If this boy did not go from this world to a higher plane, to something better, then ... then I think we're all lost" (56). Bosch has no formal religion to sustain him, just what some cops call the "blue religion." It allows him to cling to the belief that Arthur's bones came out of the ground "for me to find, and for me to do something about. And that's what holds me together and keeps me going" (185).

The subject comes up again during a conversation with Julia Brasher. The events on September 11 have obviously been on Bosch's mind and it has begun to affect his thinking about the case he's working on: "Suicide terrorists hit New York and three thousand people are dead before they've finished their first cup of coffee. What does one little set of bones buried in the past matter?" (214). "Don't go existential on me, Harry," Brasher replies. "The important thing is that it means something to you. And if it means something to you, then it is important to do what you can. No matter what happens in the world, there will always be the need for heroes" (214). "Maybe," is the only response he can muster. And then at the end of the novel he quits his job.

Early in the novel Bosch made the statement that "in every murder is the tale of a city" (35). Connelly's novels usually feature crimes that are cruel and deliberate acts of evil. But what does the murder of a twelve-year-old boy by a thirteen-year-old schoolmate over a skateboard tell us about Los Angeles? Arthur Delacroix's senseless murder seems to emphasize a point once made by Raymond Chandler: "It is not funny that a man should be killed, but it is sometimes funny that he should be killed for so little" ("Simple" 991).

Lost Light (2003)

Lost Light is one Connelly's most political novels. It's also filled with several dramatic new turns in Bosch's life. It's been eight months since his abrupt decision to retire from the LAPD and at age fifty-two he's torn between relief and regret over his decision: "For almost thirty years of my life I had been part of an organization that promoted isolation from the outside world, that cultivated the 'us versus them' ethic. I had been part of the cult of the blue religion and now I was out, excommunicated, part of the outside world. I had no badge. I was no longer part of us. I was one of them" (22).

He's made a few changes in his new life. He bought a used Mercedes Benz ML 55 SUV and has begun taking saxophone lessons from a musician named Quentin McKinzie whom he first saw play on a Bob Hope tour in Vietnam in 1969. (An expanded account of that performance and how he came into possession of McKinzie's sax many years later can be found in the short story "Christmas Even," published in 2004.) He also obtained his private investigator's license from the state. But he's restless and still feels a powerful sense of mission: "My job in this world, badge or no badge, was to stand for the dead" (23). A phone call from a former colleague provides him with the mission he's been looking for.

Four years earlier, Bosch was investigating the murder of Angella Benton, a young production assistant at Eidolon Productions who was gunned down in her apartment building. Bosch always looks for a personal reason to fire him up. This time it's the dead woman's hands, which looked to him like the hands in a Renaissance painting, "reaching heavenward for forgiveness…. I could not forget her hands. I believed they were reaching to me. I still do" (14).

Unfortunately for him, the case was reassigned to a pair of detectives in the Robbery-Homicide Division, Jack Dorsey and Lawton Cross. But before they could solve her murder, both were shot during an armed robbery at the bar where they had stopped for lunch. Dorsey was killed and Cross was paralyzed by a bullet to the neck. Now, four years later, a phone call from Cross about the cold case gives Bosch a reason to resume his search for Angella Benton's killer.

During his initial investigation into her murder, Bosch had visited the production company where the woman worked. At the time a movie was being filmed there about a burglar who steals a suitcase containing two million dollars, not knowing it belongs to the mob. The director had insisted that he needed the full two million in real money to ensure the scene's realism. As the armored truck arrived with the cash a bank agreed to lend for the filming, a gang of armed robbers suddenly appeared and began shooting. They got away with the cash, but two bank employees were shot, one fatally, and one of the fleeing robbers was also shot by Bosch, who had rushed to the scene. Now he wonders whether there could be a link between the daring robbery and the murder of Angella Benton.

During his years on the LAPD, Bosch often butted heads with an interfering bureaucracy. In this case, it's the FBI that makes his life difficult. It too is interested in the fate of the stolen two million dollars, especially after the female agent who was tracking the location of the eight hundred marked bills that were included in the bank's money suddenly disappeared. The FBI suspects that the stolen money might be used to fund terrorist activities, which prompts an examination in the novel into the role of the FBI in the aftermath of 9/11.

The FBI orders Bosch to cease investigating the case immediately. To show they mean business, agents begin following his every move. From agent Roy Lindell, who previously appeared in both *Trunk Music* and *Angels Flight,* Bosch learns that under the new Homeland Security directives, the FBI has formed a REACT (Rapid Response Enforcement and Counterterrorism) squad. It is, Lindell tells Bosch, a BAM squad (By Any Means) and adds: "The rules went out the window September eleventh, two thousand one. The world changed, so did the bureau. The country sat back and let it happen. They were watching the war over there in Afghanistan when they were changing all the rules here" (110).

The prospect of giving the FBI new authority to circumvent the rights and freedoms of those they suspect of just about anything was worrisome to Connelly: "I viewed the Patriot Act as something that gave the government too much leeway and too much power" (Davies 170). Two scenes in the novel illustrate the problem. In the first, Bosch is arrested by a trio of FBI agents who handcuff him and then deliberately slam his head into the door frame of the car they're shoving him into. They take him to the federal building where he is tossed into a barren cell alongside three others containing men of Middle Eastern descent. The following morning he's given an ultimatum by Special Agent John Peoples: cease investigating or he will end up back in the same cell and no one will ever know he's there.

Bosch reminds Peoples that America used to be a free country, to which Peoples retorts, "It's not the same country it used to be. Things have changed" (167). Bosch counters with a reminder of Friedrich Nietzsche's warning that "whoever is out there fighting the monsters of our society should make damn sure that they don't become monsters themselves. See, because then all is lost. Then we don't have a society" (170). Peoples tells Bosch he almost got the quote right, to which Bosch retorts, "Getting the quote right isn't what matters. It's remembering what it means" (170).

The second scene is far more chilling. Thanks to a video camera Bosch had secretly hidden in Lawton Cross's room to confirm his accusation that his wife has been mistreating him, he gets shocking evidence of physical abuse. But it doesn't come at the hands of his wife, it comes from the FBI. Two agents from the bureau's anti-terrorism unit are shown barging into Cross's home at 12:10 a.m. They begin interrogating him about what he has told Bosch. When he refuses to talk, one of the agents crimps his air-supply hose, cutting off his oxygen, nearly killing him. When they're finished with him, they leave him sitting alone in the dark, sobbing like a wounded and helpless animal.

"Do you think this is what the attorney general and the Congress of the United States wanted when they enacted legislation that changed and streamlined the bureau's rules and tools after September eleventh?" (207) asks the defense attorney Bosch shows the videotape to. "No," he replies, but he contends they should have known what could happen. This isn't some Middle-Eastern terrorist they are waterboarding, he notes, but an American citizen, a paralyzed retired cop who took a bullet in the line of duty.

Rather than make the tape of the FBI's torture of Cross public, Bosch uses it to get the agent who tortured Cross fired and to force the bureau to return all the files and other evidence they confiscated from him. He is now free to continue his investigation, which produces some surprising twists. It turns out the cash heist was an inside job, masterminded by Linus Simonson, the bank employee who was wounded while delivering the money to the film set. He and a trio of friends planned to use the cash to open a string of clubs in L.A. They killed Angella Benton in an attempt to throw suspicion for the theft onto the studio where she worked. But they didn't kill Martha Gessler, the missing FBI agent. That was done by Cross and his partner, who had become accomplices of Simonson. They were in turn double-crossed by him and gunned down in the bar.

Everything leads to a heart-pounding conclusion where Bosch first has to survive an encounter with Milton, the FBI agent who is waiting in his home to kill him to get revenge for having gotten him fired for assaulting Lawton Cross. Then he has to battle Simonson and his three partners, who shoot Milton and then try to kill him. In the end, armed only with a length of an old iron pipe, in true action-hero fashion he ends up the last man standing surrounded by four dead bodies and one seriously wounded one.

There's only one other matter to clean up. Bosch pays a final visit to Lawton Cross, not to thank him for giving him the chance to get justice for Angella Benton but to inform him that he has figured out that he has been using him the whole time to get revenge on Simonson and his buddies for leaving him paralyzed. When Cross won't tell him where he and his partner buried the body of Martha Gessler after they killed her, Bosch angrily reaches toward Cross's face with the intent of doing to him what Agent Milton had done earlier. This time, however, the victim isn't the innocent person he first appeared to be but a crooked cop guilty of the cold-blooded murder of an FBI agent who also nearly got him killed. Only the timely intervention of Cross's wife saves him from going over the edge of the abyss himself.

Shortly after completing *A Darkness More Than Night*, Connelly wrote "Cielo Azul," a short story for his newsletter that was an expanded account of the case Bosch and McCaleb worked on together that is mentioned in that novel. He decided that because the story was meant only for subscribers to his newsletter, he'd try something different and for the first time he made Bosch the narrator of the story. He decided to use first-person again in *Lost Light* as a way of highlighting the change in Bosch's life from cop to private eye. It also gave him an opportunity to pay tribute to two of his favorite crime writers, Raymond Chandler and Ross Macdonald, whose novels are narrated in first-person.

Connelly admitted to at first being afraid of using first-person for it's harder to hold things back. It's as if you are whispering your thoughts to the reader, who will feel cheated if you withhold important information. Using third-person allowed Connelly to describe the action through Bosch's eyes and to tell us from time to time what he's thinking, but he was also able to finesse how much to tell and what to hold back so the reader isn't always sure what's going on in his head. This helped maintain a bit of mystery about the character.

First-person, on the other hand, gives the reader a closer look into how Bosch's mind works than we have been previously given. For example, while being questioned by the FBI about how Milton managed to gain access to his home the night he was killed, we get to listen in as Bosch considers his options: should he tell the truth and create another problem for the FBI, or lie and say he invited Milton to his home? When he lies and says the latter, we fully understand his reasons for doing so.

What he reveals about himself isn't always flattering. After persuading his FBI friend Roy Lindell to run a search for a Nevada license plate without being honest about the real reason he's doing it, he makes this confession: "Guilt washed around me like the waves hitting the pylons under the pier. I might be able to fool Lindell with the request but not myself. I was running a check on my former wife. I wondered if I was capable of doing anything lower" (267). There are also a few instances where it might have been better if he had kept some thoughts to himself, as in this boastful description of his mission after he recalls listening to the jazz classic "Lush Life" with a friend: "I left him to his memories of a lush life while I headed out into the night to see a king about a stolen life. I was unarmed but unafraid. I was in a state of grace. I carried the last prayer of Angella Benton with me" (296). Sometimes it's more effective to let your actions speak for themselves.

The most revealing use of first-person involves Bosch's feelings about Eleanor Wish. Although they have stayed in touch by phone once or twice a year, he has not seen her in person in three years. She's now living in Vegas, doing well at her professional poker-playing job. But his longing for her prompts him to invent excuses to visit Vegas, where he hopes she will pick him up at the airport or perhaps join him for dinner. But he wants much more than this, and what he confesses is revealing from the man with the usual stoic demeanor: "She had pierced me through and through. There were other women before and other women since but the wound she left was always there. It would not heal right. I was still bleeding and I knew I would always bleed for her. That was just the way it had to be. There is no end of things in the heart" (126).

Bosch becomes increasingly suspicious about Eleanor, who is closemouthed about her current life. She won't invite him to her home, even refuses to open the trunk of her car to let him put his luggage in. Fearing that there may be another man in her life, he turns into something of a stalker. When he unexpectedly shows up at her front door one afternoon, she reluctantly invites him in and says, "This is not how I wanted to do this" (357). Then she leaves the room and returns moments later holding hands with a four-year-old girl. "This is Maddie," she says, introducing him to a daughter he never knew he had. Torn between anger at not having been told about the child and joy at feeling that this is the place "where lost light came from. My lost light" (359), he kneels down and introduces himself, then he presses her tiny fists to his closed eyes and speaks the uplifting final lines of the novel: "In that moment I knew all the mysteries were solved. That I was home. That I was saved" (360).

The Narrows (2004)

The Narrows cleans up some unfinished business, incorporates several characters from a pair of non–Bosch books into the series, and allows Bosch to spend much of the novel in Las Vegas so he can get to know his daughter while he mulls over an offer to return to the LAPD. Unlike the usual Bosch novel, the plot is straightforward with very little mystery to solve as much of the action occurs before the novel begins.

The book is a sequel to *The Poet*, published eight years earlier. At the end of that novel, serial killer Robert Backus, known as the Poet for his habit of leaving quotes from Edgar Allan Poe at the scene of all his murders, eluded capture. Connelly said he did this intentionally to emphasize the reality that not all murders are solved or killers caught. But then, "As I watched my young daughter grow it began to bother me that I had created a fictional world where a killer like [the Poet] could walk free" (Anderson, *Triumph* 187). So he decided to kill off Terry McCaleb, the chief pursuer in *The Poet*, and give Bosch the job of tracking the Poet down this time.

Terry McCaleb's transplanted heart failed him and he died while out at sea on his boat. But his widow Graciela believes he was murdered. She has discovered that someone had tampered with his meds by replacing two drugs in the capsules he needed to take to stay alive with a harmless powder. She asks Bosch to investigate. Despite McCaleb's declaration to Bosch at the end of *A Darkness More Than Night* that he no longer wanted to be friends with him, Bosch accepts the assignment.

Though dead, McCaleb does become Bosch's silent partner for the first third of the novel during which he pores over McCaleb's files looking for anything that might give him a clue to a suspect in his murder. He eventually zeroes in on a mysterious man who showed up on McCaleb's boat a few days before he died. He also finds several photographs sent to McCaleb anonymously that show someone following his wife and family. The evidence begins to point to Robert Backus, the infamous Poet who was once McCaleb's boss at the FBI. Did the Poet kill McCaleb?

Meanwhile, the FBI has received a package containing a GPS reader with a site marked in the Nevada desert. The fingerprints on the device also match those of Robert Backus. When agents visit the location and begin digging, they find multiple bodies buried in the desert. Another site on the GPS reader is named "Hello Rachel," an apparent greeting to Rachel Walling, the FBI agent who shot him, which resulted in her demotion to the FBI office in Rapid City, North Dakota. The FBI invites her back to Quantico to observe the bureau's renewed search for the Poet.

Soon Walling and Bosch combine forces to track down the Poet. Backus was a fascinating villain in his first appearance. Here, not so much. We learn about all the new murders he has committed since he resumed killing—five men in Amsterdam's Red Light District over a two-year period and eleven men killed while he was working as a driver for a brothel in the Nevada desert—but he does little in the way of action this time out. In *The Poet* we got to spend several chapters trapped inside his twisted perspective. In *The Narrows*, he's given only a handful of chapters and they add little to what readers of *The Poet* already know. For those who haven't read *The Poet*, it may be difficult to understand just how twisted and clever he really is.

Bosch and Walling eventually track Backus to a house in Canoga Park where he is lying in wait to kill Ed Thomas, a bookstore owner and former cop who was one of his intended victims in *The Poet*. As Walling enters through the front door, she overhears Backus order Thomas to copy down some lines from another poem by Edgar Allan Poe. But before she can do anything, Backus has his gun pressed against her neck. Fortunately Bosch, who has entered from the rear, arrives in time to get the drop on Backus. When he's momentarily distracted by something Waller says, Backus escapes by jumping through a window. The Poet is once more on the run.

In both *A Darkness More Than Night* and *City of Bones*, water played a redemptive role for Bosch, who thought of it as baptismal as it washed over his face. In *The Narrows* it assumes a much more dangerous role in the exciting finale. Located just a short distance from the house where Backus jumped through the window is the Los Angeles River, which is normally a mere trickle. But a heavy rainstorm like the one now falling would "awaken the snake and give it power" (372), turning the lazy river into a raging torrent. To control the flooding, years earlier the city decided to line the river with concrete walls. Where the walls narrow, the river becomes deadly.

Bosch chases after the fleeing Backus and despite the warning he remembers from his mother to "stay out of the narrows," referring to the fast-moving water trapped between the concrete walls it flows through, the two of them end up being swept away by the raging river. Bosch manages to grab onto a large tree rushing by long enough to be rescued by a helicopter. Backus isn't so lucky. The Poet is finally dead.

Connelly has one more surprise for the reader. The Poet didn't kill McCaleb. No one did. He committed suicide. He was told his transplanted heart was failing and he needed another one. Rather than incur the financial burden another operation would place on his family, he doctored the pills himself and hoped no one would figure out what he had done, for that might cost his family his insurance and pension benefits. Bosch is angry to learn that Rachel Walling knew what McCaleb had done and kept it from him so he would become involved in the case, which torpedoes the professional and personal relationship that had developed between them during the course of the novel.

Connelly has given his previous novels plenty of authenticity by, among other things, incorporating references to real events like the O.J. Simpson trial and the 1994 Northridge earthquake. In *The Narrows* he goes even further in blurring the line between the real and the fictional. One way he accomplishes this is by bringing Buddy Lockridge, McCaleb's marina buddy and charter-fishing partner, into the novel. He's a bit of a comic character who acts like an annoying kid brother who constantly pesters his older brother to let him tag along when he goes off to his job, and then pouts when he's told he can't come along. But he's also useful in bringing Clint Eastwood's film version of *Blood Work* into *The Narrows*. In Eastwood's version, the identity of the killer was changed to the Buddy Lockridge character, which the real Buddy Lockridge (or at least the fictional version of the real Buddy Lockridge) is still upset about. He's unhappy about having been made to look like a creep in the movie.

While reading through McCaleb's files, Bosch notices that he had been taking notes on several real-life cases that were in the news in 2002: the disappearance of pregnant Laci Peterson from her California home on Christmas Eve; the kidnapping of fourteen-year-old Elizabeth Smart from her home in Salt Lake City; and the arrest of actor Robert Blake in the murder of his wife, who was shot in a car parked outside a Studio City restaurant. A number of real people also make appearances in the novel. Bosch has a phone conversation with Hollywood Division homicide detective Tim Marcia, one of the cops Connelly regularly consults with about material for his novels. Clint Eastwood attends the funeral for Terry McCaleb, the character he played in the movie. Even gum chewed by mass murderer Ted Bundy plays a role; Backus, who had saved it after an interview he conducted with Bundy years earlier, planted it in the grave of one of his victims as his calling card.

The Narrows marks the end of Bosch's brief stint as a private detective and as a first-person narrator. He has filed the papers that will allow him to return to his job with the LAPD and the narration in his next appearance will return to its usual third-person. While first-person gives the reader greater access to the inner Bosch, Connelly found that writing that way was a struggle for him. He wanted to pay tribute to Philip Marlowe's narration, which he often did effectively. But some similes, like this description of a closing door—"The loud snap of steel on steel had a finality to it that ricocheted through me like a tumbling bullet" (253)—don't quite hit the mark, forcing him to concede that "it's hard to do Harry in the first person without coming off as a cheap Marlowe imitation" (Feldman).

The Closers (2005)

After writing two books about Bosch as a private detective, Connelly realized he had made a mistake. Bosch needed to be a cop. Then he learned that William J. Bratton, the former head of the New York Police Department who had just become the new LAPD commissioner, had recently instituted a program to bring veteran detectives (over 900 of whom had recently retired) back to the department. Those within three years of their retirement could return without having to go through the police academy. Over 150 detectives took advantage of the opportunity. One of them was Harry Bosch.

Bosch is thrilled to be back: "Like the prodigal son returning, he knew he was back in his place now. He was baptized again in the waters of the one true religion. The church of the blue religion" (20). The new chief (who is unnamed in the novel but is clearly based on Bratton) gives Bosch his old badge back and welcomes him home. He is also happy to be reunited with his former partner Kiz Rider, whom he considers the most skilled and intuitive partner he had ever worked with. His new assignment is to look into cold cases, or what the new commissioner prefers to call Open-Unsolved cases: "Every one of them is like a stone thrown into a lake," he reminds Bosch. "The ripples move out through time and people. Families, friends, neighbors.... Those aren't cold cases, Detective. They never go cold. Not for some people" (7).

His first case involves the kidnapping and murder of sixteen-year-old Rebecca Verloren seventeen years earlier in 1988. She was abducted from her home in Chatsworth and her body was later found in the nearby hills. The daughter of a white mother and a Black father, she was popular with friends and teachers in school, and seemingly had no enemies. She wasn't sexually assaulted and her death was staged to look like a suicide. The one surprising fact is that no one, including her parents, knew that she had had an abortion a few weeks before her murder.

Abel Pratt, the officer in charge of the new Open-Unsolved Unit, reminds his officers of the challenge they face with 8000 unsolved cases since 1960: "We're like the guys they bring in in the bottom of the ninth inning to win or lose the game. The closers. If we can't do it, nobody can. If we blow it, the game is over because we're the last resort" (16). The problems Bosch and Rider face are that there are few leads and the murder weapon is missing. Their one piece of evidence is some blood and tissue found in the hammer of the gun that has been preserved.

Although he's been gone from the department for only three years, Bosch has plenty of catching up to do, especially when it comes to advancements in science and technology. It is now possible to identify the person whose DNA was originally found on the murder weapon: it belongs to Roland Mackey, who was eighteen at the time of the murder. When Bosch suggests they check the DMV to find his address, Rider informs him that's so old-school. The department now uses Auto Track, a computer database that is able to provide an individual's entire address history. They learn that Mackey now lives in Chatsworth and works there as a tow-truck driver.

What they don't have is any connection between Mackey and Becky Verloren, and no idea about the possible motive for her murder, so Bosch focuses on the gun used to kill her. He learns that it was previously stolen during a robbery at the home of Sam Weiss. Weiss is Jewish and the police suspected it might be the work of a local gang of racist skinheads called the Chatsworth Eights. One member of the gang, Billy Burkhart, was a neighbor of Weiss who was later arrested for burning a cross on a Black family's front lawn and vandalizing a synagogue. When Bosch learns that Mackey and Billy Burkhart are now living in the same house, the murder of the biracial Becky looks like it might have been a hate crime.

During Bosch's previous time with the department, Deputy Chief Irving was frequently his nemesis. In his new position, he figures he no longer has to worry about Irving, especially after learning that he was pushed out of his high position by the new police commissioner and given a meaningless assignment. So he is surprised when Irving stops by to thank him for resurrecting him in the department. Bosch wonders what he means. "You are a retread," Irving tells him. "But you know what happens with a retread? It comes apart at the seams.... You will fuck up—if you will excuse my language. It is in your history. It is in your nature. It is guaranteed" (41). Bosch's certain failure will be Irving's ticket back into power in the department because it will reflect badly on the new commissioner who rehired him.

Bosch later learns that in 1988, Irving headed the department's Public Disorder Unit, which was trying to stop a rise in hate crimes that year. The eight in the Chatsworth Eights refers to the eighth letter of the alphabet, H, which represents Hitler; 88 would refer to both "Heil Hitler" and to the year 1988, when the racist attacks were occurring. Did Irving's unit shut down the investigation into Becky Verloren's murder because of its racial implications? If so, Bosch would be facing what cops call "high jingo," a case of possible corruption and coverup carried out by their own department.

Bosch determines that his best hope for an answer is Roland Mackey, so he comes up with an elaborate plan to smoke him out. He plants a story with a local newspaper reporter about how the new technology will now enable the police to identify the DNA of the person whose blood and tissue were found on the murder weapon. Then he and Rider convince a judge to approve a wiretap on Mackey's phone. Thanks to new technology, cops no longer have to camp out in a cramped van parked outside a suspect's place of residence. Listen Technologies, a private contractor now used by all the agencies in Los Angeles County, operates an air-conditioned facility where police can monitor as many as ninety wiretaps at a time. Then after getting a makeup artist to paint temporary white supremacist tattoos on his neck, Bosch calls for a tow truck he knows will be driven by Mackey. During the ride to the garage, Bosch tests Mackey with leading questions that confirm his racist views.

The trap is set. And then everything goes wrong. While Bosch waits to see how Mackey will respond to the newspaper story that has just appeared, he is called out to tow a disabled car. Bosch follows him but by the time he gets to the location of the service call, Mackey has been fatally injured by the car he was supposed to tow. Someone else—the likely killer of Becky—set a trap aimed at silencing Mackey.

It's now back to square one. Bosch re-examines all the details of the case and discovers a pair of small details he had overlooked that eventually lead him to the killer: Gordon Stoddard, a former teacher of Becky's who is now principal of the school she attended, began sleeping with the sixteen-year-old girl. When she became pregnant by him, he pressured her to get an abortion. When she later tried to break up with him, it drove him to kill her with the gun he had obtained from Roland Mackey, who traded it for a grade in the class Stoddard was tutoring him in at the time.

In addition to solving the murder, Bosch also gets a measure of revenge against Deputy Chief Irving for calling him a retread and claiming he would be his ticket back to power in the department. Bosch originally thought that Irving had shut down the investigation into Becky's murder in order to avoid further inflaming racial tensions in L.A. in the late 1980s. But then he discovers a far less civic-minded reason when he learns that the leader of the Chatsworth Eights was the son of Richard Ross, head of the LAPD's Internal Affairs Division. The real reason Irving stopped the investigation was to keep Ross's son out of the spotlight, which then gave him control over Ross and the entire

Internal Affairs Division. Without Irving's interference, the case might have been solved, sparing Becky's family seventeen years of pain. Irving doesn't get his old job back. Thanks to the information Bosch dug up about Irving, the new commissioner is able to use it to force Irving to retire from the department.

The Closers is a return to the classic police procedural. It takes the reader through Bosch's step-by-step investigation while bringing into play all the latest advances in science, technology, and police techniques. While there are no dramatic car chases, shootouts, encounters in tunnels and the like, the novel is nonetheless compelling reading thanks to the artful way everything is carefully constructed. The revelation of the killer's identity is both surprising and credible.

The novel's emotional impact comes from the way Connelly weaves together issues of loss, grief, and guilt that arise over the murder of a sixteen-year-old girl. Without having to contend with a serial killer or a complex case with multiple twists and turns, Connelly has the time to devote to the human cost of crime. Becky Verloren is not simply another cold case statistic; hers is the tragic story of a promising life cut short, leaving her family to deal with the devastating consequences each and every day in the seventeen years since her murder.

In the first of three scenes designed to illustrate how her death affected others, Bosch and Rider pay a visit to Becky's school, where they hope to find someone who might remember if Roland Mackey also attended while Rebecca was there. They speak with Gordon Stoddard, Rebecca's science teacher, and another teacher who had been friends with Rebecca since first grade, about what she meant to them. As they page through several school yearbooks, they observe the awkward eighth-grader with pigtails and braces blossom into the pretty and confident sophomore member of the student council. "She was going to be a heartbreaker," Bosch comments. "Maybe she already was," replies Rider. "Maybe she picked the wrong one to break" (93).

Bosch and Rider also visit the Verloren home to speak with Becky's mother, Muriel. She tells them that her husband, unable to deal with their daughter's death, left her years earlier. She now lives alone with her cat and her memories. She seldom leaves the house. Each day she enters her daughter's bedroom, which she has left unchanged since the morning Becky went missing, and often lies on her bed. At night she reads from Becky's journal as if it were her Bible. When Bosch mentions before leaving that he, too, is the father of a young daughter, she passes along the hard lesson life has taught her: "Never let her out of your sight" (115).

The saddest story of all is that of Becky's father, Robert. The last Muriel knew, he was homeless and living in an area of missions. Bosch tracks him down at the shelter where he is now in charge of preparing breakfast each day for as many as 160 people. The death of his daughter knocked him into a black hole. "You are like an empty bottle tossed out the window. The car keeps going but you are on the side of the road, broken," he tells Bosch (189). He began drinking heavily and eventually lost the popular Malibu restaurant he once owned. Though he's now been sober for three years, he still remains haunted by grief over the loss of his daughter and guilt over the belief that he might have been the reason for Becky's murder if she was killed by white supremacists because her father was Black.

Bosch's return to the LAPD hasn't been a smooth one: he botched one interview and neglected to turn off his phone, which rings at a key moment while he is trying to secretly get close to a house. He knows he's on probation and rookie mistakes like these could cost him his job. And while he and Kiz Rider immediately fall back into the easy rhythms of their prior partnership, he hasn't learned from his shabby treatment of his former partner Jerry Edgar. On a number of occasions he fails to inform her about what he is planning to do and in one instance publicly embarrasses her deeply by mentioning information about the investigation to a group of cops that makes it obvious that he never told her about it in advance.

On Bosch's first day on the job, Abel Pratt had warned him to be prepared for what he called "the toll of violence over time" (17) in unsolved cases. Bosch learns the truth of that when solving a seventeen-year-old cold case sadly produces violent new ripples that claim two more lives and further destroy another. Bosch's effort to smoke out Roland Mackey by the publication of the newspaper article about the case led directly to his murder by Stoddard, who needed to silence him about how he got the gun from him that he used to kill Becky Verloren. And when Robert Verloren learned about Stoddard's arrest for his daughter's murder, he immediately started drinking again. He was soon arrested for assaulting the cop who tried to arrest him on a drunk-and-disorderly charge. He pleaded guilty and was sentenced to a week in the same jail where Stoddard was being held. This gave him the opportunity to finally get revenge against his daughter's killer by stabbing Stoddard to death with a shiv he made from a sharpened spoon. All a shocked Abel Pratt can say to Bosch is, "How's that for closure?" (403).

The Lincoln Lawyer (2005)

After the eleventh Bosch novel, Connelly took another break from the series to introduce yet another new character, an L.A. criminal defense attorney named Mickey Haller. Instead of describing the relentless mission of a veteran detective to arrest the bad guys and put them in jail, this time he would show the other side of the coin and focus on someone who makes his living trying to keep those people out of jail.

The character was inspired by a man dressed in a business suit working on his computer whom Connelly met on opening day of the baseball season at Dodger Stadium. David Ogden turned out to be a criminal defense attorney who worked out of the back seat of his Toyota, not because he couldn't afford an office but because it was a better use of his time as he traveled around to the forty different courthouses spread out all over L.A.

Mickey Haller is called the Lincoln Lawyer not because he resembles Honest Abe in any way but because he conducts his practice from the back seat of a Lincoln Town Car. The car, which sports the license plate "NT GLTY," is driven by a client who owes him for getting him probation on a cocaine sales conviction. (When he was once flush with cash, Haller actually bought four such cars in order to get a fleet discount; as soon as the odometer on one hits 60,000 miles, he sells it to a limousine service.)

The novel begins with a quote attributed to J. Michael Haller—"There is no client as scary as an innocent man"—that announces the theme of the novel we are about to read. Haller, we learn, was a legal legend in L.A. whose clients included gangster Mickey Cohen and the Manson girls. But his son Mickey is not that kind of lawyer. He's a slick operator, but after fifteen years of practice, he's become cynical and disillusioned. "There was nothing about the law that I cherished anymore," he confesses (25). "The law school notions about the virtue of the adversarial system, of the system's checks and balances, of the search for truth, had long since eroded like the faces of statues from other civilizations. The law was not about truth. It was about negotiation, amelioration, manipulation. I didn't deal in guilt and innocence, because everybody was guilty. Of something" (25). In his view, the law is simply "a large, rusting machine that sucked up people and lives and money. I was just a mechanic. I had become expert at going into the machine and fixing things and extracting what I needed from it in return."

It's this attitude that was the primary cause of his divorce from his first wife, Maggie McPherson, a prosecuting attorney known as Maggie McFierce for her relentless approach in court. On an intellectual level, she could handle being married to someone whose job was to keep his clients, many of them guilty, out of prison, but in reality it was more than she could bear. To their eight-year-old daughter, Hayley, whom he loves but admits he's too busy to spend enough time with, Maggie is a hero for putting bad people in jail. "What could I tell her was good and holy about what I did," he says, "when I had long ago lost the thread of it myself?" (50).

His primary motivation is the money he can make from his clients—"I work on green inspiration" (13)—who are mainly drug dealers, motorcycle gang members, and hookers rather than the famous clients his father worked for. The main job of his case manager Lorna Taylor (who is the second of his ex-wives) is to screen all potential clients—most of whom call after seeing one of his thirty-six ads scattered on bus benches located in high-crime areas—for their ability to pay before they ever get to meet him. And his message to potential clients is not the traditional, "Don't do the crime if you can't do the time," but "Don't do the crime if you can't pay for my time" (19).

One day, Haller gets an unusual client: Louis Roulet, a young man from a prominent Beverly Hills family who just might turn out to be what he calls a "franchise client," one who ends up paying him as much as he ordinarily makes in one year. The police seem to have an airtight case against Roulet. He was arrested in the apartment of a woman named Reggie Campo who was badly beaten. Her blood was on his hand and a bloody knife with his fingerprints was found nearby. She claimed he broke into her apartment and began attacking her. She managed to escape by clobbering Roulet in the head with a bottle of vodka, then fled to a neighbor's apartment to call the police. Two of those neighbors then immobilized Roulet until the police arrived.

His story, however, is quite different. According to him, after agreeing to meet the woman, whom he had just met at a bar, at her apartment, she knocked him out as soon as he entered. When he awoke, he found himself handcuffed with blood on his hand. He claims he was being set up by the woman, who hoped to cash in on a big payoff by suing him for the assault.

Haller expects all his clients to insist they're innocent. What worries him about Roulet is that he fears he might be telling the truth. He remembers what his father said about innocent clients, especially his warning that "if you fuck up and he goes to prison, it'll scar you for life" (90). The possibility that Roulet may actually be innocent unsettles him: "I was always worried that I might not recognize innocence. The possibility of it in my job was so rare that I operated with the fear that I wouldn't be ready for it when it came" (75).

Haller's investigator Raul Levin is charged with determining the credibility of Roulet's story. He obtains a copy of a surveillance tape made by a bar owner that shows Reggie Campo giving a note to Roulet with her address on it that seems to confirm his story of what happened.

But Haller has to be careful what he does with the evidence because if he uses it to get the charges against Roulet dismissed, he will forego much of what he intended to charge his client's family for his services.

Then the case takes an unexpected turn. As Haller takes a closer look at the photographs of the battered face of Reggie Campo, he realizes that the uninjured half of her face closely resembles that of another woman he remembers. Two years earlier, Martha Renteria was the victim of another client of his named Jesus Menendez, who was charged with raping and stabbing her to death in her apartment. The details of that case, including similar knife wounds on the neck, are eerily similar to the Roulet case. Even though the police had plenty of evidence against Menendez, including his DNA on a bathroom towel, he insisted he was innocent. Like Roulet, he claimed the woman was a prostitute who accepted his offer of 500 bucks and invited him into her apartment.

Haller travels to San Quentin, where Menendez is serving a life sentence; he has brought with him six photographs of his clients and asks Menendez if he recognizes any of them as the man he saw with Martha Renteria when he first met her. Without hesitation he points to the one of Roulet. Suddenly, Haller's worst fears are confirmed: "I had been presented with innocence but I had not seen it or grasped it" (173). He had convinced Menendez, whose case he took pro bono for the free publicity, to plead guilty to the murder rather than go to trial and risk the death penalty, even though Menendez tearfully begged him to believe in his innocence. Although it was Menendez who uttered the word guilty to the judge, Haller is now the one left feeling "as though it had been me, his own attorney, holding the knife of the system against his neck and forcing him to say it" (167).

The only way to prove Menendez's innocence is to prove that Roulet, the client he assumed was innocent, is actually guilty of the crime that sent an innocent man to prison for life. Now bound ethically to defend Roulet, Haller cannot reveal what he suspects about his previous crime; he also now suspects he was hired because Roulet knew that even if his connection to the Renteria murder was exposed, Haller was the kind of lawyer that wouldn't walk away from a case that would earn him a six-figure bonanza.

Raul Levin, who has continued to delve into Roulet's past, comes up with some disturbing information that suggests that Roulet may have committed several other murders. But before he can inform Haller, he is gunned down in his office. To make matters worse, a bullet found at the scene reveals that the gun used to kill him is the exact same model of the gun Haller's father once gave him. When he goes to retrieve it from the gun box in his closet, it's gone. From a previous scene we know that Roulet has a key to his house. It's now obvious that the man he once thought was innocent is instead pure evil.

This clever set-up ensures that there will be plenty of drama when the action moves to the courtroom. The suspense comes not from whether or not Roulet is guilty, for just as the trial is about to begin, he confesses to Haller that he has killed before, including Martha Renteria. But he has placed Haller in a bind. He knows that thanks to attorney-client privilege, Haller is bound to secrecy and can't tell the police about any of his murders. And if Haller fails to get a decision of not guilty, Roulet still has his gun, the one used to kill Levin, which he will turn over to the authorities.

Even if Roulet doesn't turn the gun over, Haller faces the very real prospect he could be arrested during the trial if the police discover that he owns the same model gun used to kill Levin and then search his house and find it missing from the gun box. To make matters worse, the gun, which was given to his father by L.A. gangster Mickey Cohen, was once tested for ballistic evidence that can still be used to connect Haller to Levin's murder.

As the trial progresses, we observe Haller calculating the effect each one of his questions has on the judge, the jury, the prosecutor, and his own client. Thanks to Connelly's use of first-person narrative in the novel, the reader is privy to what's going on in Haller's mind at all times. (The original title of the novel was *Confessions of the Lincoln Lawyer*.) Haller's not above playing by crooked rules, as for example when he sets a trap for the inexperienced prosecutor trying the case by paying another of his clients, a drug addicted prostitute, $25,000 to feed information to a jailhouse snitch the prosecution is forced to use. The scam works, enabling Haller to undercut the snitch's testimony, which includes Roulet's confession that he killed Martha Renteria, by producing a newspaper report that he committed perjury during another murder trial in Arizona. Because of prosecutorial misconduct, the state has no choice but to dismiss all charges against Roulet.

But the drama is far from over. The police immediately arrest Roulet on suspicion of murder in the Renteria case. But when Haller later opens his front door, he is greeted by Roulet's mother, who points a gun at him and shoots him in the stomach. He falls backward but manages to fire his gun, killing the woman before she can get another shot off. It turns out the gun she used to shoot him is his own gun, proof that she was the one who killed Levin in an effort to protect her son. Though no longer a suspect in Levin's murder, Haller is in no mood to celebrate.

He undergoes three surgeries during his five-month stay in the hospital and his law license is suspended for ninety days. Roulet is awaiting trial in the Renteria case and will likely spend the rest of his life in prison, that is if he isn't executed, but the six-figure payment Haller received for defending him has been eaten up by medical expenses and legal fees for defending himself against malpractice suits by both Roulet and Menendez. Thanks to his efforts Menendez has been released from prison, but Haller will also have to live with the fact that his client merely traded one life sentence for another: he is dying of AIDS he contracted in prison. Despite all this, the novel ends with him about to return to work, which is indeed good news for readers looking for an opportunity to meet him once again.

Haller's a complicated character. At first, he appears to be your stereotypical shyster lawyer, a street-smart con artist who knows how to play all the angles. But underneath that slick exterior is a savvy lawyer who, like Sam Spade, isn't as crooked as he appears to be. As Spade reminded Brigid O'Shaughnessy just before he turned her over to the police at the end of *The Maltese Falcon*, "Don't be too sure I'm as crooked as I'm supposed to be. That kind of reputation might be good business—bringing in high-priced jobs and making it easier to deal with the enemy" (215). Behind Haller's reputation lurks a good and decent man. As his ex-wife says to him, "You're a sleazy defense lawyer with two ex-wives and an eight-year-old daughter. And we all still love you" (291). And when he realizes what he has done to Jesus Menendez, he does whatever he can to make amends.

Haller isn't the brooder that Bosch is, nor is he a loner like him; he has loyal friends (including several return clients) and two ex-wives who still love him. He has a sense of humor, and can even joke about himself. One of his favorite jokes—what's the difference between a catfish and a defense attorney? One's a bottom-feeding scum sucker and one's a fish—is a putdown directed at lawyers like himself. And his taste in music isn't the mournful jazz Bosch prefers but the music of rappers like Tupac Shakur, which he says helps him understand his clients better.

Another significant difference between the two is that Haller is the narrator of the action. This gives the reader a closer relationship to his character because we are allowed access to his thoughts and concerns. We hear his reaction to what others do and say, which he often expresses in comic ways: "Dobbs looked at me like I hadn't used mouthwash in a month" (39). And even his descriptions of inanimate objects—"San Quentin is over a century old and looks as though the soul of every prisoner who lived or died there is etched on its dark walls" (168)—offer us a glimpse into a side of him others rarely see.

Connelly also uses Haller to illuminate some truths about the justice system in America. Darius McGinley, one of Haller's regular clients, has been dealing rock cocaine since he was eleven years old. He's what Haller calls an "annuity client," a repeat offender who becomes a repeat customer, at least as long as he defies the odds and keeps on living. But he also understands the nature of the world he was born into, one where he'd never had a shot at anything but thug life in the first place. "He'd never known his father and had dropped out of school in the sixth grade to learn the rock trade. He could accurately count money in a rock house but he had never had a checking account. He had never been to a county beach, let alone outside of Los Angeles. And now his first trip out would be on a bus with bars over the windows" (95). Like millions of young Black men in America, the society he lived in intersected with mainstream America only in one of the forty courthouses spread across L.A. County "like Burger Kings ready to serve them—as in serve them up on a plate" (91). He was simply "fodder for the machine. The machine needed to eat and McGinley was on the plate" (95).

The Lincoln Lawyer turned out to be far more than a simple respite for Connelly from his Bosch series. It is a confident entry into the legal thriller genre that combines the courtroom drama with an exploration into how our legal system works. Connelly shows as much expertise in this area as he does with the ins and outs of police work. And Mickey Haller has the same kind of complex personality and drive that Bosch has.

In the final draft of the novel, Connelly made one very important change. He came to realize he wasn't finished with his lawyer character and enjoyed writing in his first-person voice. He began looking for a possible way to link the character with Harry Bosch. And then he remembered a scene he wrote in *The Black Ice* where Bosch attends the funeral of J. Michael Haller, the father he never knew. At the funeral he spotted a man he assumed was Haller's son and thus his half-brother. So Connelly changed the name he had originally given the Lincoln Lawyer to Mickey Haller. Though Haller doesn't yet know he has a half-brother, the two will soon meet and begin a fruitful relationship that connects the novels of both characters.

Echo Park (2006)

The novel opens in 1993 with a scene set in a location that pays tribute to Connelly's favorite author, Raymond Chandler. Bosch and partner Jerry Edgar are called to the High Tower apartments, which are built into the granite hills behind the Hollywood Bowl. The property's landlord has discovered an abandoned car parked in a garage belonging to a vacant apartment. On the front seat of the car, Bosch spots the neatly piled clothes and underwear belonging to a twenty-two-year-old woman named Marie Gesto, who has been missing for ten days. He and Edgar take the elevator in the tower outside the building up to the top floor and cross the outdoor walkway to the vacant apartment to speak with the landlord in hopes of finding some connection to the missing woman.

Viewers of Robert Altman's film version of Chandler's *The Long Goodbye* will recognize the apartment as the one where Philip Marlowe (played by Elliott Gould) lived. Connelly himself lived in the apartment for a spell and wrote *The Lincoln Lawyer* there. He enjoyed the scenic view of Hollywood, but found the lack of air-conditioning in the summer to be a major inconvenience. Those interested is seeing the actual apartment can view a short film on Connelly's website based on the opening chapter of the novel that was shot there.

The unsolved Gesto case has obsessed Bosch for the past thirteen years. His only suspect all that time has been Anthony Garland, son of a wealthy oilman, whose lawyers eventually obtained a restraining order preventing Bosch from questioning him anymore. Then one day in 2006, he gets a phone call from another homicide detective named Freddy Olivas regarding a man named Raynard Waits, who was stopped by police for a possible license plate violation. When the officers spotted some plastic garbage bags dripping blood in the back seat of his van, he was arrested. Inside the bags were the dismembered remains of two women he murdered.

Waits's attorney has offered prosecutors a deal: his client will plead guilty to the murders of the two women in his car and also provide information about seven other murders he committed between 1992 and 2003; in return, the state will neither seek the death penalty nor file charges in the homicides he provides information about. Olivas contacted Bosch because Waits has offered to show police the location where he says he buried one of his victims—Marie Gesto.

The case is especially important to Rick O'Shea, who runs the Special Prosecutions Section of the District Attorney's office. He is currently running for the office of DA and clearing seven unsolved murders would boost his chances for election. But this puts Bosch in a bind. He's torn between providing comfort to the families of all those victims who have been living with uncertainty about the fate of their loved ones and being put in the position of working to save the life of a guy "who cuts women up and keeps them in the freezer until he runs out of room and has to take them out like trash" (56).

But as he learns more about Raynard Waits, he discovers something else that is deeply disturbing: Robert Sexton, a name Waits once used, is listed in the murder book he and his partner compiled about the killing of Marie Gesto in 1993. He now fears he may have been guilty of committing the one mistake that is every detective's worst nightmare: overlooking a name that might have solved the 1993 murder. He may have allowed that murderer to quietly kill nine more victims over the next eleven years. Connelly's novels have featured serial killers before, but they were braggarts who taunted the police by leaving behind quotes from Edgar Allan Poe or references to the paintings of Hieronymus Bosch. Raynard Waits is an under-the-radar killer who wants no publicity about what he does. Bosch's first face-to-face interview with him is especially chilling. The most striking thing about him is how ordinary he looked. Slightly built with an everyman's face, he is "the epitome of normality" (125). That is, until he begins talking about his murders. He killed his first victim, a male security guard, by setting him on fire. His motive: "I wanted to see if I could. I had been thinking about it for a long time and I just wanted to prove myself" (127).

The rest of his victims were young women. When Bosch asks him if he had sex with them after death, he jokes, "I always say a woman is at her best when she is dead but still warm" (139). He describes looking for a good place to bury Marie Gesto, eventually finding "a nice private spot to plant my little flower" (141). The publicity about her murder did teach him a valuable lesson: he now had to be more careful and select victims that would draw less attention. His comments leave Bosch speechless. "It was moments like these that made him feel inadequate as a detective, moments when he was cowed by the depravity that was possible in the human form" (139).

The dramatic centerpiece of the book comes when Waits leads a four-vehicle caravan followed by a media helicopter hovering overhead on a field trip to Beachwood Canyon in the Santa Monica Mountains where he claimed he buried the body of Marie Gesto. Bosch and three other armed cops accompany Waits, whose arms are shackled to his waist, as they proceed down a slippery slope. They are forced to stop at a ten-foot drop-off to wait for a ladder so they can descend further. When they reach the bottom, Waits points to the area where he buried the body.

As they prepare to ascend the ladder, Waits's lawyer insists he will not allow his client to climb up it with his arms chained to his waist, so they are unshackled. Waits then heads up the ladder to where Kiz Rider, Bosch's current partner, and Freddy Olivas are waiting for him, when the unthinkable happens. As Olivas reaches down to grab Waits's hand, there is a scuffle. Suddenly, Olivas's body comes crashing down onto

Bosch, who has started to climb up, knocking him to the ground. Shots ring out and Bosch feels the impact of two bullets hitting Olivas's body, which acts as a shield, saving his life. By the time he scrambles to the top, he realizes that Waits had grabbed Olivas's gun when he reached down to take his hand. Olivas and an armed deputy now lie dead at the foot of the ladder. Kiz Rider is bleeding profusely from a bullet that hit her carotid artery. And Waits has escaped.

Bosch now finds himself in the middle of a complicated mess. Rider survives the attack, but confesses to Bosch that she froze when Waits grabbed Olivas's gun and did nothing to stop him. She has decided to quit the LAPD. Deputy Chief Irving, Bosch's longtime nemesis, goes on TV to charge that bringing him back to the department is an example of the new chief's ineptitude and the department's moral corruption. The videotape that O'Shea arranged to have taken so he could use it in his political campaign turns up missing. When it's found, scenes of O'Shea running in terror when the shots rang out and giving the order that Waits's handcuffs be removed have been edited out. The edited tape now makes it looks like it was Bosch's idea to remove the handcuffs from Waits's wrists. A serial killer is now on the loose in L.A. And to top it all off, Bosch is eventually forced to conclude that Waits was lying: he never killed Marie Gesto but was pressured by his lawyer to claim he did. That means the real killer is still out there.

The novel now becomes a search for two killers: Waits and the real murderer of Marie Gesto. Connelly finds yet another way to get Bosch back into a dark tunnel when he locates the garage where Waits, who has kidnapped a new victim, is hiding. At the rear of the garage, he notices an opening into a tunnel dug into a hillside embankment, which prompts this reminder of his fate: "He had come many years and many miles but it seemed to him that he had never really left the tunnels behind, that his life had always been a slow movement through darkness and tight spaces on the way to a flickering light. He knew he was then, now, and forever a tunnel rat" (320).

Bosch creeps through the thirty-foot-long tunnel to the room where Waits has a gun pointed at the head of the young woman he had just abducted. Scattered on the ground around him are the bones and decaying flesh of his previous victims. Waits confirms that he didn't kill Marie Gesto. His lawyer ordered him to convince Bosch that he was her killer in order to get him off the trail of her real killer, though he claims to have no idea who that person might be. In the end Bosch has no choice but to shoot Waits before he can kill his female captive, whom he then brings to safety.

One piece of business remains—finding the mastermind behind

the plan. At first, Bosch suspects Rick O'Shea for having orchestrated the scam, but then he learns that once again, the villain is someone close to him—his boss Abel Pratt, head of the Open-Unsolved Unit. Why, he asks himself, would a man who is only three weeks away from retirement from a job where he spent twenty-five years chasing down bad guys help one go free? Easy. He was paid a million bucks by the wealthy father of Anthony Garland to protect his son, who was Bosch's original suspect in the murder. Pratt and Garland both conveniently end up dead in a shootout in a restroom in Echo Park. The good news is that all three killers are now dead.

Despite having broken off his relationship with Rachel Walling at the end of *The Narrows*, Bosch contacts her for assistance in his current investigation. Now a member of the FBI's Tactical Intelligence Unit in L.A., she returns to play her usual role as Bosch's investigative and romantic partner for most of the novel. But once again, the relationship ends on a sour note, this time because she decides that Bosch has proven to be too reckless in his actions for her taste. And after the shootout in the Echo Park restroom, she also accuses him of knowing what was likely to happen and doing nothing to stop it. The one positive note at the end of the novel is that Kiz Rider has reconsidered her decision to quit the department and decides to return to her job in the chief's office, where she promises to act as Bosch's guardian angel.

Aside from the fact that he's traded in his Mercedes SUV for a Mustang and now needs reading glasses, there's little new to report about Bosch in *Echo Park*. Nevertheless Connelly manages to come up with new ways to complicate his life and give the now fifty-four-year-old detective plenty of opportunities to prove he still has what it takes.

The Overlook (2007)

The Overlook differs from Connelly's other Bosch novels in that it was written for a different purpose and a different audience, at least in its original form. In 2005, *The New York Times Sunday Magazine* invited several popular authors of crime fiction to each write a serial novel that would appear in weekly installments over the course of several months. The project was inspired by Charles Dickens, who wrote many of his classic novels in serial form, with individual installments published as soon as he finished them.

This time, the authors would be able to complete the writing of their short novels before they began appearing in the magazine, but they were required to abide by the directive that each chapter needed to be as close to 3000 words as possible. Following in the footsteps of Elmore Leonard, Scott Turow, and Patricia Cornwell who preceded him, Connelly accepted the challenge. On September 17, 2006, the first of sixteen installments of *The Overlook* that would appear over the next four months was published.

Because of the nature of the assignment, each chapter needed to end in a way that would make the reader look forward to the next one. Consequently, plot took precedence over character, and the focus shifted more in the direction of a thriller rather than a complicated detective story. Connelly decided to dust off a mystery plot he had previously used in *Trunk Music* and adapted it to incorporate the potential threat of a terrorist plot directed at Los Angeles.

Harry Bosch has another new position in the LAPD—he's now a member of the Homicide Special, part of the prestigious Robbery-Homicide Division that was created to handle murders with political, celebrity, or media implications. He also has a new partner, Ignacio ("Call me Iggy") Ferras, an inexperienced Cuban-American rookie cop he is supposed to mentor. After spending the past two novels solving cold cases, Bosch gets his first new case when he is called out at midnight to the scene of the murder of a doctor named Stanley Kent. He was shot twice in the back of the head beside his Porsche Carrera, which was parked on the scenic overlook above the dam on Mulholland Drive.

In *Trunk Music*, Bosch was summoned to the scene of another murder on Mulholland Drive. The victim in that case was Anthony Aliso, a small-time movie producer who, like Kent, was shot twice in the back of the head, mob style. Missing from his Rolls-Royce was a briefcase containing $480,000 in cash. In Dr. Kent's case, what's missing from the open trunk of his car is far more dangerous than money. Bosch's former lover FBI agent Rachel Walling surprises him by showing up at the murder scene shortly after he does. She informs him that Kent was a medical physicist whose name was on an FBI watch list of individuals who had access to radioactive materials used in the treatment of certain cancers. She suspects that what might have been taken from his car are several tubes of cesium, the by-product of the fusion of uranium and plutonium, the same toxic material that was released into the air in the Chernobyl nuclear explosion in 1986. If the cesium fell into the hands of terrorists, they might use it to detonate a deadly bomb blast somewhere in L.A. that would send shock waves across the country.

Her suspicions are confirmed when they visit Kent's home to inform his wife Alicia about his death. They find her naked, gagged, trussed up and lying on her bed in a pool of urine. She tells Bosch that two masked men, one of them speaking what sounded to her like Arabic, burst into her home. After tying her up they then took photographs of her on the bed. A search of her computer reveals that the photos were sent to her husband along with the warning that if he didn't bring all the cesium available to him to the Mulholland overlook by eight o'clock, his wife would be raped, tortured, and then killed.

The remainder of the novel alternates between the FBI's race to locate the missing cesium and Bosch's search for Kent's killer. The FBI claims priority in the case, but Bosch, as usual, stubbornly refuses to be pushed aside: "This is a homicide and nobody, not even the FBI, brushes me off a case" (107). The ensuing action is confined to a twelve-hour period and Connelly balances the two investigations effectively, with both providing plenty of suspense for each installment.

Thanks to his attention to even the smallest detail, Bosch figures out the truth of what really happened. In the end, like the mob in *Trunk Music* that Bosch initially believed was behind Aliso's murder, the terrorist threat in *The Overlook* is a red herring. And like *Trunk Music*, the culprit is the murder victim's wife, who partners up with another rogue FBI agent, Rachel Walling's former partner Cliff Maxwell. The motive for the murder had nothing to do with terrorism; that was a smokescreen to cover their tracks. As Bosch explains it, "Sex plus money equals murder. That's all" (204). The two of them, who had fallen in love, concocted a way of diverting attention away from a scheme to rid Alicia of her husband in order to get her hands on the money from his insurance and his half-ownership of a prosperous medical business. Instead, both of them end up dead in the end.

Because of length restrictions, Connelly needed to find a way to use some of his characters for dual purposes. For example, Jesse Mitford, a twenty-year-old witness to the shooting of Kent, had just hitchhiked to L.A. from Canada. He was hiding behind the trees near a mansion only a hundred yards away that was once owned by Madonna. He was there, he said, to get an autograph to send to his mother, a big fan. He found the address on a map to the homes of the stars he had just purchased, though the information it contained was long out of date. He claims to have heard a voice say something about Allah just as the gunshot rang out. Bosch assumes that what the voice said was "Allah Akbar" ("God is Greatest"), which is what the terrorists in 9/11 were heard to exclaim. That seems to confirm that terrorists are involved. However, it turns out Bosch heard what he wanted to hear, for after zeroing in on Kent's wife Alicia as the person behind the murder, he realizes what young Jesse probably heard as the shot rang out was the name Alicia, not Allah.

Connelly also uses Jesse's appearance in the story as an opportunity to work in some commentary about one of his favorite subjects, notably what Hollywood represents to so many people lured there in hopes of realizing their dreams. Jesse Mitford was like thousands of others who got off the bus every month or thumbed it into town with "more dreams than plans or currency. More hope than cunning, skill or intelligence. Not all of those who fail to make it stalk those who do. But the one thing they all share is that desperate edge. And some never lose it, even after their names are put up in lights and they buy houses on top of the hills" (84).

Bosch's new partner Ignacio Ferras also serves to illuminate Bosch's character for those readers of *The New York Times* who are unfamiliar with him. A by-the-book new recruit, Ferras is shocked to see how his veteran partner does his job. For example, he can't believe Bosch would lie to Rachel Walling when she asks him what he has done with Jesse Mitford. Bosch has to explain that when dealing with the FBI, it's important to hold some information back so you can later trade it if you need to. To someone schooled in proper police procedure like Ferras, it's difficult to accept how Bosch simply ignores the idea of going though channels. To the frustrated new recruit's complaint, "We shouldn't be doing it this way" (115), the seasoned veteran offers this helpful advice: "Watch and learn" (107).

Connelly admitted that writing in such a tightly prescribed manner wasn't easy. "Writing this way," he said, "is rather like having a boss watching over your shoulder yelling '3,000 words, 3,000 words, 3,000 words'" (Karim). What he did find enjoyable, however, was the opportunity he had several months later to revise his story for novel publication. This allowed him to expand the material, restore some cuts he made, and even introduce a new character, Captain Don Hadley, commander of the local Office of Homeland Security, whose trigger-happy attack on a reputed terrorist supporter's home demonstrates why he has earned the nickname Captain Done Badly.

Given its restrictions, *The Overlook* is a minor entry in the series. Despite being almost 20,000 words longer than the *Times* version, the book version is still over forty percent shorter than the usual Bosch novel. Although it succeeds as a slick crime thriller, it lacks the depth of character and sense of place that distinguish Connelly's best work.

The Brass Verdict (2008)

It's been a rough three years since Mickey Haller's debut appearance in *The Lincoln Lawyer*. His recovery from the gunshot wounds he suffered at the end of that novel was slowed by several setbacks, including a botched operation aimed at fixing a problem. He also developed an addiction to the pain pills he was taking that required a stint in rehab. Now after a year's absence from his law practice, he's ready to return.

Lorna Taylor, ex-wife number two, is still on the job as his case manager, and he continues to work out of the back seat of one of his three remaining Lincoln Town Cars (this one sports the license plate "IWALKEM"). He has a new investigator, Dennis Wojciechowski, who goes by the name Cisco, and a new driver, Patrick Henson, with whom he shares a past history of addiction to pain pills. He even has a new ringtone on his phone, the "William Tell Overture," that makes him feel like the Lone Ranger riding out again, only in a black Lincoln instead of on a white horse.

He planned to return to work gradually but that changes dramatically when attorney Jerry Vincent, a longtime colleague, is shot twice in the head in the parking garage near his office and his briefcase, cell phone, laptop computer, and some important files he was working on were taken. Bosch is summoned to the office of Judge Mary Holder, chief judge of the Los Angeles Supreme Court, who informs him that according to a document Vincent had filed years earlier, he has inherited Vincent's practice. Thirty-one cases have suddenly been dropped in his lap.

One stands out. Big-time movie producer Walter Elliot, chairman of Archway Pictures, is set to go on trial in one week for murdering his wife Mitzi and her German lover Johan Rilz in his Malibu weekend home. He's currently out on bail of twenty million dollars. Despite the presence of gunpowder residue on his hands and a powerful motive (his wife announced she was divorcing him the day after their prenuptial agreement went into effect, entitling her to upwards of a hundred million dollars), Elliot insists he is innocent and demands that his trial not be postponed. If Haller can convince him he is capable of taking over his defense, he will also inherit the hefty fee Elliot will pay. He gets the case.

Things become complicated when he is introduced to the homicide detective in charge of investigating Vincent's murder, a brusque cop named Harry Bosch. The two get off to a rough start when they get into an argument over who is better qualified to look through Vincent's files to identify possible suspects in his murder, the veteran lawyer or the seasoned detective. Bosch is hoping to learn anything he can from Haller that might help him solve the murder. He also provides updates about developments in the case. That's how Haller learns that Vincent had received several phone calls from the FBI on the day he was killed and that he had earlier made a suspicious withdrawal of $100,000 in cash from Elliot's client trust account. Bosch suspects the money might have been used to bribe a juror in his trial. He also scares Haller by showing him a photograph of an armed man entering the building near where Vincent was murdered and warns Haller that he could be the killer's next victim.

In addition to worrying about ending up dead like Vincent, Haller's ego is dealt a serious blow by news about a bribed juror. That would explain why Elliot didn't want the trial postponed and is so extremely confident he will be acquitted. That also means Haller wasn't hired for his expertise. If the fix is in, it doesn't matter how good he is. Any lawyer would do. "I was simply a lawyer who would work in the scheme of things. In fact, I was perfect. I was pulled out of the lost-and-found bin. I had been on the shelf and was hungry and ready. I could be dusted off and suited up and sent in to replace Vincent, no questions asked" (164).

Despite these concerns, Elliot has convinced him he's innocent so he forges ahead with a masterful display of his courtroom savvy. But when juror number seven, the one who was bribed to deliver a not-guilty verdict, fails to show up in court one day and is replaced, Elliot's surefire acquittal is no longer guaranteed. Now everything depends on Haller's defense. Fortunately, he has discovered what he calls a magic bullet, the real explanation for the gunshot residue on Elliot's hands. When the police arrived at the murder scene, they handcuffed him and placed him in the back seat of a police car whose previous occupant had just fired ninety-four shots. The residue came from that seat.

Shortly before the verdict is announced, Elliot surprises Haller by confessing that he did indeed kill his wife and her lover. This isn't the first time Haller has been bamboozled by a guilty client. It happened in *The Lincoln Lawyer*. What irritates him is how he had been used so well and for forgetting the basic rule he mentions in the first sentence of the novel: "Everybody lies. Cops lie. Lawyers lie. Witnesses lie. The victims lie" (3). And now thanks to his skillful defense, a cold-blooded murderer is going to go free.

And then Haller is nearly killed by juror number seven, whose name he learns is David McSweeney. Posing as a cop, McSweeney phones Haller to tell him he has arrested a friend of his but he's willing to give her a break if Haller will come and get her. Only the timely arrival of Bosch, who with the FBI has been following McSweeney, saves Haller's life when he arrives at the remote spot on Mulholland Drive where McSweeney is lying in wait for him.

Haller eventually puts the pieces together and concludes that the mastermind behind the murder of Jerry Vincent, the bribery of David McSweeney, and his attempt to kill him is Judge Mary Holder. He visits her office to tell her what he knows about her role and informs her that McSweeney has been arrested and is talking to the FBI about her role in the whole scheme. The FBI arrests her the next day.

But Elliot doesn't get away with the murders after all. It turns out there is another kind of magic bullet, one that is loaded in a gun that can be used to obtain street justice, what the cops call a "brass verdict." Johan Rilz's German relatives, who have been attending the trial, take matters into their own hands and shoot Elliot and his female executive assistant, who had helped in the murders of Mitzi Elliot and Johan Rilz, the night before he would have been acquitted in their murders.

Despite the courtroom drama and clever twists, the most interesting aspect of the novel, certainly to readers of the Bosch series, is the relationship between Bosch and Haller. (Connelly has said that the scenes between the two of them were the most enjoyable parts of the book to write.) From our reading of *The Lincoln Lawyer* and the Bosch books, we know what makes each one tick and how they operate. But because they know nothing about each other (aside from the fact that Bosch knows Haller is his half-brother), they are wary when they first meet.

Bosch, the more suspicious of the two, had concocted a phony story about the photo of Vincent's killer in hopes of scaring something out of Haller that would point him in the right direction. Haller, however, is savvy enough to realize he's being scammed and calls Bosch out on it. Bosch admits to what he did and, uncharacteristically, apologizes for his actions. "So now that we have that out of the way," he then asks Haller, "will you help me?" (239). After they discuss possible ways of shaking things up in the investigation, Haller agrees to help.

Though there are some obvious differences between the two men— Bosch puts bad guys in jail, Haller tries to get them out; Haller likes to talk, Bosch is tight-lipped; Haller wants to be liked, Bosch doesn't care if he is or isn't—they are flip sides of the same coin. Both are skilled at what they do. Both have a troubled past. Both live in houses with decks overlooking the city, although they are appropriately enough located on opposite sides of the Hollywood Hills, with Haller's looking down on the Sunset Strip and Bosch's overlooking Universal Studios. Both are divorced (Haller twice) and have young daughters they love. Like Bosch, Haller even encounters a dark tunnel he must go through to the light on the other side, only in his case the tunnel is at the end of the freeway that leads to the ocean.

The most important thing they have in common, especially from Bosch's point of view, is that they are kindred spirits who both like to color outside the lines, to cross legal and/or ethical boundaries when they deem it necessary. For example, despite risking being charged with jury tampering, Haller tells Bosch that he was the person who sent the anonymous note to the judge informing her that juror number seven wasn't who he pretended to be and needed to be checked out. (He wanted the bribed juror removed so he could prove he could still win the trial on his own merits without any help.) And despite being warned by the FBI not to tell Judge Holder what he knows about her role in the case, he immediately informs her in order to force the FBI to move against her without delay.

In addition to watching the interaction between Bosch and Haller, thanks to Haller's first-person narration we also get a running commentary about Bosch's behavior and demeanor. Haller pays particular attention to Bosch's facial expressions: "He grinned at me again without any warmth, giving me that cop's practiced smile of judgment. His brown eyes were so dark I couldn't see the line between iris and pupil. Like shark eyes, they didn't seem to carry or reflect any light" (44); "Bosch smiled like he was dealing with a child" (107); "Bosch looked like he might be about to jump over the desk at me" (232). The only time Haller notices a genuine smile on Bosch's face is when he is introduced to his daughter.

At their final meeting, Bosch compliments Haller for doing the right thing when he broke the rules by sending the anonymous letter to Judge Holder and informing her about what the FBI knew. But he says nothing about his blood relationship to Haller. It turns out he doesn't have to. Haller has already guessed it. From the beginning, he sensed something familiar about Bosch. Only after looking at some photographs of his father did he notice his resemblance to Bosch. Recalling the reproduction of Hieronymus Bosch's *The Garden of Earthly Delights* that hung on the wall of his father's office confirmed it. When asked why he didn't reveal it, Bosch said he didn't want to rock anyone's boat with a surprise like that. However, he does confess that he did show up at the hospital after Haller was shot in case he needed blood.

The ending is a bit of a tease. Haller tells Bosch he's decided to quit being a lawyer, and after Bosch leaves, he expresses doubt that he'll ever see him again. But Connelly obviously enjoys writing about his two heroes too much to ever allow that to happen.

The Scarecrow (2009)

Reporter Jack McEvoy made a name for himself in *The Poet*, where he and FBI profiler (and lover) Rachel Walling teamed up to track down a serial killer nicknamed the Poet (real name Bob Backus), though he managed to escape capture at the end. He wrote a bestselling book about the case, sold the film rights for a hefty sum, and even appeared on *Larry King Live*. The Poet was eventually tracked down eight years later by Harry Bosch and Rachel Walling in *The Narrows* (2004), where he died after being swept away by the raging Los Angeles River.

McEvoy was not involved in that novel, but he did pop up in *A Darkness More Than Night* (2001), the second Terry McCaleb book, where he was first introduced to Harry Bosch. At that time, he was living in L.A. and working as a freelance reporter for the *New Times*, an alternative weekly. He also made a brief appearance in the second Mickey Haller novel, *The Brass Verdict*, where he was now a crime reporter for the *Los Angeles Times*.

He returns as the main character for the second time in *The Scarecrow*. When he first joined the *Times*, it was known as "the Velvet Coffin," a place so pleasurable to work that you would stay there till you died. But times are changing and so is the *Times*—McEvoy is being let go as a cost-cutting measure by the paper's corporate owners. Even worse, in return for being allowed to stay on his job for two more weeks, he has to train his replacement, a beautiful and ambitious young reporter named Angela Cook. She's what he calls a *mojo*, a mobile journalist who could file text and photos for the website or paper and video and audio for television and radio. And she'll work for far less money than veteran reporters like him are being paid.

McEvoy would like to go out in a blaze of glory with one last memorable murder story. It looks like he may have found it in the case of a sixteen-year-old Black drug dealer named Alonzo Winslow, who the police claim murdered a white exotic dancer named Denise Babbit when she came to his crime-infested neighborhood to buy drugs. According to the police, he sexually tortured and strangled her, then dumped her body in the trunk of her car and drove it to a beachside hotel twenty miles away in Santa Monica. At the prodding of Winslow's grandmother, McEvoy agrees to take another look at the case and begins to see the possibilities for a story about how a sixteen-year-old became a cold-blooded killer.

But once he starts examining the evidence, especially the transcript of the nine-hour interview the police conducted with Winslow, he comes to believe the boy is innocent. The transcript confirms that Winslow did confess to stealing money from Babbit's purse and driving her car to Santa Monica after he discovered her body in the trunk, but he repeatedly denies killing her. In journalism, proving a supposedly guilty person innocent is as good as it gets. McEvoy may have his story.

Meanwhile Angela Cook, who has been searching Google to find stories about trunk murders, finds one that is remarkably similar to that of Denise Babbit. An exotic dancer in Las Vegas named Sharon Oglevy was sexually assaulted, strangled, and dumped in the trunk of a car belonging to her ex-husband Brian, who despite his denials was convicted of killing her. After reading the story, McEvoy heads to Vegas to investigate. The crime scene photographs he examines of Oglevy's murder reveal that not only were the details of her death similar to Babbit's, the women could have been sisters: both were blonde, long-legged exotic dancers who were suffocated with a plastic bag tied with a cord around the neck. It appears that a previously unknown serial killer is on the loose and McEvoy is now hot on the trail of an even bigger story.

He makes arrangements to visit Brian Oglevy at the state prison in Ely, Nevada, where he is serving a sentence for murder. But he begins to suspect that something is amiss when his credit cards and phone service are cancelled, his Internet service is blocked, and his bank accounts emptied out. At the hotel where he's staying, a stranger in a cowboy hat befriends him and later follows him down the hallway to his room. The man abruptly departs when he hears a woman's voice coming from inside McEvoy's room say, "Hi, Jack."

The voice belongs to McEvoy's former lover, FBI agent Rachel Walling, who has flown to Nevada out of concern for his safety after receiving a phone call from him earlier in the day asking for her help in the case. It turns out she may have saved his life, which they realize only when the two of them return to McEvoy's home in L.A. After making love, McEvoy happens to look under the bed for a missing sock and sees the body of Angela Cook with a plastic bag tied over her head like the other two victims. The stranger he met in Ely might have intended to kill him, too.

Connelly's previous serial killers were distinguished by the unusual clues they left behind, like quotes from Edgar Allan Poe and details from Hieronymus Bosch's paintings. Wesley Carver, the serial killer in *The Scarecrow*, is by contrast a bit of a dud. Raised by a stripper mother who ended up having to wear braces on her legs, he now murders exotic dancers and attaches leg braces to their long legs before killing them. Why? No one really knows. The only interesting thing about him is how he uses the Internet to carry out his darkest plans.

The Internet has changed our lives in countless positive ways. However, like many technological advances, it can also be used for evil purposes. It can, for example, make life easier for a serial killer. Carver, a graduate of M.I.T., is chief technology expert at Western Data Consultants, a colocation center in Mesa, Arizona, that backs up and secures data for almost a thousand clients. The clients, many of them law firms, maintain ownership and control of their servers, which are managed and protected by the company on a day-to-day basis. As its chief threat engineer, Carver works in an underground bunker where he oversees forty server towers lined up in neat rows like crops in a field. The place is called the farm and Carver has been dubbed "the scarecrow" for his job of "keepin' all the dirty, nasty birds off the crops" (296).

But the isolated bunker is also where he manages his own private operation that uses the Internet to identify and recruit like-minded disciples like Freddy Stone, who shares with him a condition called abasiophilia, a psychosexual attraction to people who wear orthopedic devices like leg braces. It also enables him to select his victims and to keep a watchful eye on anyone who might show an interest in his private activities. Carver has created a fake web page that sends him a message when anyone attempts to access it. This is how he first comes across the name of Angela Cook. It doesn't take him long to gain entry to all her emails and Google searches. But what's so disturbing about Carver is what he does with this information: he uses it to arrange for Angela's murder and the foiled attempt to have his partner kill McEvoy.

Carver is a clever opponent, but Connelly is equally clever in creating the way he is identified. Carver has tricked McEvoy and Walling into believing they are looking for two killers—Freddy Stone, Carver's disciple, and Declan McGinnis, the CEO of Western Data Consultants. Both soon end up dead—Stone kills McGinnis, who has nothing to do with the murders, and then dies when he tumbles down an elevator shaft during a fight with McEvoy. The case now appears to be closed. But out of the blue comes a clue that cracks the case wide open. The killer known as the Scarecrow is done in by another Scarecrow, this one played by Ray Bolger in *The Wizard of Oz*.

As McEvoy is leaving his office for the last time, Dorothy Fowler, one of the paper's editors, invites him into her office for a final goodbye. Hanging on the wall is a photograph of the Scarecrow from the famous film, a joke gift from a friend who gave it to her because she, too, is a girl named Dorothy from Kansas. The photo reveals that the Scarecrow's face is formed by a burlap bag pulled over the head and tightly cinched by a rope at the neck, precisely the way the killer's victims looked like when they were found. The detail that leads McEvoy to Carver is the name of the artist who did the original illustrations for the L. Frank Baum book *The Wonderful Wizard of Oz* (1900)— William Wallace Denbow, the same name he remembers Carver had used for one of his websites. But unlike what happened at the end of *The Poet*, this time the killer doesn't get away. He is doomed to spend the rest of his days in a deep coma as a result of being shot in the head by Rachel Walling.

Jack McEvoy is both the unluckiest and the luckiest crime reporter in the business. In just two books he has managed to become entangled with four serial killers, each of whom tries to kill him. Both experiences, however, have brought him fame and fortune: from *The Poet*, a best-selling book and a film about the case; and this time an advance of a quarter of a million dollars for a book about the Scarecrow and a novel he's long been interested in writing. And though he's offered his old job back, he decides to join the enemy, writing investigative stories on subjects of his own choosing for an online news site named velevetcoffin.com.

One other victim of the Internet featured prominently in *The Scarecrow* is the newspaper business. McEvoy's loss of his job isn't personal, he's simply a casualty of a dying business. "Like the paper and ink newspaper itself, my time was over," he declares. "It was about the Internet now. It was about hourly uploads to online editions and blogs. It was about television tie-ins and Twitter updates. It was about filing stories *on* your phone instead of using it to call rewrite. The morning paper might as well be called the *Daily Afterthought*. Everything in it was posted on the web the night before" (12).

It's not only the loss of jobs for experienced reporters that concerns Connelly, it's the cost to the readers. As he notes, the American newspaper is irreplaceable: "The newspaper is a community tent pole. It is a center of information, discussion, and debate. And when the center is broken up and shifted to websites and blogs that can go unseen and ignored, then the tent comes down" (Taylor). Without a watchdog like the newspaper, Dorothy Fowler warns McEvoy, "Corruption will be the new growth industry" (29).

For ex-reporter Connelly, the death spiral of newspapers also represents a painful personal loss. This description of a newsroom from the novel serves as an epitaph to a profession he loved for fifteen years:

> At one time the newsroom was the best place in the world to work. A bustling place of camaraderie, competition, gossip, cynical wit and humor, it was at the crossroads of ideas and debate. It produced stories and pages that were vibrant and intelligent, that set the agenda for what was discussed and considered important in a city as diverse and exciting as Los Angeles. Now thousands of pages of editorial content were being cut each year and soon the paper would be like the newsroom, an intellectual ghost town [259].

He also bemoans the fact that journalism will no longer be able to provide the kind of training he received on his path to becoming a novelist. "Many of us cut our teeth in the newspaper business," he says, "so

I think that we will lose a whole school of training. I learned the craft of writing at a newspaper. It also put me in close proximity to crime scenes and detectives and victims and just about everything I write about now. I would not be doing this if I had not been a reporter on the crime beat" (Taylor).

Connelly often deals with topical issues, but real-life events threatened to render *The Scarecrow* outdated even before it was published. The day after he turned in the finished book to his publisher, the corporate ownership of the *Los Angeles Times* filed for bankruptcy, which required him to make some changes. And then three days before the novel was scheduled to go to the printer, the *Rocky Mountain News*, McEvoy's former newspaper that had offered him his old job back, abruptly ceased publishing, requiring additional last-minute alterations. Sadly, the downward spiral of the newspaper business described in *The Scarecrow* has in the years since the novel's publication turned into a death spiral. Since 2004, over 2000 newspapers in the U.S. have shut down.

Nine Dragons (2009)

Nine Dragons is a pivotal book in the series for it brings Bosch to an important crossroads in his life that both costs him dearly but sets him on a promising new path. It all begins, as so many of his novels do, with what appears to be a straightforward case. Because of a temporary shortage of detectives in the South-Central Bureau, Bosch and partner Iggy Ferras are dispatched to the scene of a shooting at a liquor store in Watts. John Li, longtime owner of Florence Liquors, has been fatally shot in an apparent robbery. Bosch ordinarily has to look for a personal connection to the victim to fire himself up, but this time that's easy.

Twelve years earlier, he was near that very location during the riots on Normandie Avenue in South Central L.A. He was transporting a crooked cop who turned out to be the killer he had been searching for when his car was hit by a firebomb. Momentarily blinded and bloodied, he managed to speed to safety, but his passenger had been dragged from the back seat of the car by an angry mob and beaten to death. He walked over to Florence Liquors in search of a cigarette, but the store had been looted and had none. The owner, John Li, the man who had just been killed, offered him his last cigarette. When Bosch went outside to light it, he noticed the fortune printed on the book of matches he had taken from the store: *Happy is the man who finds refuge in himself.* Believing that he is a man who has found refuge in himself, he has kept that book of matches in his pocket ever since. Now he has a chance to repay the man for his kindness.

The obvious suspect in Li's death is a young shoplifter who was heard threatening to kill him a few days earlier, but Bosch is always skeptical of the obvious. Li was shot three times in the chest, indicating that the killer was methodical, not acting out of any personal vendetta. So he does what he does best: he begins looking for clues. Although the killer had removed the store's surveillance tape that recorded the murder, Bosch spends twenty-two hours reviewing older tapes before seeing Li handing over $216 to an Asian man exactly one week earlier and at about the same time that he was gunned down. David Chu of the department's Asian Crimes Unit tells Bosch that half of $216 dollars is $108, a number that has great significance to the triads, secret Chinese criminal organizations now operating extortion and protection rackets in the U.S. (The first triads were formed by five monks who survived an attack that killed 108 of their comrades.) Once Bosch is able to determine the man on the tape's identity, he tracks him down and arrests him just as he is about to flee to Hong Kong.

In the middle of interrogating his suspect, Bosch gets a phone call from a man with an Asian voice who promises him there will be consequences if he doesn't immediately cease his investigation. Then it gets even more personal. His thirteen-year-old daughter Maddie has been living in Hong Kong for the past six years with her mother (and Bosch's ex-wife), Eleanor Wish. He is sent a video from her cellphone that shows her gagged and tied to a chair. At one point, one of her abductors attempts to fondle her breasts. The message is clear: back off the case or he will lose his daughter. Armed only with some digitally enhanced photos taken from the cellphone video, he hops on the first flight he can get to Hong Kong.

The Hong Kong portion of the novel is a fish-out-of-water/damsel-in-distress thriller that rockets along at breakneck speed, leaving a bloody trail in its wake. It begins the moment Bosch arrives at the Hong Kong airport, where he is met by ex-wife Eleanor and her security guard (and current lover) Sun Yee. They begin following the clues on the photos Bosch brought with him until they finally arrive at a hotel in Kowloon where he believes Maddie is being held. (A ten-minute video available on Connelly's website shows him walking the route he created for Bosch during a trip he made to Hong Kong.) When Bosch busts through the door of the room, it's empty. There is evidence that Maddie has been there, but she's gone. Where?

As Bosch and Eleanor are leaving the empty room, two armed men approach them. He pulls the gun that Sun Yee had managed to get for him and begins firing at them as he pushes Eleanor to safety. He kills both men but is horrified by what he sees next. Eleanor has been struck in the head by one of the bullets fired at them and is dead. Even though they were divorced, Bosch has always hoped they would eventually grow old together. But now she's dead. Even worse, it's because of a mistake he made that got her killed. The dead men aren't Chinese and couldn't possibly be triad members. Bosch had flashed a big wad of bills when he was told he had to pay for a room in order to be allowed to enter the upper floors of the hotel. The men had only intended to rob him.

As Bosch resumes his search for Maddie, more dead bodies pile up. He first discovers the bodies of Maddie's friend He and her family. Later he shoots and kills two men during a frantic search for his daughter aboard a ship that is about to leave port. In the end, he finds her in the trunk of a car and immediately whisks her back to L.A. with him. The title of the novel refers to the nickname for Kowloon, an area of Hong Kong where much of the action takes place. (The name Kowloon supposedly comes from the Song Dynasty's Emperor Bing, who named the area for its eight tallest mountains. The ninth dragon was the emperor himself.) But the novel could have also been titled *Nine Bodies*, for that is the number of people killed in less than twenty-four hours.

The action in the final third of the novel returns to L.A. where Bosch needs to get his daughter settled into her new life, which involves such parental tasks as finding a school for her and buying new clothes and school supplies. But his troubles are far from over. A pair of Hong Kong detectives come to L.A. to question him about all the dead bodies that were discovered. Fortunately, Bosch has a sharp lawyer—Mickey Haller. Although he appears in only one scene, Haller sends the cops packing by turning the tables on them, accusing the Hong Kong police of failing to act when Maddie was kidnapped. He threatens to get his newspaper friend Jack McEvoy to write a story about their incompetence. Haller's parting shot is like one of his summations to a jury: "Thirteen-year-old American girl kidnapped in China for her organs and the police do nothing. Her parents are forced into action and the mother is killed trying to save her daughter.... Every paper, every news channel in the world will want a part of this story. They'll make a Hollywood movie out of it. And Oliver Stone will direct it!" (336).

Bosch then gets some new information that points him in a fresh direction. Before dying, Li had managed to hide in his mouth a shell casing from one of the bullets fired at him. Thanks to a technological advance called electronic enhancement, a fingerprint on the bullet has been identified as belonging to Henry Lau, a young screenwriter who is currently involved in the making of a movie starring Matthew

McConaughey (who played Mickey Haller in *The Lincoln Lawyer*). McConaughey can even provide an alibi for where Lau was at the time of the murder. The only link Bosch can find between Lau and John Li is that his son Robert Li was Lau's roommate in college. Robert Li and a friend come to Lau's apartment every week to play poker. While there, his friend stole Lau's gun, which was used to kill John Li.

Nine Dragons is more than an action-packed thriller; it also tells the story of three family tragedies. The first involves Bosch's own family. His effort to save his daughter results in the tragic death of her mother and the love of his life. To make matters worse, Maddie reveals that she herself triggered the whole bloody mess when with the help of her friend He she faked her kidnapping in an attempt to convince her mother to let her move to L.A. to live with her father. But then she became a real kidnapping victim when He's older brother saw an opportunity to cash in on the situation by trying to sell Maddie on the black market to someone willing to pay to get her organs. His plan backfires, resulting in the murders of his mother, his sister, and himself.

The murder of John Li also turns out to be a family matter, not a gang killing. Li had adamantly refused to listen to his son's pleas to stop paying over $800 a month in needless protection money for his two stores and to sell the one in Watts so he could open another one in a more promising location. Li's daughter Mia, who resented her traditional father for forcing her to drop out of college and move back home to cook and clean house for her parents, cooked up a plan with her brother to murder their father and make it look like a triad killing.

Perhaps the saddest of all these family tragedies involves Bosch's partner Iggy Ferras. While Bosch admires Ferras's skill in handling all the paperwork the job entails, he has become increasingly frustrated with him for being overly cautious. The father of a toddler and newborn twins, the victim of a previous shooting that required nine months of physical therapy and rehab, and the husband of a wife who is constantly fearful about his safety and demands his help with their three young children, Ferras is understandably nervous about dangerous assignments.

He and Bosch get into a heated argument over which one of them should have checked some phone records that ends with Bosch telling Ferras, "You've been letting the whole job slide, partner." To which Ferras retorts, "And you are full of shit, partner. You mean because I'm not like you, losing my family to the job and then *risking* my family to the job, that I'm letting it slide? You don't know what you're talking about" (322). Stung when he learns that Bosch has requested a new partner, he angrily complains that he should have been given one more chance to prove himself. He sees an opportunity to do that by not waiting for Bosch and arresting Robert Li by himself. Tragically, he ends up dead, shot four times by Mia Li before she turns the gun on herself, leaving behind a grieving wife and three young children who will never get to know their father.

Although *Nine Dragons* has obvious parallels to the film *Taken* (2008) starring Liam Neeson about a CIA agent who has to travel to France to rescue a teenaged daughter who has been kidnapped, Connelly's novel was written before the movie came out. The seeds of his novel were planted several years earlier in *Lost Light* when Bosch first learned he had a daughter. Bosch has since then tried to arrange his life in order to become what he calls bulletproof: "He needed to build himself and his life so that he was invulnerable, so that nothing and no one could ever get to him" (173). *Nine Dragons* shows just how vulnerable he really is. Connelly waited to tell this story until Maddie was old enough to be able to engage with her father like an adult and so he could draw upon his own experiences of raising a daughter the same age as Maddie.

Nine Dragons also solved another problem for Connelly. Because Bosch ages at the same rate we all do, the question arises as to how many more years he can realistically continue to be a cop. One way of giving him a new purpose in life is to have him become a full-time father. Thus Eleanor needed to be sacrificed in order to eliminate the main impediment standing in the way of Maddie being allowed to move to L.A. to be with her father.

Maddie gets her wish, but not in the way she intended. At the tender age of thirteen, she has encountered the darkness in the world that her father has been fighting all these years. Now she must deal with the emotional consequences of her actions, which she feels caused both her mother's death and that of her friend and her family. All Bosch can do to comfort his daughter is to offer this advice: "We all make mistakes. Everybody. Sometimes, like with my partner, you make a mistake and you can't make up for it. You don't get the chance. But sometimes you do. We can make up for our mistakes here. Both of us" (374).

Nine Dragons received decidedly mixed reviews, a rare occurrence for one of Connelly's novels. Many reviews were positive, like this one from Bill Ott, who called the book "the most wrenching Bosch novel yet.... The jagged intersection between a cop's personal and professional lives is a recurring theme in many crime novels, but never has it been portrayed with the razor-edge sharpness and psychological acuity that Connelly brings to the subject." But other reviewers felt the opposite. Two of them, both of whom ordinarily championed Connelly's novels, didn't even review the novel but only mentioned it in passing in a subsequent review of one of his later books: Janet Maslin in *The New York Times* dismissed *Nine Dragons* as "a slow boat to China" that was "disappointingly flat and gimmicky"; in the *Washington Post*, Patrick Anderson, who had previously called the Bosch books "the finest crime series anyone has ever written" (*Triumph* 189), deemed it one of his lesser efforts, being "too obvious, pulp material" ("Michael").

Despite the starkly different reactions to the novel, everyone can likely agree that Bosch's life has been dramatically altered as he suddenly goes from being a father four weeks a year to having sole responsibility for raising a teenage daughter. Will he be up to the challenge? Will being a full-time father change him and affect how he does his job? Will this new responsibility make him overly cautious like Ferras? The next books in the series will answer some of those questions.

The Reversal (2010)

The title of the third Mickey Haller novel has multiple applications in the book: it refers both to the reversal of a criminal conviction and to the switch in Haller's position from defense attorney to prosecutor. The novel also teams him up with both his ex-wife Maggie and his half-brother Harry Bosch, both of whom also reverse their usual roles.

L.A. District Attorney Gabriel Williams comes to Haller with an unusual proposition: he wants to hire him on a one-time basis to be special prosecutor in the re-trial of a man named Jason Jessup. Jessup was convicted twenty-four years earlier of abducting and murdering twelve-year-old Melissa Landry. Recent advances in DNA testing have determined that the semen found on the dead girl's dress was not Jessup's, which led the California Supreme Court to reverse his conviction.

Jessup has now filed a civil suit seeking millions in damages for his twenty-four years of false incarceration. The only way to fight that is to retry him on the original charge and prove him guilty again. The attorneys in the DA's office are disqualified from the case, forcing Williams to find an outside attorney. Haller is his choice. Haller agrees to take the case under two conditions: (1) that he be autonomous and (2) that he gets to choose his second chair and investigator. Williams agrees and Haller asks his ex-wife Maggie McPherson, a skilled prosecutor known for her relentless drive as Maggie McFierce, and Harry Bosch to join him.

All three of them have a personal reason for getting involved in the case. Haller hopes to curry favor with his daughter Hayley, who has never been impressed by his job of defending the guilty. Maggie

McPherson is promised a promotion to Major Crimes if Haller can secure a guilty verdict. And despite his own misgivings about his half-brother's chosen profession, Bosch can't turn him down for one compelling reason: "He knew there were certain kinds of evil in the world that had to be contained, no matter the hardship. A child killer was at the top of that list" (14).

The evidence against Jessup appears to be strong: though it wasn't his DNA on Melissa's dress, he was identified by her thirteen-year-old sister as the man who abducted her from the front yard of their house while they were playing a game of hide-and-seek; several strands of her hair were found in Jessup's truck; and the dumpster where her body was found is located in close proximity to the parking lot of the towing company Jessup worked for. There are, however, some hurdles the prosecution faces: the semen on Melissa's dress was found to have come from her stepfather, which gives the defense an alternative suspect in her murder; there is no way of determining how Melissa's hair got into Jessup's truck, so it could be argued that it was planted by the cops; and the only witness, Melissa's sister Sarah Gleason, has a well-documented history of crystal meth use, which the defense will argue can cloud the memory.

The trial is the dramatic highlight of the novel. As skilled as Haller is as a defense lawyer, this is his first trial as a prosecutor, so he's fortunate to have Maggie McPherson sitting beside him, especially since his courtroom opponent, Clive ("Clever Clive") Royce, is one of the best in the business. And the stakes are high, because a not-guilty verdict might cost the city millions of dollars in a civil suit.

Even before the proceedings begin, Haller surprises everyone by not objecting to Jessup's request for bail during the trial. He does this in the hope that Jessup might do something incriminating that would give the police, who would have him under constant surveillance, evidence he could use against him in court. On several nights he has been spotted driving to deserted canyons on Mulholland Drive where he would sit quietly and often light a candle. He is observed receiving an object wrapped in a towel from a convicted gun dealer. And he has been hiding canned goods in a locked storage room under the Santa Monica Pier. What is he up to? And why is he sitting in a parked car late one night in front of Bosch's home?

As Haller's investigator, Bosch performs several important functions. He does the footwork outside the courtroom, tracking down missing witnesses like Melissa's sister Sarah Gleason and traveling to a small town in Washington state to try to convince her to return to L.A. to testify. During the trial he is asked to read the sworn testimony of key witnesses at the original trial who are now deceased. He even spends some of his free nights with members of the LAPD's elite surveillance team who are charged with constantly monitoring Jessup's every move whenever he's not in court.

The trial comes down to the testimony of the defense's key witness, Sarah Gleason's drug-dealing ex-husband Edward Roman, who claims to have damning evidence against her. But Bosch has managed to track down the woman he has been living with. She's too strung out to testify to anything, so Haller uses her as a silent witness whose presence in the courtroom unsettles Roman so much that he ends up telling the truth about what he knows rather than giving the damaging testimony he promised the defense he could offer. It looks like a sure victory for the prosecution.

Haller and his team enjoy a celebratory lunch in anticipation of the verdict they expect to hear when they return to the courtroom, but Connelly has a few surprises up his sleeve. During the lunch break, Jessup has obtained a gun and shoots his lawyer and three other innocent victims, including one of the cops following him. Bosch needs to find him before he can harm other targets, including his and Haller's daughters. Thanks to his own nighttime surveillance of Jessup, he has figured out where he is likely hiding. When the police arrive to arrest him, they kill him when he begins shooting at them.

Justice is served, but there is little to celebrate. The judge has no choice but to declare a mistrial, meaning no decision in the proceedings. And then Haller learns that all his work would have been wasted because one juror, who was selected in the first place because of his mistake, announces that he would have voted for acquittal. This would have produced a hung jury and Jessup would have gone free. And because Haller failed to get a conviction in the case, Maggie doesn't get the promotion she was promised. Haller is also left feeling guilty over the thought that it was his decision to allow Jessup to be granted bail during the trial that led to all the killings.

Haller knows he's going to take heat for being the one who let Jessup roam free, so he looks forward to returning to his old profession as a "defender of the damned" (3). Bosch also looks forward to returning to his regular job after a silver bracelet with a graduation charm is dug up at one of the locations where Jessup was seen lighting a candle. This could be evidence of another young girl Jessup might have killed. Once again, he becomes a man on a mission.

By alternating the chapters between Haller and Bosch, Connelly was able to tell two dramatic stories: one that details what goes on in the courtroom from pre-trial motions and jury selection to final arguments;

the other what happens outside as we follow both Bosch's investigation and Jessup's mysterious nighttime activities. The trial itself runs smoothly as Haller does a masterful job of countering every one of Royce's moves, which thanks to his own experience, he anticipates and is ready with countermoves. Connelly effectively maintains suspense in both stories for despite what is revealed about Jessup's suspicious nocturnal activities, the reader never knows until the very end whether he did in fact kill Melissa.

One of the novel's attractions is watching what happens when Connelly places three strong-willed characters on the same team. There are inevitable tensions and conflicts. Maggie, whom Haller calls the best prosecutor he knows, resents playing backup to a novice who has never prosecuted a case. She and Bosch also clash. The two of them travel together to visit Melissa's sister Sarah Gleason in the state of Washington where she now lives. When Bosch spots smoke coming from the chimney of a barn on her property, he immediately concludes, based on the woman's history as an addict, that she's cooking meth. Maggie advises caution and wants to call the police, but Bosch insists on inspecting the scene on his own. Fortunately, before he can make a mess of things, he discovers she isn't cooking meth, she's a glassblower. When Haller asks Maggie upon her return to L.A., "How was Bosch today?" all she needs to say is, "He was Bosch" (102).

For his part, Bosch has always had an instinctual distrust of lawyers, whom he believes often try to manipulate the law to their advantage. "His part in the process was pure. He started at a crime scene and followed the evidence to a killer. There were rules along the way but at least the route was clear most of the time. But once things moved into the courthouse, they took on a different shape. Lawyers argued over interpretations and theories and procedures. Nothing seemed to move in a straight line. Justice became a labyrinth" (190).

Working with two of them on a case feels like another reversal, this one of the way he ordinarily does his job: "We start with the bad guy already in prison and we take him out" (80). Given his relentless nature, however, nothing can stop him from investigating on his own. He spends several days when he's not in court looking for other cases of abducted and missing young women, potentially other victims of Jessup. But when he presents his findings to Haller, he all but shrugs them off. "Here we go," Haller says. "Look, man, I don't know why you're giving me the attitude," Bosch replies angrily. "You pulled me in as an investigator on this thing and I'm investigating. Why don't you just let me tell you what I know? Then you can do with it whatever you want" (165).

Although *The Reversal* is listed as a Mickey Haller novel, we see very little of his private life, as he spends most of his time in court. Instead we get an update on the progress Bosch is making as a full-time parent. The action of the novel takes place four months after Bosch rescued his daughter from her kidnappers in Hong Kong and brought her back to L.A. to live with him. We learn that she has been undergoing therapy to help her deal with the sudden death of her mother, but we don't see much in-person interaction between her and her father. He's so busy, both day and night, that his main fatherly duty is largely limited to scrambling around to find a babysitter. The fact that one he finds is the assistant principal at Maddie's school becomes a sore point between them because the woman makes her do homework that isn't even due for a week. And like fathers of fourteen-year-old daughters everywhere, he'd better get used to hearing the familiar whine, "Daaaad!"

The Fifth Witness (2011)

In *The Reversal*, Mickey Haller had to adapt to a new role as a prosecuting attorney. In *The Fifth Witness*, it's the distressed economy he needs to adjust to. Crime hasn't declined but the number of clients who can afford to hire him has, forcing him into a new branch of law, home-foreclosure defense.

During the Great Recession in 2008, millions of Americans faced the loss of their homes. The problem began when banks and other lending institutions made it far too easy for people who couldn't afford it to buy a home. When the economy later went sour, people lost their jobs at the same time that the value of their homes plummeted. Millions could neither pay their mortgages nor sell their homes, which were now worth less than what they owed on them. People turned to foreclosure lawyers like Haller to help them keep their homes. Thanks to his ads running on Spanish radio stations, he is forced to hire a new associate, Jennifer Aronson, who is fresh out of law school, to help him handle his ninety new clients.

One of his foreclosure clients now faces a much more serious problem than losing her home. Lisa Trammel, a thirty-five-year-old high school social studies teacher and mother of a nine-year-old son, lost her home after her husband left her. She has become increasingly agitated, especially since she also lost her teaching job. She has become so fixated on the bank that foreclosed on her home that it obtained a restraining order requiring her to stop picketing in front of the bank and to stay a hundred yards away from the property and its employees altogether. When Mitchell Bondurant, the bank's senior vice-president directly in charge of the home-loan division, is found murdered in the bank's parking garage and Trammel is spotted by a witness a block away only minutes after the murder, she is arrested. She now needs Haller to defend her against a murder charge.

Lisa Trammel turns out to be what Haller calls a "nuisance client," one who pesters him with daily phone calls for updates, questions his decisions, and ignores his advice. He soon comes to understand why her husband left her. But he also sees in her case a chance for a big payday. He knows that this could be *the* signature story about the country's biggest ongoing financial catastrophe. He has her sign a contract that gives him the right to have his Hollywood agent solicit book and movie deals, which would cover the $150,000 fee he charges but knows she can't pay.

Just before the trial begins, his life is complicated by two things. Lisa has made a deal with a small-time Hollywood producer named Herbert Dahl to pay her bail and find a film deal for her, totally ignoring the terms of the contract she had just signed with Haller. He manages to get that problem settled, but his second problem is more serious. While walking to his car in the parking garage, a pair of thugs approach and beat him viciously, leaving him with thirty-eight stitches in his head, nine fractured ribs, four broken fingers, two bruised kidneys, and one severely twisted testicle. Someone wants him off the case, but he refuses to let his injuries slow him down.

The prosecution has some pretty damning evidence against Trammel: she was seen near the murder site at about the time of the murder; and Bondurant's blood is found on a hammer, now missing from its normal place in her garage, and on a pair of her shoes. Haller hopes to counter this with the fact that Bondurant, who is ten inches taller than her, was killed by a hammer blow to the top of his head, which seems all but impossible for the much shorter woman to have done. His best defense strategy is to come up with an alternate theory, what he calls building "the hypothesis of innocence" (82). The key piece of evidence here is a letter Bondurant sent to Louis Opparizio, owner of the company handling the paperwork in Lisa's foreclosure, in which he threatens to expose him for fraudulent behavior. That just might convince the jury that Lisa Trammel wasn't the only one with a motive for killing Bondurant.

Connelly's challenge in the novel is making a trial without much drama interesting to the reader. He does this in part by finding clever ways for Haller to describe the proceedings. For example, he characterizes the sometimes-tedious process of selecting a jury as a simple matter of finding the twelve strangers each side hopes they can "mold into our own soldiers of justice" (153). He attaches names like "the hunter-gatherer stage" and "the science day" to each step in the prosecution's case. We are schooled in the importance of choreographed moves—like having his client reach out to touch his arm at a previously arranged moment—and time management strategies. At the end of the day, with say thirty minutes remaining, which witness do you choose? Do you want one whose testimony will fit into the time slot, or one who will give the jury something to think about overnight before that witness resumes the next day?

Haller also uses several sports references to describe his various courtroom moves. Questioning one witness has him "bobbing and weaving, jabbing with the left when he was expecting the right, a hit-and-run mission" (218). Sometimes it's a move borrowed from a game of football: "When you're a defense lawyer you have to be like a cornerback. You know you're going to get burned from time to time. It's just part of the game. So when it happens you have to pick yourself up, dust yourself off and forget about it because they're about to snap the ball again" (373). He even throws in a baseball metaphor when he can't believe the judge hasn't chastised a witness for what he just said: "I looked at the judge and spread my hands like a baseball manager who just saw a fastball down the pipe called a ball" (221).

Connelly also creates a certain amount of suspense by giving some of the chapters cliffhanger endings. For example, as Haller heads to the judge's chamber to discuss a motion, he says, "I was confident that I was about to tilt the case in the defense's direction or I was headed to jail for contempt" (232). But the real suspense comes at the end of the trial after Haller plays his ace in the hole: the fifth witness. That person is Louis Opparizio, his fifth defense witness and the one he succeeds in forcing to invoke the Fifth Amendment against self-incrimination when Haller begins asking questions about his family's connection to the Gambino mob in New York. The witness is dismissed and the trial ends. Surprisingly, the jury comes back quickly with its verdict—not guilty.

While Haller and his team are attending a celebration/fundraising affair that Lisa has put together, he watches as she begins to inflate some helium balloons for the kids in attendance. Suddenly, the truth hits him. She did it! She used a helium-filled balloon to get Bondurant to tilt his head way back to look up, enabling her to hit him directly on the top of his head with her hammer. "She had me wired from day one," Haller now realizes. "Everything was part of her plan" (416).

In the final chapter, Haller's mood has lightened. It's been three weeks since Lisa's party and he's sitting in the back seat of his Lincoln listening to Eric Clapton's "Judgement Day" as his car comes out of the tunnel and into the bright sunlight. He has achieved a measure of redemption by anonymously phoning the police with a suggestion that they should dig up the garden in Lisa's back yard, where they discover the body of her murdered husband. He left her, but not in the way she claimed. When Lisa asks him to defend her on her new murder charge, he declines: "I'm changing my life. I'm tired of being around people like you" (419). Instead, he decides to run for district attorney.

In addition to being a compelling legal thriller, the novel also offers the fullest portrait of Mickey Haller to date. Unlike in *The Reversal*, where the narrative shifted back and forth between Haller and Bosch, this time the focus remains entirely on Haller. (Bosch is limited to a single brief appearance when he and his daughter show up at Haller's birthday party.) We are given further insight into Haller's professional side when his attempts to educate the idealistic Jennifer Aronson about the real ways of the world force him to articulate (and even question) his own beliefs about what being a defense attorney really entails.

While Aronson believes it's important to know if your client is innocent, Haller tries to tell her the truth: "You never ask your client if he did it. Yes or no, the answer is only a distraction. So you don't need to know" (83). Sometimes knowing things limits you, he says. "Not knowing them gives you more latitude in crafting a defense" (57). When she's disturbed by what appears to be a lie Haller tells while questioning a witness, he defends himself by splitting hairs semantically. "Don't go growing a conscience on me," he warns her. "I've been down that road. It doesn't lead you to anything good" (84). But as the trial continues, she continues to struggle with the ethics of what he does. "I felt sympathy for her," he admits, "but not too much. Idealism dies hard with everybody" (239).

Despite his confident manner in the courtroom, in private Haller has always been a more vulnerable, more introspective, and less assured character than Bosch, and in his first-person narrative, he's willing to share those fears and doubts, especially about his personal life. He's at the point where he can't shake the dream that he and Maggie and their daughter will one day live together again as a family. But whenever he presses Maggie about getting back together, she resists, knowing as she does that the primary reason for their breakup—i.e., that they are both people who bring their work home with them—hasn't changed. She seems comfortable with their current relationship as good friends, parents with a shared interest in the welfare of their daughter, and occasional bed partners. That's not enough for Haller, but he's afraid that if he pushes her too hard to make a choice—marriage or end the relationship—she'll choose the latter. And his deepest fear is what his life would be like with her completely gone from it.

As a defense lawyer, Haller hasn't been able to forget the warning his famous lawyer father once gave him that "there is no client as scary as an innocent man." That lesson hit him hard in *The Lincoln Lawyer* where he caused one innocent client to go to prison because he refused to believe in his innocence and freed another client because he mistakenly believed in his innocence and let a guilty man go free. Not wanting to know whether or not Lisa is innocent may have helped him craft a strategy to win her case, but was it the right thing to do? And he keeps wishing he could do something that would make Maggie and Hayley proud of him.

Maybe Haller shouldn't have been so critical of Aronson for growing a conscience, for he may now be doing the very same thing. Instead of her following his advice—she decides she doesn't like criminal defense anymore and wants to return to foreclosure cases—it is he who follows her example in leaving criminal defense behind to run for district attorney. Is this simply a desperate ploy to win his ex-wife back or a step in a new direction? Only time (and the next Haller novel) will tell.

The Fifth Witness won the Harper Lee Award for Legal Fiction in 2012, which is only fitting considering how important *To Kill a Mockingbird* was to Connelly. When asked by *Esquire* magazine, "What is the one book every man should read?" he answered, *To Kill a Mockingbird* (Perri). One of his most prized possessions is an inscribed copy of the novel. And he honored the librarian in the Fort Lauderdale library who first put the novel into his hands when he was thirteen years old by dedicating *The Overlook* to her.

The Drop (2011)

Bosch has a pair of unrelated cases to solve in *The Drop*, a situation Connelly compares to a double helix, with the strands winding around each other but not intersecting. Each case, however, offers further reflections on two of Bosch's recurring concerns: high jingo and the nature of evil.

Bosch and partner David Chu are assigned a case dating back to 1989, when nineteen-year-old Lily Price was raped and stabbed to death. Thanks to new technology, the DNA found on a drop of blood on her neck has now been identified as belonging to Clayton Pell, who has spent six years in prison for rape and is currently living in a halfway house. The only problem is that Pell would have been eight years old at the time of the murder. Was there a mix-up in DNA testing at the state forensic lab or some other possible explanation for how his blood ended up on Lily Price?

The story Pell recounts when Bosch meets up with him at the halfway house is truly horrifying. He reveals that at age eight, he was regularly sexually assaulted and frequently beaten by his mother's boyfriend, a man he knew only as Chill. Bosch concludes that the belt the killer used to strangle Lily Price was likely the same belt he used to beat Clayton Pell. That's how his blood got on her neck. Now he has to find the man named Chill.

In his second case, long-time nemesis Irvin Irving has asked him to investigate the death of his son George. A consultant for hire who uses his connections to his father to get his clients access to important people in City Hall, he died after falling from the balcony of his room at the Chateau Marmont hotel. Hours earlier, he had checked into room 704, where he and his wife had celebrated their honeymoon (and where Connelly wrote much of the novel). Since being forced out of the department, Irving has been elected to the city council, where he has sought to get revenge against his former department by voting against every proposal to raise salary and to cut one hundred million dollars from the overtime budget. He also has enough muscle to get Bosch assigned to the case. Even though he doesn't like him, he respects his relentlessness and integrity. Bosch immediately suspects the case will involve high jingo, i.e., political pressure. Does Irving intend to use what he finds out about his son's death against the department?

George Irving's death appears to be a simple case of suicide until Bosch finds a series of four crescent moons, each about two inches high, on his shoulder. He recognizes the pattern as one often left by the large military watches worn by many of the LAPD cops who employed the chokehold to render a person temporarily unconscious. That technique was later banned by the department after it was linked to several deaths. Bosch soon has a suspect and a motive for a possible murder: a former LAPD cop who was fired for overusing the chokehold. He is now part-owner of a taxi business that is losing its Hollywood taxi franchise to another company that paid George Irving $100,000 to ensure that the L.A. City Council approve the switch. If Irving's father was in on the deal, the blowback will be intense.

(Many of Connelly's novels have a ripped-from-the-headlines immediacy about them; in this case, it took a decade for that to happen, thanks to the nationwide furor over the death of George Floyd by a police chokehold in 2020. No one who has seen the chilling video that ends with his dying words, "I can't breathe," can fail to see the deadly consequences of the practice. Connelly, however, points out one of the ironies of the ban in L.A. Police were now required to carry batons and a Taser. It was the Tasing and beating of Rodney King by batons in 1991 that led to the devastating L.A. riots in 1992. A simple chokehold might have rendered him unconscious and avoided the tragic aftermath.)

In the Lily Price case, Bosch finally tracks down the man Pell called Chill, whose real name is Chilton Hardy. He pulls a gun and threatens to kill Hardy in order to force him to confess. It works. Hardy admits to killing Lily Price as well as thirty-six other victims: "You're going to be famous, Bosch," he tells him. "You caught the goddam record holder.... I planted thirty-seven crosses" (325). What Bosch sees next shakes him to the core.

The walls of Hardy's apartment where he carried out his killings are covered with photographs of his victims and accounts of his murders from newspapers around the country. The upstairs bathtub still has a brownish ring around it from all the blood that had been washed off there. Bosch also finds a stash of Polaroid photos, VHS tapes, and DVDs of his victims, indications that the killings took place over many years. All of this leaves Bosch gasping for air. (The case is based on the real-life story of the Grim Sleeper that is mentioned in the novel. Lonnie David Franklin, Jr., was arrested in 2010 for murdering at least ten victims in L.A. between 1985 and 2007. Found in his home were over 1000 photographs and hundreds of hours of video of naked women, many of them his murder victims.)

The resolution of this case echoes that in *The Closers*, where the father of a murdered girl deliberately gets himself arrested so he can kill his daughter's murderer. This time it's Clayton Pell who assaults a cop in order to get arrested and taken to court on the same bus he learns Hardy will be on. He seeks revenge against Hardy for turning him into the sexual predator he has become. This time, however, Bosch figures out what Pell is planning and manages to stop him while he's in the midst of strangling Hardy with the chain around his waist. But he's not sure that saving the life of such a monster was the right thing to do. He robbed Pell of a final chance for redemption; instead, he'll be sent back to prison and the man who ruined his life will get to live. Hardy may at some time in the future face execution, but in the meantime he can bask in his newfound celebrity status. As for Bosch, "he knew he would carry the guilt for his actions of the day for a long time" (382).

Kiz Rider, Bosch's former partner who now works in the chief's office, had earlier asked him to slow down the case against Hardy for a month until after the next city council election. She argues it's "for the good of the department," six words Bosch knows "never added up to anything but high jingo" (386). She fears that Irving will use that case as evidence that the department failed for years to recognize a serial killer on the loose. The department plans to use the appearance of Irving's complicity in a pay-for-play scam with his son (based on false information they created) to get him defeated in the upcoming city council election. Bosch now realizes it was Kiz, not Irving, who was hoping to use him for political gain.

During the course of the novel, Bosch makes several decisions he comes to regret but is able to correct. The first involves David Chu, his partner of two years. It's not easy being Bosch's partner; even Kiz Rider, his favorite, judged him to be an "asshole" of a partner. Bosch likes to go it alone and routinely keeps his partners out of the loop. Most end up feeling like his employees rather than trusted equals. "Is this how it's always going to be, Harry?" Chu complains. "You just tell me what to do and when to do it. I never get a say" (286)? Things come to a head when Bosch reads a story in the newspaper that contains compromising information that could have only come from Chu. Chu confesses but defends himself by saying, "If you had treated me right, I never would have done it!" (245). Bosch responds by telling him that as soon as their current cases are over, so is their partnership.

But unlike Bosch's previous partner Ignacio Farras, who was tragically killed trying to prove to Bosch that he was a worthy partner, Chu is more successful in achieving redemption. He and Bosch are summoned to a meeting with the chief of police and Irvin Irving, during which Bosch takes some heat. This triggers an outburst from Chu—"Harry Bosch has more integrity than anybody I've ever met. Anybody in this room" (292)—which leaves everybody shocked, including Bosch. It is also Chu whose digging produces the address that leads to Hardy's capture. Later Bosch tries to make up with his partner. "I just wanted to say you did good today. We did good as partners," he says, and then adds, "So never mind all that stuff from before, okay? We'll just start from here" (356).

Bosch also changes his mind about keeping his job. According to the terms of the Deferred Retirement Option Program (DROP), cops like him who return to the department are allowed one renewal period of up to five years. (The title of the novel refers not only to that program but to the drop of blood found on Lily Price's neck and the fatal drop from the top of the Chateau Marmont hotel that killed George Irving.) Initially he's happy to hear he's been given an extension on the job for thirty-nine more months. However, the Irving case forces him to wonder whether he's losing his edge, and he tells his daughter it might be time to retire. But after witnessing the horrors of what Hardy has done, he decides to stay, especially after being offered a full five-year extension. "Two days ago he didn't think he could leg out the last thirty-nine months of his career. Now he wanted the full five years" (339). What he has come to realize is that his mission is not over. There is more work to be done. He'll remain a cop for another five years.

He makes another decision that is more personal. His initial meeting with Dr. Hannah Stone, the rehabilitation program director at the halfway house where Pell is staying, doesn't go well as he makes it clear he doesn't believe that predators can be rehabilitated. Later, he feels embarrassed by his arrogance and admits that in many ways, she was doing more good than he was by trying to stop crimes before they happened. He returns to apologize and before long they are enjoying lunch and each other's company. Soon the relationship becomes a romantic one.

A dinner conversation between the two of them unexpectedly moves from small talk to the knotty problem of evil. "Where does it come from?" Hannah asks. "How do people become evil? Is it in the air? Do you catch it like a cold?" (199). Bosch is at first reluctant to answer questions like these. He believes it's his job to find evil and take it out of the world, not worry about where it comes from. But she persists, and they move on to the nature-versus-nurture argument. Bosch acknowledges that in the case of Clayton Pell, evil was nurtured by the actions of his mother's boyfriend. But he also points out that not everyone in his situation becomes a monster. All he can say is that his job and hers come into play only after the damage is done. And then she reveals the reason behind all her questions: her son is serving time in San Quentin on a rape charge. Is he evil? Who is responsible?

The first night they spend together in bed makes Bosch feel that Hannah just might be the right woman to bring into the life he was now sharing with his daughter. But when she brings up her son again, warning lights go off and he starts to wonder if perhaps she is only using him as a "means to a hopeful end that was about her son and not them" (222). Has his loneliness and need for connection caused him to make a mistake with Hannah? This relationship appears doomed.

The novel's theoretical discussion of evil is countered by a scene that depicts the horrifying presence of real evil, no matter the cause. What Bosch sees on one of Hardy's videos is more gut-wrenching and horrible than anything he's ever encountered. It shows Hardy raping and torturing a woman, who begs him to kill her to put her out of her misery, which he does by strangling her while smiling. Later, Bosch finds a photo of what appears to be a naked Lily Price lying on a dirty blanket, though it's not clear whether she's alive or dead. He makes a positive identification by comparing it to her smiling face in her high school yearbook, further evidence of how easily a promising life can be snuffed out by a monster.

If there's one bright spot in Bosch's life, it's his daughter Maddie and the relationship that is developing between them. She's showing definite signs of becoming a chip off the old block by declaring she wants to be a cop like her father and has even begun taking shooting lessons. She also displays some of the skills every cop needs. When she notices an important detail he overlooked in a video her father shows her of Irving checking into the hotel, he is impressed by her powers of observation. She's also canny enough to smoke out information about Bosch's new girlfriend by asking him to explain the lipstick on one of the two wineglasses she found in the dishwater. After he comes clean, she confesses she just bluffed him; there was no lipstick. "You know something, kid?" he says. "Someday you're going to be the one they'll want in the interview room" (269).

So where does a father like Bosch take his daughter on an outing? To Catalina Island, and not for the scenery. Maddie, whose marksmanship puts his to shame, has entered a pistol-shooting competition at a local gun club. The only girl in the contest, she wins her first match although is eliminated in the second. The proud father has to put on his sunglasses so no one can see the look in his eyes: "Most parents were raising citizens of the future. Doctors, teachers, mothers, keepers of family businesses. Bosch was raising a warrior" (301).

The Black Box (2012)

The Black Box had special significance to Connelly. It was his twenty-fifth novel and also marked the twentieth anniversary of the publication of his very first one. Two thousand twelve was also the twentieth anniversary of another major event, this one far less joyous—the destructive riots in South Los Angeles following the not-guilty verdict in the trial of the four white L.A. cops who were caught on video savagely beating a Black man named Rodney King.

The riots also had personal meaning for Connelly, and not only because he was thunderstruck by what was happening to his city. He was covering the story for the *Los Angeles Times* when the not-guilty verdict was announced. Everyone expected a guilty verdict and shock quickly turned to anger and then to violence. Connelly was suddenly caught in the middle of an angry mob and had to be rescued by the timely intercession of a Black man wearing a t-shirt with the word LOVE on it who led him safely to his car. The novel is dedicated to that unknown man.

The action begins on the third day of rioting when Bosch and partner Jerry Edgar are dispatched to the scene of the riots where "the acrid smell of burning rubber and smoldering dreams was still everywhere. Flames from a thousand fires reflected like the devil dancing in the dark sky" (4). Their job involves hopping from one crime scene to another under the protection of the National Guard, gathering evidence, documenting the scene, and collecting the dead. Then on to the next murder.

After quickly handling the case of a man shot by the owner of the store he was looting, Bosch and Edgar move on to an alley off Crenshaw where the body of a white woman has been found. They quickly determine she wasn't a victim of random violence but had been deliberately shot at point-blank range execution style sometime within the past twenty-four hours. A press card on her chest identifies her as Anneke Jespersen, who they later learn was a photojournalist for a Danish newspaper. The only piece of evidence Bosch finds is a brass bullet casing on the gravel near the body. Suddenly, the sound of gunfire forces them to duck for cover. Edgar notices that when Bosch ducked down, he shielded the dead woman's body as if she were still alive. Before leaving Bosch whispers to her, "I'm sorry," a sure sign he won't rest easy until the killer of this woman is brought to justice.

Twenty years later, to commemorate the anniversary of the riots, the Open-Unsolved Unit is assigned the task of taking a fresh look at all the unsolved murders from the riots. Bosch, who has always felt he had abandoned Anneke Jespersen, requests that case. It's a long shot because it lacks a black box which, like the one recovered after a plane crash, contains enough information to identify its cause. The sole piece of evidence he has is that single shell casing. But based on what we've seen Bosch do over the past twenty years, there's little doubt he'll find the killer.

Connelly usually creates difficult hurdles Bosch must overcome in order to continue his mission. This time there are two. The first comes from the chief of police, who asks him to slow down his investigation. He fears the political consequences if the only murder during the riot that is solved is that of a white woman possibly killed by a Black gang member. The other comes as a result of Bosch's relationship with Dr. Hannah Stone, the therapist with whom he had become romantically involved in his previous novel. Thanks to the latest technology in DNA testing, the murder weapon has finally been traced to a man named Rufus Coleman, a Crips gang member now serving a sentence for murder in San Quentin. He was in prison at the time of the murder, so Bosch travels to San Francisco to try to get him to name the person he claims he gave the gun to. He also has time to pay a brief visit to Hannah's son

Shawn, who is also there serving a sentence for rape. Before leaving, he generously deposits $100 into his prison canteen account. But once his boss finds out about this, he's in trouble.

Bosch's new boss, Lt. Cliff O'Toole, is the kind of administrator Bosch hates, a numbers cruncher rather than a cop's cop. The two are at odds from the very beginning. "You are the worst kind of police officer," O'Toole tells Bosch. "You are arrogant, you are a bully, and you think the laws and regulations simply don't apply to you" (187). To which Bosch retorts, "You left something out, Lieutenant.... You forgot that I close cases" (187). O'Toole now sees a way to rid the department of Bosch when he learns about his visit to Hannah Strong's son at San Quentin. He formally requests that Internal Affairs investigate him for conducting personal business at taxpayer expense. According to the terms of his DROP contract, Bosch can be dismissed if such a complaint is sustained. On top of everything, he now has to worry about keeping his job.

What follows is largely a conventional police procedural, with Bosch and partner David Chu conducting a slow-and-steady, step-by-step investigation. Unlike the situation in many of his previous novels, this is the only case Bosch is working on and there is little drama for most of his investigation. He needs to investigate two main questions: (1) who owned the gun that killed Jespersen and (2) why was she in L.A. at the time of the riots? The answer to both involves another major event from the early 1990s, Operation Desert Storm. Bosch learns that Jespersen was a correspondent during the war and by chance found herself on a cruise ship where U.S. soldiers were enjoying a few days of rest and relaxation. There she met up with a group of National Guardsmen from central California who, as luck would have it, were deployed to riot duty in L.A. one year later. In fact, one of them, J.J. Drummond, now a county sheriff in Modesto, was the guardsman who led Bosch to Jespersen's body.

It initially appears that Jespersen might have been investigating the soldiers for some sort of war crime, but while the crime did occur during the war, Bosch learns it was personal. He requests a week of vacation time so he can travel to Modesto where all the Desert Storm soldiers who knew Jespersen still live. He has no evidence, only a hunch that he might find some answers there. He tracks down one of the soldiers, Reggie Banks, whom he arrests (though he has no legal jurisdiction) and brings him back to his motel room, which he has arranged to look like an interrogation room. He reads him his rights and scares him into talking. Banks confesses that he and three of his buddies drugged and gang-raped Jespersen while they were together on the ship. She was murdered the following year in L.A. by J.J. Drummond, the guardsman who led Bosch to her body. He is the driving force behind a conspiracy to keep their crime hidden, especially now that he is planning to run for Congress.

At this point, Drummond suddenly shows up at the motel room and forces Bosch and Banks at gunpoint to come with him. Drummond brings the two men to a remote location where he shoots Banks but then leaves, giving Bosch time enough to escape. He uses the pin from Banks's watch buckle to open the handcuffs binding his wrists, although he's unable to open the locked doors to the barn where he's being held. But then Nancy Mendenhall, the Internal Affairs detective who had been assigned to investigate him, suddenly shows up to open the bolted door for him.

Her explanation for being there—that she followed him to Modesto on her own simply because she was curious about what he was doing—doesn't make a whole lot of sense. Meanwhile Drummond, who years earlier had killed another of his soldier buddies to silence him, shoots the two remaining members of the group as soon as they arrive. He attempts to flee the scene by helicopter, but it crashes into the blade of a wind turbine on the property, leaving him paralyzed from the neck down.

Although Bosch left the impression in *The Drop* that his relationship with Hannah Stone was over, she returns in *The Black Box*, but almost entirely for plot purposes. It is Bosch's visit to her son in prison that first creates a major complication for him, for it turns out he was the one who initiated the complaint against him. He feared he was losing his mother's attention and was hoping to drive a wedge between her and Bosch. She also serves a useful purpose as a convenient babysitter for Maddie, which allows Bosch to go off freelancing in Modesto to solve the case on his own time.

Connelly's plots are usually well-oiled efforts whose individual parts fit together smoothly, but some of the plot machinery in *The Black Box* creaks awkwardly. Despite these rare hiccups, *The Black Box* is another reminder of what has made Bosch such a popular character with readers. Only someone with his single-minded determination could against all odds achieve justice for a murder, even if it takes him twenty years to accomplish the task. As a bonus, we are also given some new insights into Bosch's past as well as several scenes with Maddie that show him growing into his new role as a loving father.

The Gods of Guilt (2013)

Mickey Haller's hopes for a happy reunion of his family are dashed when he loses the election for district attorney because of the actions of one of his clients. Shortly after he gets a drunk-driving charge against the man dropped on a technicality, his client kills two people while driving drunk. Haller's sixteen-year-old daughter Hayley cuts off all contact with him because the victims were a classmate of hers and her mother, who was also her homeroom teacher. On a far less serious note, Haller is also not entirely happy about the success of *The Lincoln Lawyer* film based on him. So many lawyers are now working out of Lincoln Town Cars that he often mistakenly sits in the back seat of some other lawyer's car.

Andre La Cosse, a digital pimp who runs the social media site for a number of hooker clients, has just been arrested for the murder of one of those clients, Giselle Dallinger. He wants Haller to take his case because the murdered woman once told him he was the best lawyer around. Who is this Giselle Dallinger who recommended him so highly? It turns out her real name is Gloria Dayton and up until seven years ago, she and Haller shared a long history.

Haller had defended Dayton at least six times over the years on drug and prostitution charges. Although they were never sexually involved, he took a liking to the young woman and several times helped her out by getting her into pretrial intervention programs and halfway houses. He hasn't seen her in seven years but assumed from an occasional postcard he got that she had straightened out her life. Now he feels angry and disappointed to learn that she had returned to prostitution. He has another reason to feel bad because he fears that her murder might be related to a deal he made on her behalf years earlier.

Hector Arrande Moya, a member of the Sinaloan drug cartel, is serving a life sentence in prison because during his last arrest on a drug charge, a gun was found under his pillow, which added a weapons charge that allowed for the life sentence. He has just filed a habeas corpus petition seeking to vacate his sentence by claiming the gun was planted by Gloria Dayton. Seven years ago, Haller did arrange a deal to keep Gloria out of prison in return for snitching on Moya, who was her drug dealer, but he knew nothing about claims that she was also working with a rogue DEA agent named James Marco to get Moya sent away for life on the gun charge. Could her murder be related to that case? If he can prove it was, that could get La Cosse acquitted on the murder charge.

The first half of the novel is largely devoted to searching for evidence of a possible conspiracy between Gloria Dayton, James Marco, and a former cop named Lee Lankford to plant the gun that got Moya sent to prison for life. Haller and Lankford also have a past history. In *The Lincoln Lawyer*, Lankford tried to pin the murder of Haller's investigator Raul Levin on him. Haller proved him wrong by solving the crime, which earned Lankford's enmity. Now retired and working for the DA as an investigator, he gets himself assigned to the La Cosse case. This gives him an opportunity to keep a close eye on Haller and to bombard him with frequent insults—his first words to Haller when they meet again are, "Well, well, well, if it isn't Mickey Mouth, great courtroom orator and defender of douche bags" (66).

Haller's a lawyer, not a detective, so all the investigating is done by Cisco, his crack investigator, and since Haller is the narrator of the novel, all that detective work takes place off stage. Sometimes, this is no problem, as for example when Cisco collects all the security camera videos of Gloria's visit to a client she was supposed to meet at the Beverly Wilshire hotel. We sit beside Haller as he views the videos and spots a mysterious man in a hat who has been following Gloria the whole time. This all takes place just hours before her death. Could that mysterious man, later identified as Lee Lankford, be her murderer?

It becomes clear early on that Andre La Cosse is innocent, especially after Haller discovers a GPS tracker on his car, which suggests that someone is closely following him wherever he goes. And that someone also wants him dead, which becomes evident when a tow truck runs his Lincoln off the freeway, seriously injuring him and killing his driver Earl. To compound his physical pain he now feels guilty for not removing the tracking device when he discovered it, enabling the tow truck to follow them. The title of the novel refers to the jurors in a trial who determine the guilt or innocence of the accused, but it also applies to the voices Haller hears inside his head who remind him of those like Gloria Dayton, Earl Briggs, and the mother and daughter killed by his drunken client, who all died as a consequence of his actions.

Cisco and his team obtain the video evidence Haller needs to prove the conspiracy between Marco and Lankford, though how they get it borders on the implausible. On his trial witness list Haller puts the name of a man who lives across the street from a house where several years earlier Marco and Lankford investigated the murders of two drug dealers. His hope is that the two of them will become suspicious when they see the name and investigate. He pays the homeowner $4000 to rent the place for two weeks, telling him it's for a film production. Cisco and his men then hide cameras all over the house and wait. Haller's hunch pays off when Marco and Lankford conveniently show up one night. Once they get inside the house, the video shows Marco planting drugs inside a pizza box in the refrigerator freezer, clear evidence of conspiracy between the two men.

As the trial winds down, Haller is hit with a pair of shocking surprises. After leaving court one day, La Cosse is viciously attacked by another prisoner with a sharpened shiv and is in a hospital fighting for his life. The prosecution demands that the judge declare a mistrial, but Haller objects. He needs the trial to continue in order to secure a not-guilty verdict for his client. To do this, he convinces the judge that he was able to get the comatose La Cosse to sign a waiver of attendance, which allows the trial to continue without his physical presence in the courtroom.

The second shock comes at the end of Detective Lankford's testimony. Once he learns that Haller has the incriminating video of what he and Marco did, he realizes he has no choice but to confess to his role in the scheme to frame Moya and help set up the murder of Gloria Dayton by James Marco. At the conclusion of his testimony, he melodramatically pulls a gun from his sock and blows his brains out in front of the shocked audience in the courtroom. The trial is over, and Haller's client is set free.

Haller is increasingly coming into his own as a character, especially in the contrast between him and Bosch. They do share at least one important feature in common: like his half-brother, Haller likes to break the rules. According to him, the law is "like soft medal ... it could be bent and molded" (15), and bend it (and sometimes break it) he often does. A good example occurs in the opening chapter of the novel. After failing to shake the testimony of a sixty-year-old woman whose car was hijacked by his client, that client angrily attacks him, leaving him with a bloodied mouth and shirt. The judge has no choice but to declare a mistrial.

But in the very next chapter we learn that the attack was orchestrated with the help of David "Legal" Siegel, Haller's late father's partner. The blood in Haller's mouth came not from a punch but from a capsule he had hidden there. He figures a mistrial will get a better deal for his client from the prosecution, which likely won't want to go through with a new trial. Haller's no saint, but like Bosch he's damned good at what he does in the courtroom, even if he doesn't always play by the rules.

But there are some key differences between the two men. Haller is not the loner Bosch is. He surrounds himself with a professional family that keeps growing. In addition to ex-wife Lorna and her husband Cisco, Bosch has a new associate, Jennifer Aronson. At one strategy meeting of Team Haller, the regulars are also joined by Bosch's driver Earl Briggs and his mentor David Siegel. Unlike Bosch, who routinely criticizes his partners, Haller listens to his associates and praises them for the good work they do.

Connelly uses Bosch's lone appearance in the novel—he and Haller meet briefly in a courtroom hallway—to remind Haller of another important difference between them: both have daughters the same age, but while Bosch's daughter still talks to him on a regular basis, his no longer does because Bosch "put bad people in jail. I got them out" (250). While Bosch has found happiness in building a strong relationship with his teenage daughter, Haller's daughter is becoming less and less a presence in his life.

Haller's unhappiness over the estrangement from his family causes him to become something of a stalker. He drives by his ex-wife's condo to look at the lighted windows and imagine his daughter in her bedroom doing her homework. He also regularly visits a park overlooking a soccer field so he can watch from a distance as she practices with her team. When she doesn't show up at practice one day, he becomes concerned, only to learn that no one had bothered to tell him that she had quit the team and taken up horseback riding. To compound his suffering, ex-wife Maggie informs him that she has taken a job in Ventura County and she and Hayley will be moving out of L.A.

The novel ends six months after the trial and Haller's situation has improved. He has won a $2.4 million dollar settlement for La Cosse, who had sued the city for the physical and mental harm caused by his wrongful arrest and false incarceration. He uses his share of the money to give big bonuses to his team and $100,000 to Earl Briggs's mother. He can also take some satisfaction in knowing that he solved the murder of Gloria Dayton when the police didn't and that a drug cartel took care of James Marco when he fled to Mexico. Above all, a favorable article about him and the case that appears in the *Los Angeles Times* re-opens communication again with his daughter.

The Burning Room (2014)

The Burning Room is a classic police procedural with one of Connelly's most satisfying investigative plots. Now in the final year of his DROP contract, Bosch is asked to look into the death of Orlando Merced, a mariachi musician who was shot in the abdomen and paralyzed ten years earlier. He has only now succumbed to the blood poisoning caused by the bullet lodged in his spine, which officially makes his death a murder. That bullet is the only clue to his killer.

The head of the Open-Unsolved Unit has decided to create new teams by pairing an experienced veteran cop with a rookie. As the oldest detective in the department, Bosch is assigned the youngest newcomer, Lucia Soto, a twenty-eight-year-old Mexican American. Bosch has a checkered history with his partners, few of whom ever live up to his high standards. In the three previous cases he and Soto investigated together, he was impressed by her work. But then she commits a cardinal sin. While working late at the office one night, Bosch texts her to ask where she is. She replies she's at home and about to go to bed. But then he discovers her in a nearby room photocopying the pages of a murder book on a case that isn't theirs. Angry at being lied to, he demands to know what she's doing.

The case she's copying dates back twenty-one years to a fire at the Bonnie Brae apartments during which nine children at an unlicensed day-care center located there perished. The rumor at the time was that some gang members started the fire because the apartment manager wouldn't let them deal drugs in the building. This isn't their case; why is she pulling these files? She answers by rolling up the sleeve of her shirt to show Bosch a tattoo of five names of friends of hers who were killed in that fire. She, too, was trapped with them in a supply closet, but was lucky to have made it out alive. Bosch now sees in Soto the same sense of personal mission that drives him. He agrees to help.

Bosch has been around long enough to have witnessed the dramatic changes in policing that have turned the job of investigation into a desk-bound activity: "Keyboards and cell phones were the main tools of the modern investigator. Detectives sat in twelve-hundred-dollar chairs and wore sleek designer shoes with tassels. Gone were the days of thick rubber soles and function over form, when a detective's motto was 'Get off your ass and go knock on doors'" (74). He's also old school enough to remind his young new partner of the dictum that says, "Cases are made with patience and little steps.... Not lightning strikes" (198). The search for the truth can be a tedious slog, but Connelly manages to make the painstaking step-by-step process Bosch and Soto follow interesting by incorporating the old and the new, the latest technology with old-fashioned shoe-leather, occasionally assisted by a stroke of luck to keep the momentum of the investigation going.

Orlando Merced was shot while relaxing with his three bandmates at Mariachi Plaza where they were waiting in hopes of picking up another job. The initial explanation is that he was accidentally hit by a stray bullet fired during a gang confrontation. But after a digital expert in the department's new Video Forensic Unit is able to enhance and triangulate videos from three different camera locations at Mariachi Plaza, an alternative explanation emerges. In a scene that echoes one in Michelangelo Antonioni's classic 1966 film *Blow-Up*, Bosch and Soto repeatedly watch the enhanced videos in slow motion on three separate screens until they begin to notice details they had missed before.

Blow-Up was also the inspiration for one of Connelly's favorite films, Francis Ford Coppola's *The Conversation* (1974), where surveillance expert Harry Caul, played by Gene Hackman, eventually hears evidence of a possible murder plot after painstakingly refining and editing the recorded conversation between two people captured on several different devices. Harry Caul was also one of the major influences on the character of Harry Bosch.

As they zoom in closer on one screen, they spot a brief flash in the window where the bullet came from. After studying the location and behavior of Merced's three bandmates at the moment of the shooting, it also becomes clear that one of them, Angel Ojeda, was the intended target, not Merced. They track Ojeda down in Tulsa, Oklahoma, where he fled following the shooting. From him they learn the motive behind the botched attempt on his life: he did not end the affair with the wife of a powerful man named Bruce Broussard, despite Broussard's threat to kill him if he didn't. When Bosch learns that Broussard is a major donor to Armando Zetas, a former two-term mayor of L.A. who is about to launch a bid for the governorship of California, he fears the worst, i.e., that the case is tangled up in politics in some way.

Bosch's daughter Maddie, who is a member of the Police Explorer Unit, a program for high school kids considering a career in law enforcement, even gets to contribute a key piece of information. Her father takes her to a shooting range once owned by Broussard, where they learn that he sold the place nine years earlier after an accident on the property. Maddie does some digital digging on her own and finds a newspaper story about the incident in which Broussard accidentally shot his best friend David Willman, the manager of the range and a gun dealer. Following up on Maddie's lead, Bosch learns that one of the guns Willman owned was the same model rifle that shot Merced and that was used in two other murders. This prompts another search, this one for the murder weapon, which Bosch finds hidden behind a gun cabinet in the garage of a home Willman once lived in.

Bosch begins his investigation into the Bonnie Brae arson case the same way he usually does, by systematically poring over all the old files and evidence gathered at the time. As he reads through some old, yellowed newspaper clips from twenty-one years ago, a story on the back of one of them about an unrelated crime—the armed robbery of EZ Bank, a check-cashing business that netted $265,000 in cash—catches his eye. He notices that the robbery occurred only a short distance away from the Bonnie Brae fire just fifteen minutes after the fire was reported. Could there be a connection?

Soto uncovers a key piece of evidence when she learns that Ana

Acevedo, the bank employee who unlocked the steel door that allowed the robbers to get to the safe, was the roommate of a woman who had an apartment at the Bonnie Brae. That woman later confirms that Acevedo was often visited by two men, one the manager of the check-cashing place that was robbed, the other a security guard who was on duty there. Could one or more of them have been in on the robbery? And was the fire at the Bonnie Brae set deliberately as a distraction to give the robbers more time to carry out the robbery?

Ana Acevedo's former employer is able to provide Bosch with a W-2 tax statement from 1993 that she asked him to send to her current address in Calexico, California. It takes only a few moments for Soto to Google the address and find it belongs to a convent there. The two of them head out on the 200-mile drive to the border town to find what they hope might explain her role in the robbery.

Bosch and Soto are rewarded for all their hard work by solving both cases, which Connelly also uses to address a favorite pair of subjects. The first is how politics often hampers justice. Bosch has always been cynical about politicians, but he takes a strong personal dislike to Zetas when he discovers he is using his personal motto—"Everybody counts or nobody counts"—as a campaign slogan. Horrified when he first sees it on a poster, he tears it down in disgust. Bosch eventually determines that Zetas knew from the beginning who shot Merced but conspired with his chief of staff to keep that information secret in order to use it for his own political gain. Nothing can be legally proven about what Zetas did, but Bosch is happy that the negative publicity surrounding the case will likely doom his chances for the governorship.

Redemption is another recurring theme in the series, and Ana Acevedo is one of Connelly's most interesting examples of it. It's clear she played some role in the robbery, but whether she was connected to the Bonnie Brae fire is unknown. What interests Bosch is how she spent the rest of her life atoning for the deaths of those killed in the fire. When she first arrived at the convent, she identified herself as Esther Gonzalez, the name of the teacher who died trying to save her students. She paid off the convent's mortgage, possibly with her share of the robbery cash, and asked to join the order. Before Bosch gets a chance to speak with her, she is killed by cartel assassins in Mexico, where she had recently gone to work with the local children. After her death a note is found requesting that the following words be placed on her gravestone: "She Found Redemption for the Children with the Children."

The novel ends on a bittersweet note. Bosch's casual disregard of rules that stand in his way finally trips him up. His supervisor has obtained a video of him illegally picking the lock to the captain's room to get access to information he needed for his investigation into the EZ Bank robbery. This infraction is enough to force his suspension and likely dismissal from the LAPD.

Bosch now faces an uncertain future, but at least he's comforted by the knowledge that he has trained someone who can carry on his mission. In many ways he and Lucy Soto are kindred spirits: both suffered childhood trauma; both saw the same department psychologist following an incident while on duty; both are workaholics who arrive at the office early and leave late; she even buys the exact kind of notebook Bosch carries. Before he departs his office for the last time, Bosch gives Soto the kind of praise he never gave any of his previous partners: "The thing you have to remember is that you are one hell of an investigator. You know the secret. So don't let the fools around here drag you down. You have things to do, Lucy" (288). In return he receives a standing ovation from Soto and from Tim Marcia and Mitzi Roberts, two of the real-life detectives who have been Connelly's source for much of the inside information he has used to create the Bosch novels.

The Crossing (2015)

Unhappy about the way he was forced to leave the LAPD, Bosch hires his half-brother Mickey Haller to file a lawsuit against the city charging that the department had engaged in unlawful tactics to force his resignation. In turn, Haller surprises him by offering him a job as his chief investigator on a murder case against a client he believes is innocent.

Thirty-eight-year-old Lexi Parks, an assistant city manager for West Hollywood, was found dead in bed by her husband, a sheriff's deputy in Malibu. She had been sexually assaulted and brutally beaten to death with a blunt object. Six weeks later, DNA found in her body was identified as belonging to Da'Quan Foster, a former gang member who denied knowing the woman and claimed he was at work in his art studio at the time, an alibi discounted by a witness. Although he has a history of drug arrests and served a four-year sentence in prison, he has seemingly reformed his life; now an artist married with two children, he teaches after-school and weekend art classes to children in the neighborhood. Mickey Haller has become convinced of his innocence and wants Bosch to help him prove it in court.

As a retired detective, Bosch finds himself in unfamiliar territory: "He used to feel like an outsider with an insider's job. From now on he would be a full-time outsider" (50). Restoring a 1951 Harley-Davidson motorcycle as old as he is isn't entirely staving off boredom, but is crossing over to the other side the right thing to do? After spending his entire thirty-year career hunting down murderers, he's now being asked to help get one out of jail. "Did he miss the work so much," he asks himself, "that he could actually cross the aisle and work for an accused murderer?" (53). Not only would this violate his principles, it would feel like a betrayal to all his former LAPD colleagues. Even his daughter responds negatively to the thought that he might be putting a bad person back out onto the streets. And yet, despite all his reservations about taking the case, he is also bothered by the thought that if in fact Foster is innocent, then there is a "killer out there whom no one was looking for. A killer devious enough to set up an innocent man" (31). (The novel's title refers both to the place where killer and victim first cross paths and to what Bosch is doing as a police investigator working for the defense.)

Bosch begins his investigation by examining graphic photographs of the murder victim. He certainly doesn't enjoy this part of his job, but is thankful he has never gotten used to it because he still needs the emotional response to the result of human inhumanity that "lit the match that started the fire of relentlessness" (64). That match gets lit when he looks at Lexi's hands, which she had used to fight off her attacker. In the photos they are raised in surrender to her killer. Bosch also notices something else; on her wrist is faint indication of a tan line where she wore a watch. That watch—later identified as an Audemas Piguet Royal Offshore worth $14,000—will be the key to the solution to her murder.

When Bosch finally meets up with Da'Quan Foster, the man admits his claim that he was working at his studio at the time of the murder is untrue. He confesses that he was actually having sex with a male transvestite prostitute named James Allen at the time. Two days later, before Allen could confirm Foster's alibi, he was murdered. It looks like somebody is going to great lengths trying to frame Foster for Lexi Parks's murder.

The novel opens with two men named Ellis and Long driving behind a motorcycle. Ellis, the driver, suddenly announces he's about to fix a problem and then pulls directly into the path of the motorcycle, causing it to crash into oncoming traffic. Only later do we learn that the victim was Haller's investigator Cisco, who was seriously injured, which prompted Haller to try to bring Bosch in to continue the investigation Cisco had begun.

The novel includes several more chapters from the point of view of the bad guys, who we later learn are a pair of vice cops who have also made a crossing, this one over to the criminal side. They never really come alive as characters, nor are we given much insight into why the two of them went from being cops to extortionists and finally cold-blooded killers who eventually murder seven innocent people—including a Hollywood plastic surgeon, two Vietnamese brothers who own a jewelry store, and a pair of porno stars—in an effort to keep their illegal activities a secret. Ellis, however, does get credit for the most ironic statement in the novel after he learns that Bosch, a former cop, is now on their trail: "Now look at him. Working cases for a douche-bag defense attorney. There was no loyalty anymore. Nobody with a moral compass" (160).

The primary interest in the novel is watching Bosch laboring to adjust to his new role, which Connelly describes as being like "a man with an umbrella struggling for balance on a tightrope" (369). He enjoys the freedom his new job gives him to follow his instincts without interference from any supervisors, but since he's no longer a member of the police department, he has to finesse how he identifies himself so he can make the person he wants to question think he's a cop. He also has to remind himself that he has no easy access to police labs nor can he ever call for backup.

And although he no longer has department higher-ups to answer to, Bosch does have a new boss and he quickly learns how his investigative actions threaten to undermine Haller's courtroom defense. For example, he poses as a potential buyer of the house where Lexi Parks was murdered so he can get a first-hand look at the crime scene. However, her husband, a deputy sheriff, unexpectedly returns home and becomes suspicious. It doesn't take him long to identify Bosch as a former cop. Haller is not at all happy when Bosch calls to tell him he may have messed up: "That's not a mess-up. That's a full-fledged fuckup. You know if the guy makes a complaint, it goes on me with the judge, right?" (143).

A few pages later, he makes another blunder. This time he is visiting the Hollywood Forever cemetery, the final resting place of such famous movie legends as Rudolph Valentino, Douglas Fairbanks, Jr., and Mickey Rooney. The cemetery is located a short distance from the motel where Foster claims he had sex with James Allen at the time of Lexi Parks's murder. One of the security cameras there is pointed at the motel and could possibly confirm Foster's alibi. Bosch no longer has a badge he can use to get access to those videos so he promises the head of security that Haller will purchase one of the gravestone facsimiles he sells as a sideline if he'll cooperate and allow him to take a look at the camera footage. Once again, Haller has to school Bosch in the danger of what he did in light of how paying a potential witness for his testimony might look to a jury in the courtroom.

The climactic showdown with Ellis, who had survived an earlier shootout with Bosch by using his partner as a human shield, takes place in Bosch's home. Ellis has come to kill him in order to put a halt to his investigation before Ellis flees the country. For the second time, Internal Affairs Detective Nancy Mendenhall comes to Bosch's rescue, this time not to open a locked barn door as she did in *The Black Box* but to shoot Ellis in the back of the head before he can kill Bosch.

Following Ellis's death, Bosch is faced with another important decision. He could lie and say he heard Ellis admit to the murder of Lexi Parks before he died, which would free Foster. But he can't bring himself to cross that line. He leaves it to Haller to do his best with the evidence he has. Haller is up to the challenge and wins Foster's release by exposing the original investigators' tunnel vision. They had simply accepted the DNA match without requesting an additional test that would have shown that Foster's DNA came from a condom, which was used to transport his semen to the murder site. Nor did they pay any attention to the photo taken at the scene of James Allen's murder that clearly showed a bowl of condoms of the same brand the special test indicated. Thanks to Bosch and Haller, an innocent man goes free, marking the first time Bosch has ever been happy hearing charges of murder being dismissed.

Although their daughters plan to live together as roommates at Chapman University when they begin college in the fall (the same school Connelly's daughter Cassie attended), their fathers may not team up again as Bosch comes to the realization that he and Haller would always have a fundamental difference in how they viewed evidence and the other nuances of an investigation: "Haller had to put things in the context of a trial and how it might be used to knock down the prosecution's case. Bosch only had to look at the evidence as a bridge to the truth. This is why he knew he had not really crossed to the dark side. He could never work a case from Haller's angle" (274). Bosch's future path remains unclear.

The Wrong Side of Goodbye (2016)

Bosch has successfully settled his lawsuit with the city over his firing, resulting in a payoff that ensures he will no longer need to work to pay the bills. With plenty of time on his hands, he has begun taking private-eye types of assignments, which gives Connelly an opportunity to write the kind of Raymond Chandler/Ross Macdonald novel that first inspired him to be a writer. The "Goodbye" in the title even pays tribute to novels by both authors, Chandler's *The Long Goodbye* and Macdonald's *The Goodbye Look*.

Bosch is offered $10,000 to meet with Whitney Vance who, like his godfather Howard Hughes, is the reclusive billionaire owner of an aviation industry powerhouse, Advance Engineering. The money is Bosch's to keep even if he declines the job Vance proposes. Bosch's visit to Vance's palatial estate brings to mind Philip Marlowe's initial to visit to General Sternwood's mansion in *The Big Sleep*, with one notable difference: where Marlowe announced he was calling on four million dollars, Bosch "was calling on six billion dollars" (19).

The eighty-five-year-old Vance is nearing the end of his life and has no known heirs. At his death, the ownership of Advance Engineering will go to its board of directors. But before he dies, he wants an answer to a question that has haunted him all his life. "I want you to find someone for me," he tells Bosch. "Someone who might never have existed" (23). In 1950, when he was eighteen, he fell in love with a sixteen-year-old Mexican girl named Vibiana Duarte. She became pregnant and his father intervened to put an end to the relationship. Their affair lasted only eight months and he never saw her again. Now he wants Bosch to determine if she had a child by him, an heir he can pass his fortune on to.

This investigation differs markedly from Bosch's previous ones. There is no murder to investigate and no one to interfere with his investigation. And while he's used to investigating cold cases, one that dates back to 1951 presents special challenges. Nevertheless, he's confident he can apply everything he knows about sleuthing to find the answers he's looking for. He begins by searching county records of births and deaths, where he learns that Vibiana Duarte died in 1951. An Internet search of the address where she was living at the time of her death reveals it to be that of St. Helen's Home for Unwed Mothers. Seventeen-year-old Vibiana had been sent there when she became pregnant with Vance's child. The baby boy was born underweight, so she kept him to nurse for fifteen days until he was strong enough to be adopted. But she had forged such a deep bond with her newborn son that when he was taken from her and given to new parents, she became so emotionally distraught she committed suicide.

Bosch now sets out to find what happened to Vibiana's son. He manages to learn his name—Dominick Santanello—but then runs into another dead end when he discovers that he, too, died, sometime in the late 1960s. Acting on a hunch that he may have been a casualty of the Vietnam War, he locates his name on the Vietnam Veterans Memorial. Suddenly, the significance of the brief scene that opened the novel becomes clear. It describes the harrowing last moments in the life of a young medic whose helicopter is hit by sniper fire and bursts into flames after crashing into a rice paddy. The young man's final words before dying are a name he whispers twice—"Vibiana."

On Santanello's remembrance page Bosch finds the names of two people, one of whom turns out to be his adopted sister. When Bosch visits her home, she invites him to look through a footlocker of items her brother mailed home before he died. He begins to feel a connection with Santanello when he learns they were both on the hospital ship *Sanctuary* in the South China Sea at the same time. The most intriguing thing he finds, however, are three film negatives hidden in Santanello's camera that depict a young woman holding a baby. Did Santanello have a child?

At this point in his investigation, Bosch gets the news that Whitney Vance has just died. Does this mean his search is over? He's already been paid $10,000, which is his to keep. But with Bosch, it's never about the money; it's about the mission. A package that turns up in his mailbox containing two documents signed by Vance convinces him to continue. One is his will, which names Bosch as executor of his estate; the other is a note asking him to continue his search for a possible heir, no matter what happens to him. Bosch now sets out to find the woman and the baby in the photograph. He tracks down the woman, whose name is Gabriela Lido. She informs him that the baby in the photo is her daughter Vibiana Veracruz, who was named after Dominick Santanello's birth mother. It was her name that Santanello was referring to with his final breaths.

Midway through the writing of the novel, however, Connelly realized he had a problem. The book was going to fall far short of his usual 100,000-word length. Padding the material to extend its length would have destroyed the momentum he had effectively created for the Vance investigation. But then a chance encounter with an off-duty cop who was providing security during the filming of a scene in San Fernando for the *Bosch* TV series provided him with a solution.

The cop, a fan of the Bosch books, mentioned to Connelly that if Harry ever wanted to return to active duty and work murders, San Fernando had a program that utilized unpaid reserve detectives. San Fernando is a 2.3-square-mile island city within the L.A. metropolis. It has its own police department, but recent budget cuts eliminated many positions. To solve the problem, the chief of police instituted a new program to bring in experienced detectives who would work part-time hours for no pay. New recruits would get a detective's badge and access to all the city's unsolved cases. It's a perfect set-up: Bosch has a new job and Connelly has a second story to tell.

Though he's the newest member of the San Fernando police department, it doesn't take Bosch long to notice an overlooked connection between several rapes. Four local women, all Latinas, were sexually assaulted in their homes by a man wearing a mask who gained entry by cutting a screen. All four victims were also linked by being assaulted during the ovulation phase of their menstrual cycles. The rapist, dubbed the Screen Cutter, must have had previous access to the victims' homes in order to have known such intimate information about them. He attempted to rape a fifth victim, but she was able to fend him off with a broom. Bosch and his new partner Bella Lourdes set out to find him before he can claim another victim.

While this second case does add a sense of urgency lacking in Bosch's search for Vance's possible descendants, there is a been-there-done-that feel to it. Once again Bosch is looking for a bad guy who turns out to be a former cop; and once again he has to rescue a damsel in distress, his partner Bella, who has been kidnapped by the Screen Cutter and is being held prisoner in an underground fallout shelter in his home. His mission is successful as usual, and while Bella takes time off to recover from her ordeal and decide whether or not she wants to return to her job, Bosch is offered her position, with a salary. "It didn't matter if his turf was two square miles small or two hundred square miles large. He knew it was about cases and about always being on the right side of things" (381). He takes the job.

The search for Vance's heirs also has a happy ending. Dominick Santanello's daughter Vibiana is now living in L.A.'s Arts District. In the 1970s, the area of abandoned factories and fruit-shipping warehouses was taken over by artists of all disciplines. However, the artists are now being forced to leave as the entire neighborhood is threatened by gentrification. Vibiana, who lives with her nine-year-old son in a building that once housed the factory where the fruit boxes adorned with colorful scenes of California were produced, struggles financially. She can't even afford the resin she needs to make her large-scale acrylic statues, one of which depicts a soldier with the face of the father who died before she ever got to know him. If she is willing to provide Bosch with a DNA sample and it matches the one Vance gave him, her life will change dramatically.

There is one major problem to overcome: the Advance Engineering Board of Directors wants to keep control of the company and will do whatever it takes to ensure that no heirs to the Vance fortune are ever found. Bosch calls upon half-brother Mickey Haller for help. Suspecting that Haller is being followed, Bosch prepares two packages of DNA to be tested; one of them a phony. Haller takes the fake package to one testing site, while Bosch surreptitiously takes the real one to another. He isn't surprised when the testing site Haller used is destroyed by arson. The DNA test Bosch had done confirms that Vibiana and her son are Vance's heirs; Haller's job is to negotiate a share of Vance's company for them.

Connelly described the way the two cases Bosch had to solve in *The Drop* were closely intertwined as being like a double helix. The cases in *The Wrong Side of Goodbye* never really cross paths. This bifurcated narrative is more like a highway where the two cars travel in neighboring lanes but move at significantly different speeds. There is, however, one important link between them and that is Vietnam.

Bosch's Vietnam memories first surface during his search through Dominick Santanello's footlocker, where he finds some of the same novels he remembers reading in Vietnam (Hesse's *Steppenwolf* and Tolkien's *Lord of the Rings*) as well as audio cassettes of the same music he listened to (Jimi Hendrix, the Rolling Stones, the Moody Blues). Most striking of all are some photos Santanello took of the Christmas Eve visit of comedian Bob Hope and his troupe of celebrities to the hospital ship *Sanctuary*, where Bosch spent four weeks recuperating after being wounded by a bamboo spear during a tunnel encounter. What Bosch remembers most vividly about the event were some encouraging words from astronaut Neil Armstrong, a heartbreaking rendition of "Both Sides Now" by Connie Stevens, and a jazz solo by Quentin McKinzie, the saxophone player he later took lessons from in *Lost Light*. It was one of his best days as a soldier. That concert first appeared in Connelly's short story "Christmas Even," published in 2004. In that story, listening to McKinzie play "The Sweet Spot" has a life-changing impact on Bosch: "He was not the same after that day" (16).

But as we learn elsewhere in the novel, not all of Bosch's memories of the war are so happy. A knife the Screen Cutter dropped when a potential victim fought him off with a broom reminds him of an incident where he was forced to use a similar knife to cut the throat of an enemy soldier in a tunnel in Vietnam. He grabbed the man from behind and tore through his throat with the knife. What still haunts him is the memory of the man's final breath against the palm of his hand and then closing his eyes as he laid him down in a pool of his own blood.

Even a simple matter like deciding where he and his daughter will eat lunch exposes something else Bosch is trying to forget. When he vetoes Maddie's suggestion that they have lunch in a Vietnamese restaurant, she accuses him of being a racist. He explains that race is not the issue. For the first time, he tells her about his experiences in Vietnam. For over two years, he ate only Vietnamese food. Now he can no longer eat it because of the bad memories it brings back.

The novel ends with Mickey Haller addressing a small crowd (which includes Dominick Santanello's widow Gabriela Lido and his adopted sister) gathered at the site of a new park in the Arts District. As the newly appointed legal advisor to the Fruit Box Foundation, funded by the estate of Whitney Vance, he is happy to announce the foundation's purchase of four historic buildings in the district that will be renovated to provide affordable housing and studio space for local artists.

His final duty is to preside over the unveiling of a new sculpture by Vibiana Veracruz, now the artistic director of the Fruit Box Foundation. Titled *The Wrong Side of Goodbye*, the twenty-foot-tall diorama depicts the figure of a young, unarmed soldier ascending to heaven from the mangled wreck of a helicopter as if being pulled by the unseen hand of God. Standing beside the wreckage is the figure of a woman holding a baby girl in her arms. After all these years, the young family is together again. As Vibiana walks past Bosch, she turns and he notices a smile on her face for the very first time.

The Late Show (2017)

As Connelly began thinking about his next novel, he realized several things: it would be his thirtieth book; it was the year he turned sixty; and he hadn't created a new protagonist in ten years. "It was about time I did something new," he declared (Burke). However, instead of following his previous practice of introducing a character who wasn't a cop—an FBI profiler, a journalist, a lawyer—he created another cop. This one, however, is a bit different from Bosch: not a homicide investigator dedicated to solving murders but a cop who works the night beat; and this cop is a woman. Her name is Renée Ballard.

There is usually a significance to the names Connelly chooses for his protagonists: Bosch, of course, was named after the famous Dutch painter; Terry McCaleb bears the maiden name of Connelly's wife, Linda; Jack McEvoy honors his mother's maiden name. In the case of Ballard, who is based on a real person, he used a symbolic name. "I chose Ballard as her last name because it suggested 'ballad' to me, the musical connotation, and I chose her first name as Renée because it can be either male or female, which I thought fit the world she works in and the role she has to play" (Corbett).

Unlike Bosch, who was an amalgam of several real cops Connelly knew plus some of his favorite fictional detectives, his new protagonist was inspired by a single individual. When Rick Jackson, one of the LAPD homicide detectives he regularly consulted with, retired, he was replaced by a female detective named Mitzi Roberts. She, too, became a regular source of information and even made an appearance in *The Burning Room*. She also worked on the *Bosch* series as a technical advisor. After listening to the stories she told about working on the graveyard shift early in her career—"she's given me gold," says Connelly (Szewczyk)—he knew he had his new character.

Like Bosch, she had to overcome a troubled childhood. She grew up with her father in Hawaii after her mother left the family. She followed in his footsteps and became an avid surfer. One day while out surfing with him when she was fourteen, she watched in horror as he went under a wave and never came up. She had nowhere to go and was homeless for a year, sleeping on the beach and occasionally on friends' couches, until her grandmother found her and brought her to her home in California.

She also shares a few things in common with Michael Connelly. Like him, after graduating with a journalism degree (hers is from the University of Hawaii), she became a crime reporter for *The Los Angeles Times*. Also like him, she employs writing skills in her new job that she first learned as a journalist: "She reacted well to deadline pressure and she could clearly conceptualize her crime reports and case summaries before writing them. She wrote short, clear sentences that gave momentum to the narrative of the investigation" (58).

Ballard is a fourteen-year veteran of the department. Two years earlier, she filed sexual harassment charges against Lt. Robert Olivas, her supervisor in the Robbery-Homicide Division, who had pushed her up against a wall at a Christmas party and forcibly tried to kiss her. Her partner of five years, Ken Chastain, chose to put his ambitions in the department ahead of loyalty to his partner, and failed to back her up even though he had witnessed the incident. The charge was dismissed and Olivas arranged to have her demoted to the late shift.

Now she works nights from eleven p.m. to seven a.m. Detectives on the night shift often work without a partner, and Connelly says he liked the idea of having a woman responding to calls by herself. These detectives usually deal with routine matters, like signing off on a suicide or looking for an Alzheimer's patient who has wandered off and gotten lost. In the case of more serious crimes, their task is to take initial reports and then turn the investigation over to the appropriate unit.

Two crimes occur that fire up Ballard's desire to investigate something of personal importance to her. The first involves the near-fatal beating of a transgender female prostitute named Ramona Ramone (born Ramón Gutierrez) who was left for dead in a parking lot. She had been savagely beaten with brass knuckles, bursting one of her breast implants, and a nipple was bitten off. The only clue to her attacker is her description of the location where she was beaten as "the upside-down house." "This is big evil out there" (19), Ballard says, "and I want to keep the case and do something for a change" (19).

She proves to be as relentless as Bosch. On her own time she begins searching through police databases looking for other crimes that match the details of the Ramone beating. Her patience is rewarded when she gets a hit for an arrest for possession of brass knuckles, a crime in California. The man's name is Thomas Trent and a search of court records produces his home address. When she checks it out, she sees that it's a two-level residence built on the side of a mountain, with the bedrooms located below the living area, an "upside-down house." She gathers even more damning evidence after she tracks down Trent's ex-wife, who gives her a key to the house she kept after the divorce. She even poses as a potential customer at the car dealership where Trent works in order to assess him with her own eyes. She feels certain she's found her "big evil."

On working days, as soon as her shift ends Ballard heads for Venice Beach with her faithful companion Lola, a dog she rescued from an abusive owner. Where Bosch found solace in jazz music, Ballard finds hers in the ocean: she spends an hour or so most days paddleboarding, then catches a few hours of sleep in a tent on the beach before heading back to the night shift. On one of her off days, she heads to her grandmother's house nearly seventy miles north in Ventura, where she goes into the garage to do her laundry and wax some of the eight surfboards she stores there. While meticulously working on her favorite, she is suddenly grabbed from behind and a bag is pulled over her head, rendering her unconscious. When she awakens, she finds herself naked, gagged, and tied hand and foot to a chair in a darkened room in Thomas Trent's upside-down house.

As everyone knows, police work is dangerous, especially for female cops. At 120 pounds, she is physically no match for a man twice her weight and size. Worse, when she awakens, she has no memory of what might have happened to her. Was she raped? Her terror only intensifies when Trent begins to sexually assault her by shoving his hand between her legs and caressing her nipple. "You're mine now" (274), he whispers before leaving to kidnap his ex-wife, who had given Ballard the key to his house.

As she had demonstrated by the meticulous way she waxed her surfboard, Ballard possesses intense focus and concentration and pays close attention to even the smallest details. She notices that the ties binding her hands and wrists are not the heavier type used by police to cuff a suspect but the household kind, which are thinner. She also knows that rubbing plastic together creates heat and that heat expands plastic. She finds the loosest tie and begins the arduous process of rubbing it back and forth until it stretches enough so she can free herself. Then she begins looking for something she can use as a weapon. All she can find are a broomstick and a piece of sharp wood she broke off from the chair she was sitting on. When Trent returns, she stuns him with the broomstick and then plunges the pointed stick into his stomach, killing him.

She must now deal with the aftermath of her trauma, which includes both the consequences of sexual assault (because she had casual sex recently, tests cannot determine for certain whether or not she was raped while unconscious) and the fact that she killed a man. She is also forced to acknowledge that there was "something inside her she didn't know she had. Something dark. Something scary" (301). During her meeting with department psychologist Dr. Carmen Hinojos, who successfully counseled both Bosch and his daughter Maddie, she gets this reminder: "If you go into darkness, the darkness goes into you. You then have to decide what to do with it. How to keep yourself safe from it. How to keep it from hollowing you out" (339).

After a brief suspension while the department's Force Investigation Division reviews her actions, she is able to resume her investigation into another case, the murders of five people who were shot dead in Dancers, a club that took its name from the one in Raymond Chandler's *The Long Goodbye*. The victims included three men sitting together in a booth; a bouncer; and a waitress, an aspiring actress who had a bit part in an episode of the TV series *Bosch*. It appears that the shooter was the fourth man in the booth, whose target was the trio of men sitting opposite him.

At the scene of the shooting, Ballard had noticed her former partner Ken Chastain picking up something from the floor and ignoring protocol by putting it in his pocket instead of the evidence bag. Shortly afterwards, he was shot in the head execution style when he arrived home from work one night. It appears that his murder may be linked to his search for the Dancers' killer. Though he had failed Ballard by not supporting her claim of harassment, he was a good partner and "nobody should put a cop down and walk away from it" (223).

Chastain was the son of John Chastain, the Internal Affairs hack who twice investigated Bosch but lost both times. Readers may remember that in *Angels Flight*, he turned out to be the killer the police were looking for. As Bosch was driving him to the station to be booked, he was dragged from the car by an angry mob of rioters and beaten to death. Once Ken Chastain learned the truth about his father, he sought to rehabilitate the family name, which he ends up doing from beyond the grave.

After his death, Ballard is informed that there is a bag of evidence with her name on it that she needs to pick up. It turns out it's Chastain's bag, which he left for her in case anything happened to him. Inside, she finds a key piece of evidence—a metal button torn loose from a shoulder holster when the shooter at Dancers pulled his gun—that leads to the identity of the person behind the nightclub massacre and Chastain's murder. Thanks to his actions, Chastain has achieved a measure of redemption, both for his father's failures and his own in not backing Ballard when she needed him. Ballard's only regret is she wishes they had been able to settle things between them before he died.

In the end, Lt. Olivas tells Ballard he wants to bury the hatchet between them. He praises her efforts in finding the killer they were looking for (yet another cop who crossed over to the dark side) and offers her old job back. While she would love to return to the full-time job of homicide investigator, she refuses to ever again work for a man like Olivas. She chooses to remain on the late show.

Ballard wasn't Connelly's first female protagonist. That honor goes to Cassie Black in *Void Moon* (2000), but she never returned for a second novel. In Ballard, it's clear he has come up with a character with the right combination of personality, drive, and intelligence to join the roster of Connelly's other series characters. The ending of the novel leaves little doubt that she will return.

Two Kinds of Truth (2017)

Although it effectively explores timely issues about truth and the justice system as well as the current opioid addiction crisis, *Two Kinds of Truth* falls just short of being a top-tier Bosch novel. The bulk of the detective work is done by others, which frees Bosch to play both an action hero who goes undercover on a dangerous assignment and a knightly hero who tries to rescue a damsel in distress. But he too needs to be rescued twice: one time to save his life, the other to salvage his reputation.

The novel opens with a case in which Bosch is the potential victim. Thirty years earlier, he helped send Preston Borders to death row for the rape and murder of Danielle Skyler. But now, thanks to DNA testing, which was not allowed in California courts at the time, semen left on the woman's clothing is found to belong to another man, a serial rapist who is now dead. Borders has filed a suit to have his conviction overturned.

The problem is that Borders's conviction rested upon an item taken from the murdered woman's apartment—a blue sea-horse pendant her mother gave her—that Bosch found hidden in Borders's apartment. If the DNA test proves that Borders didn't kill the woman, then how did that pendant get in his apartment? The obvious conclusion is that Bosch must have planted it there. If that's true, his whole public reputation will be ruined: "You open the door to this guy," he complains, "and you might as well open it for every one of the people I sent away.... It taints everything" (19).

Bosch turns to half-brother Mickey Haller for help. It's Haller's investigator Cisco Wojciechowski who first notices a person lurking in the background of a video documenting the opening of the sealed evidence box containing Danielle Skyler's clothing with the DNA that is the key to Borders's freedom. He quickly learns the man's name, Terrence Spencer, and that he works as a property officer at the LAPD Property Control office. Lorna Taylor, Haller's office manager and Cisco's wife, gets in on the action by digging up evidence that Spencer is in deep financial trouble: he's about to lose his home to foreclosure, and his foreclosure lawyer just happens to be married to Preston Borders's attorney. Armed with this information, Mickey Haller then heads to court and uses his wizardry to expose the scheme cooked up by Borders's lawyer to force Spencer to plant the DNA evidence in Danielle Skyler's supposedly secure evidence box in order to get his client set free and to bring a multimillion-dollar suit against the LAPD for false imprisonment.

Police departments across the country have had to deal with the embarrassing and damaging consequences caused by evidence being planted by cops or, in this situation, even those charged with ensuring the purity of the evidence. Thanks to advances in DNA testing and the emergence of organizations like the Innocence Project, many falsely imprisoned individuals have been freed and have collected millions of dollars in damages from cities where such miscarriages of justice have taken place. The shameful truth Connelly exposes in *Two Kinds of Truth* is how a husband-and-wife team of lawyers have discredited honest efforts to correct a failure of the justice system. Their crime exemplifies one of the two kinds of truth the title refers to: not the "unalterable bedrock" kind, but the "malleable truth of politicians, charlatans, corrupt lawyers, and their clients, bent and molded to serve whatever purpose was at hand" (128).

The other case in the novel gives Bosch, who is still working for the San Fernando Police, an opportunity to investigate a live murder for the first time in several years. He and partner Bella Lourdes, who has returned after a lengthy injury-on-duty leave, are summoned to the bloody scene at a local pharmacy where the owner, José Esquival, and his son, José Jr., have been shot to death. Unlike the father, who was killed with one shot, José Jr. was shot three times, including once in the rectum, indicating to Bosch that his murder was some kind of payback.

Lourdes quickly identifies a possible motive for the murder of José Jr.—he had recently made a complaint to the Medical Board of California about another pharmacy that had been overprescribing oxycodone. This leads Bosch to the state medical board investigator, who turns out to be his former partner Jerry Edgar. He fills Bosch in on the scam that cost the Esquivals their lives.

The illegal trafficking in prescription drugs in America is big business. Too many Americans are becoming hooked on prescription drugs after being prescribed pain medication for treatment of an injury. And the death toll from accidental overdose is truly staggering. According to the Centers for Disease Control (CDC), between 1999 and 2019, nearly 247,000 Americans died from an overdose of prescription opioids. One reason for so many deaths is that, thanks to the money that can be made from them, deadly drugs are so easy to get.

Bosch ordinarily investigates crimes like murder that involve individual acts of evil. Now he is facing a much bigger evil, a collective one carried out by thousands. As Jerry Edgar explains to Bosch, "So many people are making money off this crisis—it's the growth industry of this country. Remember what they used to say about the banks and Wall Street being too big to fail? It's like that. But too big to shut down" (103). The case that Bosch is now investigating illustrates just one instance of how such criminal enterprises work.

A Russian-Armenian gang has been using homeless drug addicts to purchase drugs from cooperating pharmacists. Gang members obtain prescriptions from doctors that have been paid off and then send the shills to pharmacies that have also been paid off to fill the prescriptions. The shills visit several pharmacies a day and are paid a dollar per pill (plus enough drugs to keep them happy). José Jr. was killed because he tried to blow the whistle on the scam, which gives Bosch the personal motive he needs to shut the operation down.

All of this serves as a set-up that allows the sixty-seven-year-old Bosch to assume the role of action hero once again. Because he's old enough to qualify for Medicare, he's a perfect choice to go undercover for the DEA and pose as one of the addicts in a group that is being bused and flown around each day to various pharmacies in Southern California. He even has the perfect coach: Mickey Haller's investigator Cisco, whose recovery from his motorcycle accident in *The Crossing* left him with an addiction to oxycodone. Cisco's experience illustrates just how dangerous the drug is and how easily one can become addicted. He eventually got clean by locking himself in a room for seven days. He's now more than happy to lend Bosch his knee brace and cane (with a hidden four-inch knife blade attached to the handle) if it will help shut the illegal operation down.

Bosch makes a convincing homeless addict, but the assignment is fraught with danger, including being forced to play Russian roulette with his own gun (which has fortunately been modified so it can't fire) and an attack from a fellow addict. But the worst comes when one of the Russian bosses recognizes him from a picture that appears in a newspaper story he sees about the Borders case. This time Bosch ends up on a small plane with the two Russian gangsters who killed José Jr. and who he knows plan to toss him out the open door once they are over the Salton Sea. He manages to kill one of them with the knife hidden in his cane; the other one simply jumps out of the plane and into the sea below.

The case was personally important to Bosch because, while some might think José Jr. was stupid or naive for being a whistle-blower, he comes to see the young man as a hero who did something noble: "People lie, the president lies, corporations lie and cheat.... The world is ugly and not many people are willing to stand up to it anymore. I didn't want what this kid did to go by without.... I didn't want them to get away with it, I guess" (289).

He also sees an opportunity to do something noble himself. One of the addicts in his group is a woman named Elizabeth Clayton. She's maybe fifty, her body ravaged by addiction. When he tries to strike up a friendly conversation with her, she rebuffs him. But after he gets into a fight with another addict named Buddy, she breaks her silence enough to warn him to be ready, as Buddy will come after him. That night he does, but Bosch is prepared and is able to fight him off. Clayton's helpful warning and part of a tattoo he notices on her shoulder that looks to him like a remembrance of someone who died young convince him that "there was still something inside her worth salvaging" (253).

After concluding his undercover stint, Bosch returns to L.A. to look for the woman who, he has learned, became addicted after her fifteen-year-old daughter Daisy's death. She was a runaway who began using drugs in junior high and was living on the streets in Hollywood when eight years ago she was tortured to death and her body tossed in a dumpster. At this point, the man who has devoted his career to acting as an avenging angel now assumes the role of Elizabeth Clayton's guardian angel.

Following a tip from Jerry Edgar, he locates her at a pill mill where she has overdosed on oxycodone, possibly intentionally. Rather than take her to a hospital, he brings her to Cisco's place, where Cisco offers to lock her in a room in the same way he beat his addiction. Bosch, now acting like a drug counselor, tries to convince Clayton that it's not too late to free herself from the dark abyss of her addiction if she wants to. He finally gets her to agree to try Cisco's cold-turkey treatment plan. Then he becomes her financial angel by using the $10,000 in cash he has stashed in a sock to serve as an emergency earthquake fund to pay for her follow-up treatment at a drug rehab facility. Why such generosity? "She had tapped into a need he had to reach out and help someone, whether they welcomed his help or not" (389).

Bosch has one more noble act in mind. The novel ends in an unusual way with him announcing what his next case will be—he'll begin searching for the killer of Elizabeth Clayton's daughter, who may still be at large.

Dark Sacred Night (2018)

Renée Ballard is called to the home of a woman whose partially naked body was found on the bathroom floor. She's been dead for several days and her face has been lacerated in several places. The cop on the scene concludes that somebody must have worked her over pretty good. But Ballard skillfully reads the scene and reaches a different conclusion: the woman accidentally fell while trying to undress and cracked her skull on the edge of the tub; the facial lacerations were caused by her cat who got hungry after a couple of days.

When Ballard returns to the deserted detective bureau to complete her paperwork, she hears the sound of a file cabinet door being opened. She gets up to investigate and finds a strange man who has been rifling through some files. The man identifies himself as an ex–LAPD cop who used to work there. He says his name is Harry Bosch. After he leaves, she finds the paperclip he used to unlock the file cabinet and the name of the detective whose file he was searching for. Her curiosity piqued, she learns that the file in question concerns the killing of Daisy Clayton, whose murder Bosch promised at the end of *Two Kinds of Truth* to solve.

The details about the teenager's death are chilling—she was violently sexually abused and tortured and her naked body dumped in an alley. As a cop, Ballard knows that murder is murder, but violent murder of another helpless woman by a man hits her hard: "There was something deeply affecting about that. Something unfair that went beyond the general unfairness of death at the hands of another. She wondered how men would live if they knew that in every moment of their lives, their size and nature made them vulnerable to the opposite sex" (379). As a cop who was working toward a specialization in sexually motivated homicides before being demoted to the late show, she's interested in Bosch's investigation.

Their next meeting takes place in Bosch's office, where Ballard is waiting for him after having gained entry the same way he did to get into the file cabinet in her office—by picking the lock. She tells him she wants in on the Daisy Clayton case. Impressed by how much she has already learned on her own about the case, Bosch tells her what he knows. Daisy's body had been washed in bleach to remove any evidence of the killer. He has determined that a mysterious mark found on her body—a two-inch circle with the letters A S P inside—is a trademark used by a manufacturer of plastic tubs. He theorizes that a twenty-five-gallon tub was used to wash the body and then transfer it to the place where it was found. The killer was likely someone who drove a van.

Bosch, an old-school detective, decides the best way to begin is by looking at the shake cards, 3 × 5 index cards patrol officers use to record every encounter they have with people on the street they stop or are suspicious about. Separately and together, the two of them spend endless hours on the tedious process of weeding through twelve boxes, each containing up to a thousand cards, looking for ones filled out by street cops about people they talked to around the time of Daisy's death.

Connelly divides the narrative in two, with the sections devoted to each character alternating throughout the book. This allows the reader to view each one through the eyes of the other. For example, Ballard describes the man she first sees rummaging through the file cabinet as having gray hair and a mustache and later on notices that he walks with a limp. Bosch provides this physical description of Ballard: "She was attractive, maybe midthirties, with brown, sun-streaked hair cut at the shoulders and a slim, athletic build" (46). A closer look leads him to correct his initial impression that her face was tanned by the sun; he now believes it to be the product of a mixed racial background, probably half white, half Polynesian.

The alternating narratives also show each of them working at their own separate jobs and living their separate lives. This is especially useful in the case of Ballard, as we get to see more of the wide range of crimes she is called upon to deal with on the night shift. The two of them turn out to have much in common. Both are lonely, relentless outsiders who act like a dog with a bone when they are on a case. Both also face multiple hurdles on the job. In Bosch's case, the obstacles are mainly incompetent, numbers-counting bosses and politicians with an agenda that often twists the truth. With Ballard, the obstacles are more pervasive and demeaning: misogyny and discrimination simply because she's a woman.

She comes to realize how much she and her male colleagues view things differently. This becomes clear when she responds to a call from the owner of a strip club who suspects a possible burglary in progress after hearing suspicious noises on the roof of his establishment. When Ballard climbs up to investigate, she discovers three fourteen-year-old boys trying to get a look at the naked dancers below. Glancing over at her male partner, she notices a smile on his face. "She realized that on some level he admired their ingenuity—boys will be boys—and she knew that in the world of men and women, there would never be a time when women were viewed and treated completely as equals" (86).

On another occasion, she is called to the Hollywood Hills home of a big movie star named Danny Monahan after a woman phoned police from the bathroom to claim that he raped her. The twenty-two-year-old woman admitted to having consensual sex with Monahan, but then she says he raped her anally against her will. Some bloody tissues Ballard finds in a wastebasket seem to support her claim. Ballard bristles when a male detective at the scene takes the man's side and delays reporting the crime because it might damage his career. But she also understands that her defense of the woman will possibly be dismissed as being biased because of the sexual harassment suit she filed.

And then she is forced to admit that she may have rushed to judgment when Monahan reveals that he secretly taped the encounter, which clearly shows that the sex was consensual. She can't decide whom she hates more—the man for secretly recording his sexual partners without their consent, or the woman for making a false claim that could undermine the credibility of real victims of sexual assault. She also knows that even though she could have arrested both of them, her actions would have been "studied and questioned by a command staff that didn't like her or want her. Some fault would likely be found and she would be further buried by the department and pulled away from the one thing she needed most: her job on the late show" (189).

Connelly has never been hesitant about making life difficult for Bosch, and in *Dark Sacred Night* he really piles the miseries on his hero's head. His latest case for the San Fernando police is the unsolved fourteen-year-old murder of Cristobal Vega, who was shot in the head while out walking his dog. Vega was known as Uncle Murda for his violent activities as a leader of one of the oldest and most violent gangs in the San Fernando Valley. Despite the man's record of violence, Bosch still feels obligated to honor his belief that everybody counts or nobody counts, so he begins looking for anyone who might have knowledge about the killing.

He locates a former member of Vega's gang named Martin Perez, whom he threatens in order to force him to provide information that leads him to suspect that a rival in Vega's gang named Tranquillo Cortez may have ordered the hit on him. But when Perez is gunned down and the business card Bosch gave him with his cell number handwritten on it is found stuffed between his front teeth, Bosch is forced to ask himself if his actions caused the man's death.

His next move also blows up in his face. He suspects Oscar Luzon, a fellow cop, of leaking the information that Perez had talked to Bosch. When Bosch confronts him about his suspicion, Luzon becomes angry and shoves Bosch into an empty cell and locks him in. Then, while Bosch looks on helplessly, he fashions a noose out of his tie, climbs up and ties it to a grate in the ceiling, and hangs himself. Though Luzon survives, this results in Bosch's termination from the San Fernando Police Department. Then he gets abducted by Vega's men and taken to a remote hilltop location where he is locked in an animal cage to await the arrival of Vega, who plans to feed him to his dogs.

Bosch may be a master of old-school methods of investigation, but fortunately for him, Ballard has expertise in the latest technology. When Bosch fails to show up for a scheduled meeting, she goes to his home and discovers he has left abruptly. She rifles through his phone bills to find Maddie's number, then calls her and asks her to use her phone tracker to find her father's whereabouts. The last location the phone recorded is the hilltop site where he is caged. Maddie sends a screenshot of the location to Ballard, who forwards it to an LAPD helicopter pilot in the area, who sends back a photograph of the abandoned animal compound where Bosch is being held, enabling Ballard to find and rescue him.

Bosch later gets an opportunity to return the favor when Ballard's search through old files turns up a possible clue to the identity of Daisy Clayton's killer. In one report, she recognizes the name of Roger Dillon, the owner of a biohazard cleaning service who was working on Sunset Boulevard the same night Daisy was murdered nine years ago. Just days earlier, she had met him when he arrived to clean up the home of the dead woman whose face was eaten by her cat. To satisfy her curiosity, she climbs up the narrow space between two buildings to get on the roof of Dillon's warehouse and enter through a skylight. Finding a van, some plastic storage containers, plenty of bleach, and a broken fingernail painted pink, she believes she has found Daisy's killer. Unfortunately, Dillon unexpectedly shows up with a gun; moments later, however, so does Bosch, just in time to save Ballard's life.

The novel's strength resides in its twin portraits of Bosch and Ballard and the different challenges each faces. For Ballard, it's the uphill battle she fights daily to prove herself to a male-dominated organization like the LAPD, where "female detectives were often treated like office secretaries" (46). In Bosch's case, his problems are caused by his own actions. Not only is he forced to acknowledge that they led to the murder of one innocent man and the attempted suicide of a fellow cop, his personal decisions also come into question.

For the past six months, Elizabeth Clayton has been living in a room in Bosch's house at his invitation, which has caused a rift between him and his daughter, who wasn't consulted about the move and refuses to visit while she is there. He even begins to question the wisdom of his decision to help her get sober, for without drugs the pain of her daughter's death is more intense and less bearable. And then one day she is gone. After a frantic search for her, his worst fears are confirmed when he finds her dead of an overdose, likely intentional.

He also has to deal with the guilty thought that he has failed as a parent by squandering the past several months as Maddie's father "trying to save a woman who didn't want to be saved" (306). Now both jobless and in a foul mood, he turns his attention to Roger Dillon. No longer restrained by lawful procedures, he feels free to do whatever it takes to force a confession from Dillon, which he does by placing a bucket filled with sulfuric acid between the man's outstretched legs. Knowing it's just a matter of time before the acid will eat through the metal and spread to his crotch, Dillon confesses to killing Daisy as well as to the murders of several other young women.

Bosch now makes another wrong choice. The father of one of Dillon's other victims happens to be the mob-connected owner of the strip club where Ballard found the boys on the roof. Bosch phones him and tells him where he can find his daughter's killer. But then his conscience kicks in and he realizes his desire for vengeance will only lead to more guilt and grief. He phones the local police and tells them to hurry to the place he left Dillon. Fortunately, the police arrive just before the vigilante father and his goons show up with a chainsaw, allowing Daisy Clayton's killer to face legal justice.

It's been a rocky road for both Bosch and Ballard, but the novel ends on a promising note. Now that he's lost his last police job, Bosch proposes to Ballard that they continue to work together as a team. "You have that thing—maybe one in a hundred have it," he tells her. "You're fierce. You keep pushing. I mean, I'd be dog food right now if it wasn't for what you've got. So let's work together. Let's work cases. Badge, no badge, it doesn't matter" (432). Ballard is interested, but has one demand. "We can work cases," she says. "But we bend the rules. We don't break them." Bosch agrees and they end up shaking hands, giving Connelly's readers the promise of another joint venture.

The Night Fire (2019)

Though he has lost his reserve officer position with the San Fernando Police Department, Bosch has more work than he can comfortably handle. But he's not in tiptop shape. He's still in plenty of pain following knee-replacement surgery six weeks earlier. He's also taking a chemotherapy pill every day after having been diagnosed with acute myeloid leukemia caused by his exposure to the radioactive cesium he handled twelve years earlier in *The Overlook*.

The novel opens at the funeral of Bosch's mentor John Jack Thompson, who taught him how to be a homicide detective thirty years earlier. Following the burial, Thompson's wife invites Bosch to her home to give him something. On Thompson's desk is the murder book of a thirty-year-old case he stole from the department when he retired twenty years earlier. The case involved the murder of John Hilton, who was shot in the back of the head while sitting in his car in an alley.

This presents Bosch with several mysteries to solve. Who killed John Hilton? Who blacked out several sentences in the murder book? And why didn't Thompson ever make any attempt to solve the case in the twenty years he had the murder book in his possession? Bosch decides he needs help and drops the murder book on Renée Ballard's desk. Though she knows the proper thing to do is return the stolen book to the department, she too likes working cases off the books on her own time and agrees to help Bosch.

Although *The Night Fire* is billed as a Ballard and Bosch book, Connelly also brings Mickey Haller into the proceedings. Bosch wants to meet with his half-brother to seek his advice about filing a workman's comp suit against the hospital where the cesium that caused his leukemia was stolen. Could it be sued for failure to provide adequate security? This brings Bosch into the courtroom where Haller is in the middle of a seemingly impossible case. Although he has chosen to stop handling murder cases, a judge has assigned him a tough one: Jeffrey Herstadt is accused of stabbing superior-court Judge Walter Montgomery to death. The problem for Haller is that Herstadt has confessed to the murder and his DNA was found under one of Montgomery's fingernails.

It's always a pleasure to see Haller in action and his livelier attitude provides some much-needed relief from Bosch's darker mood. He succeeds in explaining away his client's confession by introducing an expert who testifies that Herstadt suffers from catatonic schizophrenia, which causes him to say whatever his questioner wants him to say. What about the DNA? Bosch agrees to look into the matter and comes up with an explanation that frees Herstadt—the EMS paramedic who treated him after a catatonic attack used an oximeter clipped to his index finger to measure the oxygen content of his blood. An hour later he used the same instrument without cleaning it on his very next patient, Judge Montgomery, inadvertently transferring one man's DNA to the other.

Instead of *The Night Fire*, the novel could have been given alternate titles with a fire motif, like *The Fire Still Burns* or *Passing the Torch*. Considering how overloaded and overextended Bosch is, it might also have been titled *Burning the Candle at Both Ends*. Not only does he have the Hilton case from John Jack Thompson to solve, he's now decided he must find the person who killed Judge Montgomery, and there are five potential suspects that need to be investigated. He also spends several all-night sessions camped out in the back seat of his car with his sore knee propped up in front of the house his daughter shares with three other girls after a creepy prowler recently broke into the place and Maddie and her roommates fear he might return. Is this any way for a sixty-nine-year-old man with cancer and a throbbing knee to be spending his retirement? Fortunately, he has Renée Ballard for a partner.

Ballard is equally overextended and sleep deprived. She has her own cases to deal with, which Connelly uses to fill in more details about her life on the night shift. She is first called to a homeless encampment where a resident named Edison Banks, Jr., burned to death when his tent caught fire, apparently after a kerosene heater was accidentally kicked over while he was sleeping. Ballard has experienced homelessness herself and also sleeps in a tent, so she has empathy for those who are forced to live like this. The scene also serves as a reminder that Hollywood is a far different place in the dark hours after the neon and glitter have dimmed: "It became a place of predators and prey and nothing in between, a place where the haves were comfortably and safely behind their locked doors and the have-nots freely roamed. Ballard always remembered the words of a late-show patrol poet. He called them *human tumbleweeds moving with the winds of fate*" (15).

Later she's called to the home where an eleven-year-old girl, still dressed in her private-school uniform, committed suicide by hanging herself. Scenes like this, which can be traumatic for the cop on the scene, also remind Ballard of her own troubled childhood and it makes her wonder, "How did one child retain hope in the darkness and another come to believe it was gone forever?" (113). Ballard's superior tries to persuade her to meet with the department's Behavioral Science Unit for psychological counseling, but she refuses. She fears that adding another "shrink sheet" to her file would turn more of the department against her. She is also aware of another pernicious double standard female cops live with: "A male officer asking for counseling was courageous and strong; a female doing the same was just plain weak" (114).

In addition to helping Bosch with his cases, she must also take a closer look into the death of the homeless man in his tent after new details arise: his blood-alcohol level was three times over the drunk-driving limit and he was apparently unaware that he had inherited a family fortune, which now goes to his brother. Could this be a case of arson and murder? At this point the reader might find it helpful to take notes as the narrative switches back and forth between all these cases, one of which requires five separate investigations.

Things finally begin to come together when Ballard discovers a link between the arson case and the Montgomery murder: a woman who was caught on video buying a bottle of vodka that was later given to Banks shortly before he burned to death bears a striking resemblance to the woman who was spotted on video walking to the courthouse on her way to jury duty just steps ahead of Judge Montgomery when he was killed. And then additional connections emerge. Edison Banks Jr.'s brother had hired a law firm to cut his homeless brother out of the family trust. He lost the case but a year later he got the money anyway when his brother died under suspicious circumstances.

It turns out that one of the same firm's lawyers was once publicly embarrassed by Montgomery, who banned him from his courtroom. A suit he later brought for defamation of character against the judge was thrown out, humiliating him even more. Too many coincidences? Connelly pre-empts the reader's possible negative complaint by having Bosch make the same point: "Bosch didn't believe in coincidences but he knew they happened. And here two detectives working different cases had just found a link between them. If that wasn't a coincidence, he didn't know what was" (344).

The killer is revealed to be a female assassin. Catarina Cava (nicknamed The Black Widow by Bosch) was hired by the law firm involved in the two cases to kill both Banks and Montgomery. Now that Bosch and Ballard know the killer's identity, they must track her down. When they do and Ballard starts to search Cava, the woman pulls a knife and slices one of Ballard's arteries and then flees. Ballard survives the attack and later has the pleasure of arresting Cava when she is tracked down a second time.

The solution of the Hilton murder also wounds Bosch, but emotionally rather than physically. He determines that Hilton was a drug addict and ex-con who was murdered by a Black gangbanger he fell in love with in prison. But he is surprised to learn that he was also the son of John Jack Thompson, who he concludes stole the murder book when he retired not to solve the case but to keep anyone else from solving it. Bosch feels betrayed by his former partner: "The man who mentored him—who instilled in him the belief that every case deserved his best, that everybody counted or nobody counted—that man had submarined a case involving his own blood" (293).

Bosch and Ballard once again prove to make an excellent team. Despite some inevitable bumps in the road—when the bleary-eyed Bosch, who fights his own sleeplessness, tells Ballard she looks tired and warns her that lack of sleep leads to mistakes, she fires back and tells him to stop treating her like a daughter instead of an equal partner—their mutual trust and admiration grows. It appears that Bosch has found the perfect candidate to whom he can pass the torch.

The novel ends with Bosch mentioning to Ballard that he has taken an interest in an unsolved murder he and Thompson worked in 1982, that of a nineteen-year-old college student who was raped and stabbed to death after attending a night class. That was where Bosch first witnessed the fierceness Thompson brought to the job, which is how he wants to remember him. Perhaps solving the case for his old mentor will ease the pain of betrayal. "If you work that case," Ballard tells him, "I work it with you" (401). "That's a deal," says Bosch.

Fair Warning (2020)

It's been eleven years since Jack McEvoy's previous appearance in *The Scarecrow*. At the end of that novel, he used some of the quarter-of-a-million-dollar advance he received for a book about the Scarecrow to purchase a new Jeep Wrangler. But times have changed dramatically since then, both in the newspaper business and his life. The odometer on his Jeep keeps reminding him "how long it had been since I was buying new cars and riding bestseller lists. I checked it as I fired up the engine. I had strayed 162,172 miles from the path I had once been on" (13).

Gone are the days when a veteran reporter like him who had worked for the *Rocky Mountain News* and the *Los Angeles Times* could find another newspaper job. For the past four years, he's been working at *FairWarning*, a small non-profit consumer-watchdog website founded by Myron Levin. In the opening lines of *The Poet*, his debut appearance, Jack McEvoy proudly announced, "Death is my beat. I make my living from it." But now, instead of writing about murders, he writes consumer-protection stories on issues like scams in the debt-collection business.

FairWarning.org is a real website and Connelly is a member of its board of directors. Levin and Connelly had known each other for twenty-five years having worked together at the *Los Angeles Times*. *FairWarning* and Myron Levin's name are used in the novel with permission. But on February 20, 2021, the board of directors was forced to dissolve the website after Twitter comments by a job applicant who didn't get the job accused Levin of making racist statements when asked about the lack of diversity among the staff. Levin denied making any such statements but acknowledged that the negative publicity affected the site's ability to continue raising the charitable contributions needed to continue its mission (Witley).

The challenge for Connelly in the McEvoy series has been to come up with a credible way for a journalist to become a person who solves a crime and doesn't just write about it. It was the murder of his twin brother that provided the reason in *The Poet*. This time it's because he himself becomes a suspect in the murder of a woman he once picked up in a bar. Christina Portrero, the woman who is murdered in the opening scene of the novel, was killed in a particularly gruesome way: she died of atlanto-occipital dislocation (AOD), the separation of the spinal cord from the skull base caused by a violent twist of her head. The police want to question McEvoy after his name was found among her contacts and his two books were on her nightstand.

McEvoy admits that a year earlier he had met the woman in a bar and they had a one-night stand, but that was the end of their relationship. He agrees to submit a sample of his DNA to clear him of suspicion. What gets his reportorial juices going again is the unusual method of Portrero's death. He begins snooping around and finds a website aimed at coroners where he identifies the names of three other women who died in the same way. Further investigation reveals another link: all four had submitted DNA to a budget genetics analysis company called GT23. Could someone have used this information to target his victims? And if so how, if the DNA submissions are supposedly made anonymously?

McEvoy faces a pair of obstacles that threaten to shut him down. The first comes from the police, who arrest him for ignoring their orders to cease his investigation. This forces him to spend a night in jail, before the charges are dropped. He also has to convince his editor that the story he's working on concerns consumers. His editor agrees that if the focus is about cyberstalking, it would qualify as a *FairWarning* story. He gives McEvoy the go-ahead and assigns fellow *FairWarning* employee Emily Atwater to assist him in his investigation.

McEvoy gets a third partner when he realizes he could use the assistance of the FBI and contacts a former profiler there he knows by the name of Rachel Walling. The two of them have a long history of both a personal and professional relationship going back to his first novel, *The Poet*. But that all ended when she lost her job at the FBI because of him. Years earlier, McEvoy spent sixty-three days in jail for refusing to identify a source in a story. Walling eventually identified herself as his source, which freed him but got her fired. Now instead of chasing serial killers, she has her own business conducting background checks for corporations. But like McEvoy, she sees an opportunity to get back in the game and agrees to help.

In his previous McEvoy novel, Connelly used a serial killer known as the Scarecrow to expose the darker side of the web by showing how he used it to find and recruit those who shared his own psychosexual attraction to women in leg braces. It also allowed him to select his victims and to monitor anyone who might be on his trail. This time the danger comes from popular Internet testing sites like GT23 that allow consumers to trace their family trees by voluntarily submitting their DNA. DNA testing has been a boon to police departments, which can more easily identify murderers they are trying to find, as well as to many falsely convicted individuals, whose DNA can prove their innocence. It has also allowed many people to find family members they didn't know they had. But what McEvoy finds disturbing is the lack of security in commercial sites that threatens to undermine confidence in the whole process.

Although the regulation of the billion-dollar genetics-analysis industry falls under the purview of the U.S. Food and Drug Administration, no procedures for oversight have yet been formulated. A budget site like CT23 makes its money by selling the DNA it collects to universities and biotech companies that use it for legitimate research purposes. But there is currently no government oversight monitoring or controlling who can purchase those DNA samples or how they are used.

From a disgruntled former employee of GT23, McEvoy learns that one of the many companies it sold its collected DNA to was a private lab called Orange Nano, which only bought female DNA and then isolated the DRD4 gene. Known as "Dirty Four," this gene has been identified as possibly being related to at-risk behaviors, including sex addiction. One other thing McEvoy finds out about the four dead women is that they were known as party girls who often went to bars to meet men.

2. The Novels   149

McEvoy discovers a website called Dirty4, which caters to incels, men who describe themselves as "involuntary celibates" who hate women and blame them for their own romantic difficulties. For a $500 annual fee, its customers can download the identities of women whose DNA contains the DRD4 gene. They are free to use that information for their own purposes. One of the co-founders of Dirty4 defends selling the women's DNA by claiming that what they did "was no different from any dating service out there.... We matched people with what they were looking for. Supply and demand. That's it" (324). Except one of his customers, who calls himself the Shrike after the bird that stalks and attacks from behind, gripping its victim's neck in its beak and viciously snapping it, uses the information he gets not to meet women but to kill them.

Connelly has said that the McEvoy books are the easiest for him to write because they are based in part on his own experience as a journalist, but the problem is that a journalist can only go so far in stopping a serial killer. McEvoy reaches the point where he acknowledges that catching the Shrike before he can kill any more women takes precedence over getting an exclusive story, so he and his partners Emily Atwater and Rachel Walling seek the help of Walling's former agency, the FBI.

The novel now turns into a thriller, as the Shrike becomes aware that the authorities are on to him. He first decides to kill the co-founders of the Dirty4 website before they can identify him to the FBI. He kills one of them by his usual method of internal decapitation. Meanwhile, McEvoy has cornered the site's other owner when he steps outside the building where he works to smoke a cigarette. Fearful that his life is also in danger, the man abruptly ends the interview and walks away. Out of nowhere, a speeding car appears and runs him over, killing him. The Shrike has struck again.

When the expected confrontation between McEvoy and the Shrike comes, it takes place in a fitting location—inside McEvoy's car. Like Bosch and Haller, McEvoy spends far too much of his time driving all over L.A. This time he discovers he has a passenger hidden in the rear storage compartment of his brand-new Range Rover SUV. It's the Shrike and McEvoy knows he intends to kill him.

When the cars in front of him suddenly begin to slow to a halt because of an accident, McEvoy has no choice but to speed past all the traffic to get back on the freeway. At this point, the Shrike clamps his arm around his neck and orders him to pull over. Hoping the rollover protection his new car promised works, McEvoy floors the Range Rover and then yanks the wheel. The SUV crashes and flips over several times as it tumbles down the freeway. Battered and bloody, McEvoy manages to crawl out of the vehicle. Underneath he sees the body of the dead Shrike.

We never learn his real identity and although several brief chapters are devoted to him, he's little more than a symbol of evil rather than a real character. The only thing notable about him is how he uses new technology to find his victims. Serial killers of women are all too common and in most novels about them, the victims are seldom fleshed out as real characters. Connelly, however, wants the reader to feel the pain of one of the Shrike's victims.

Four months earlier, twenty-nine-year-old Gwyneth Rice met a man in a bar. After going home with him, the man we now know was the Shrike attacked her. He broke her neck, threw her down the stairs, and left her for dead. She didn't die, but is now a quadriplegic doomed to live the rest of her life hooked up to machines that keep her alive. McEvoy and Walling pay a visit to the rehab facility where she now lives. She can no longer talk, but is able to communicate using a mouth-stick stylus that allows her to use her teeth and mouth as a kind of keyboard. From her we learn that like the other victims of the Shrike, she, too, had sent her DNA to GT23. She also reveals some of her painful memories about the sexual encounter that almost left her dead. As McEvoy and Walling are leaving, she repeats a request she had made earlier that is spelled out in bold letters on the screen: DON'T TAKE HIM ALIVE.

Though he's moved by the extent of her suffering, McEvoy also experiences reporter's guilt following the interview: "I knew that Gwyneth Rice would become the face of the story. A victim who would likely never recover, whose life path had been violently and permanently altered by the Shrike. We would use her to draw readers in, never mind that her heartbreaking injuries would last well beyond the life of the story" (313).

Connelly says *Fair Warning* was inspired by two things. He became interested in DNA testing after reading a report that the Pentagon had directed all members of the military not to do DNA kits due to concerns about the security issues they pose. And he wanted to write about McEvoy again because of how he saw journalists coming under attack. As McEvoy knows only too well, it isn't a good time to be a journalist: "It was the era of fake news and reporters being labeled by those in power as enemies of the people. Newspapers were folding right and left and some said the industry was in a death spiral. Meanwhile, there was a rise in biased and unchecked reporting and media sites, the line increasingly blurring between impartial and agenda-based journalism" (47).

Connelly wanted to show how reporting has changed with the decline of print journalism and the rise of the Internet by focusing on one place where former reporters could still practice their profession after so many newspapers have closed. He also wanted to remind his readers of the importance of real journalism in today's world and to show how dedicated journalists like McEvoy can still play a key role in the public interest.

At the end of the novel, McEvoy has returned to the spotlight. He and Emily Atwater make several appearances on national TV and have been profiled in the *Washington Post*. Both have also left *FairWarning*, Atwater to write a book about the Shrike case, and McEvoy to follow Connelly's example and host a true-crime podcast about it called *Murder Beat*. (Connelly's podcast is called *Murder Book*.)

McEvoy does have one big regret. Once again, he has torpedoed his relationship with Rachel Walling by accusing her of doing something she vehemently denies doing. But he sees a way to get her back, at least professionally. He has decided he no longer wants to be an outsider reporting about crimes; he wants to start solving them. He invites Rachel to join him in a new podcast where they can combine their skills and try to solve cold cases. Their story may not be over yet.

The Law of Innocence (2020)

The Law of Innocence is an informative primer on the basics of the American justice system from arrest to the jury's verdict as seen through the eyes of the accused. In this case, however, the stakes are unusually high as the accused is defense attorney Mickey Haller himself. It's been seven years since the last Haller novel and Connelly said he missed the sound of his narrative voice. It's that distinctive voice that takes the reader on a roller-coaster ride through another tense courtroom drama.

After leaving the party celebrating his latest courtroom victory, Haller is pulled over by a cop for failing to have a license plate on the back of his Lincoln. Somebody has stolen his personal plate. But then the cop notices something liquid dripping out of the car's trunk. When he opens it, he finds a dead body. Haller awakens the next morning at his new address—cell 13, level K-10, Twin Towers Correctional Facility—following his arrest on the charge of murdering the man in his trunk, Sam Scales. Further investigation confirms that Scales was shot in Haller's garage. His bail is set at five million dollars.

Sam Scales was a con man dubbed "The Most Hated Man in America" in a newspaper account of his crimes. His specialty was setting up websites to collect donations for survivors of such tragedies as earthquakes and school shootings and then pocketing the money. Haller had previously defended him several times, but he drew the line when Scales was charged with keeping the donations meant to purchase coffins for children killed in a childcare massacre (and also because Scales had stopped paying the $75,000 he owed him). He hasn't seen him since then until he turned up dead in the trunk of his car.

Unlike his previous cases, where neither the reader nor Haller was certain about his client's innocence, this time there is no doubt. Someone else killed Sam Scales and is framing Haller for the murder. He's fully aware of the old adage that a lawyer who defends himself has a fool for a client, but he refuses to put his future in the hands of anyone but himself. And this time Haller needs more than a not-guilty verdict. He needs to be declared innocent, and that's not the same thing. As he notes,

> The law of innocence is unwritten. It will not be found in a leather-bound codebook. It will never be argued in a courtroom.... It is an abstract idea and yet it closely aligns with the hard laws of nature and science. In the law of physics, for every action, there is an equal and opposite reaction. In the law of innocence, for every man not guilty of a crime, there is a man out there who is. And to prove true innocence, the guilty man must be found and exposed to the world" [105].

We have witnessed Haller in his previous courtroom appearances doing the seemingly impossible by mounting a defense that against all odds results in his client being set free at the end. The task this time is made much more difficult because he must prepare his case while he's confined to jail. His experience behind bars, however, allows Connelly to give the reader an up-close-and-personal look at what Haller calls "the underbelly of the justice system" (22).

It begins with the shame of being seen wearing prison blues by friends and family. Then there's the challenge of trying to sleep on a three-inch-thin mattress amidst the constant noise of steel doors slamming and "the random echoes of desperate men calling out in the dark" (364). A daily diet of a baloney sandwich and an apple for breakfast and lunch is guaranteed to slim you down. (Haller drops thirty pounds.) A prison rash, which Haller gets all over his body, makes everything even more uncomfortable. And a jail with 4500 inmates can be a dangerous place, requiring him to pay a fellow inmate $400 a week for protection.

After several weeks of confinement, he wants out. Prior to sending co-counsel Jennifer Aronson into court to argue a motion for a reduction in bail, the always crafty Haller arranges a phone call to her from jail. Jailhouse authorities are forbidden to monitor attorney-client conversations. To test whether that prohibition is being honored, Haller and Aronson have concocted a non-existent money deal in Mexico to discuss. When Deputy D. A. Dana Berg brings up the Mexico trip in court as a reason why lower bail should not granted, Haller plays the recording he secretly made. Infuriated that Haller's private conversation with his attorney was illegally monitored, the judge immediately punishes the prosecution by reducing Haller's bail from five million to $500,000. Thanks to a pair of benefactors—Andre La Cosse, the client for whom he won a seven-figure settlement for unlawful incarceration seven years earlier in *The Gods of Guilt*, and half-brother Harry Bosch, for whom he won a million-dollar settlement from the city for unlawful termination of his job and took no fee—he makes bail and is released.

Haller takes full advantage of his freedom, dining out at his favorite restaurants and spending time with his daughter Hayley. But his freedom is short-lived, for the prosecution brings a new charge against him. Prosecutor Berg argues that Haller killed Scales for financial gain—that he hoped to get the $75,000 Scales refused to pay him from his estate after his death. A first-degree murder charge under these special circumstances prohibits bail being granted. Haller is re-arrested and returned to jail. Not only is he forced once again to prepare his defense from jail, he is attacked and nearly killed by a fellow inmate while traveling on the bus taking them to court. It appears that this is payback for exposing a jail employee for illegally monitoring his phone call with Jennifer Aronson.

In addition to his usual team—Lorna Taylor, Cisco Wojciechowski, and Jennifer Aronson—Haller is assisted by two familiar figures. One is Harry Bosch, who not only helped pay his bail but identifies a likely suspect in the murder Sam Scales. He has learned that one of the owners of a biodiesel refinery called BigGreen Industries is a man named Louis Opparizio. Nine years earlier in *The Fifth Witness*, Haller's line of questioning forced Opparizio into a trap that left him no choice but to plead the Fifth Amendment during the murder trial of Lisa Trammel, which led to her being freed on a murder charge. His testimony also led to revelations about his mob connections, which resulted in the collapse of a multi-million-dollar merger deal he and his mob backers had arranged.

Bosch also learned that the autopsy on Sam Scales yielded scrapings from underneath his fingernails that contained vegetable oil, chicken fat, and sugarcane—unusual for a man whose previous career was limited to white-collar crimes. However, those are the ingredients used in the making of biofuel, linking Scales and Opparizio. Could Opparizio have killed Scales and then used his body to frame Haller for his murder as payback for what he did to him nine years earlier?

Haller's co-counsel Jennifer Aronson is forced to leave town when her father suddenly becomes ill, felled perhaps by a mysterious new virus from Wuhan, China, that people are beginning to talk about. Her sudden departure opens up a slot on his defense team that is filled by ex-wife Maggie "McFierce" McPherson. Although she is a career prosecutor, at Haller's urging she agrees to take a leave from the District Attorney's Office and cross over to the dark side as his co-counsel. He's thrilled that his daughter Hayley can finally get to see her parents together on the same side in a courtroom. He also finds himself falling in love with Maggie all over again, and begins imagining a future after Hayley graduates from law school when mother, father, and daughter can hang out a shingle that reads, "Haller, Haller, and McFierce, Attorneys-at-Law."

The second half of the novel is largely devoted to the trial itself, which Haller reminds us will be a brutal battle: "There's nothing pure about the law when you get inside a courtroom. It's a bare-knuckle fight and each side uses whatever it can to bludgeon the other" (232). The wily Haller has to be on his toes, ready for everything, including the surprise appearance on the stand of Lisa Trammel, the client he got off on a murder charge by forcing Louis Opparizio into invoking the Fifth Amendment. Only after he won her freedom did he discover she was really guilty. He managed to get justice by alerting the police that they might find the body of her missing husband buried in her backyard. They did, and she's now serving a fifteen-year prison sentence for manslaughter. She's a polished liar who will say whatever it takes to get revenge against Haller. Fortunately, he's up to the challenge and outfoxes her.

At various times during the course of the trial, the presiding judge takes time out to remind us of the importance of some of the fundamental elements of our legal system, e.g., why the jury is a cornerstone of our democracy and why the Fifth Amendment against self-incrimination must always be honored. But the best part of the trial is listening to Haller as he shares his thinking about how he can best bend and twist the rules of the court to his own advantage. We are also schooled in such practical matters as how to question potential jurors in order to suss out any prejudices that might reveal whether they lean toward the prosecution or the defense; and how to delay the prosecution so it is unable to wrap up its case on a Friday, thus preventing the jury members from having two full days with only the prosecution's case in their minds.

In the end, we learn the whole story about Louis Opparizio, Sam Scales and BioGreen once the FBI becomes involved in the case. BioGreen was engaged in a scam in which it was bilking the federal government out of thousands of dollars a week it paid in subsidies for recycled fuel. The company collected payment for every truckload of biofuel driven out of the factory but in truth was driving the same truckloads of restaurant grease back and forth and simply changing the labels on the trucks. Scales was an FBI informant who was secretly running a version of the scam on his own, which was why Opparizio killed him. He in turn was later killed by his mob bosses. To protect its own investigation, the FBI steps in to demand that the state drop all charges against Haller and hold a press conference proclaiming his innocence.

At the end of the novel, Haller has much to be thankful for. Because of the pandemic that has finally arrived, he's frustrated at the lack of items like toilet paper and bottled water on the shelves of the supermarket when he goes shopping. But at least he's able to shelter at home with Maggie and Hayley and is no longer confined to a jail cell where there is no escape from the deadly virus. He can also be thankful when he gets to his car in the supermarket parking lot that the FBI has been secretly following him and is thus able to shoot Opparizio's assassin, who was waiting there to kill him. Best of all, he's happy to see that his missing license plate with the words "NT GLTY" is back on his car.

Connelly began writing *The Law of Innocence* during the height of the COVID-19 pandemic and for the first time in his career experienced writer's block. The country was in a lockdown and the courts were all closed. How could he continue to tell a story about a trial under these conditions? For a full month he found he couldn't write a word. But as he re-thought the novel, he solved his dilemma by moving the action back a few months to pre-pandemic time. This allowed him to have a trial under normal conditions while also being able to chronicle the coming of the pandemic from the first appearance of someone wearing a mask up to the shutdown at the end of the novel. This gave the novel a sense of impending doom on a national level that mirrored Haller's fears about the uncertainty of his own future.

The Dark Hours (2021)

The Dark Hours is the most appropriately titled of all of Connelly's books. He often uses his novels to provide an update on what's happening at the time of their writing, but his latest state-of-the-nation update is particularly bleak. It begins with the arrival of the COVID-19 pandemic, which has dramatically changed lives. Not only was Renée Ballard sidelined for three weeks with the virus, she's been forced to move into an apartment after the beach where she often slept has been closed.

Restaurants and popular tourist attractions are also shut down and people are beginning to mask up and hoping for a vaccine. The only positive benefit of the pandemic is that it's much easier to get around L.A. since there are far fewer cars on the road.

It has also been a year filled with social unrest and violence. Like many police departments, the LAPD had been vilified, and she along with it. "She'd been spat on, figuratively and literally, by the people she thought she stood for and protected. It was a hard lesson, and a sense of futility had set upon her and was deep in the marrow now" (4). The year 2020 can't end soon enough for Ballard.

The story begins on New Year's Eve as Ballard and her new partner Lisa Moore are nervously awaiting the "gunshot symphony" to begin when revelers fire their guns at the sky at midnight to celebrate the arrival of the new year. Smart cops like Ballard park themselves beneath an underpass for protection from bullets falling back to earth. Shortly after the shooting begins, a man named Javier Raffa is found dead of a bullet wound to the head, presumably by one of those stray bullets dropping from the sky.

But when Ballard examines the body more closely, she finds burnt hair and gunpowder specks around the wound, indicating that this was not an accident but the first murder of the year. Meanwhile, she and her partner have another case to deal with. Over a five-week span, a pair of tag-team rapists Ballard dubs the Midnight Men have broken into two houses late at night and sexually assaulted the women in their beds for several hours. They video their assaults and then before leaving cut off a chunk of the women's hair.

The obstacles Ballard faces in investigating both cases come from her own department, which is suffering from a double whammy. It's been a tough year for many police departments, especially after the nationwide protests following the death of George Floyd from a chokehold at the hands of a white cop in Minneapolis. Multiple other incidents of white police gunning down unarmed Black men have also brought renewed attention to policing methods and prompted calls for the defunding of police departments.

Because of the extra expense incurred in dealing with all the local protests, the LAPD has already suffered de facto defunding as it has run out of money, resulting in hiring and promotion freezes and the disbanding of entire units. Morale has plummeted. The LAPD is now largely made up of "officers stripped of the mandate of proactive enforcement and waiting to be reactive, to hit the streets only when it was requested and required, and only then doing the minimum so as not to engender a complaint or controversy" (30).

Ballard has always felt like an outsider in the department because of her gender, but now her refusal to succumb to the "why-should-we-care disease" (61) isolates her even more. "She was not popular in the office after a year of cajoling and then demanding intel and help in her investigations from people bent on doing as little as possible" (33). Even her new partner Lisa Moore, who tries to avoid doing as much work as she can, accuses her of giving the rest of the department a bad name: "Just stay in your lane," she advises her. "Nobody moves, nobody gets hurt, right?" (40). Fortunately, Ballard enjoys working on her own and these two cases will consume all her waking hours, both on and off the job.

Ballard learns that the bullet that killed Javier Raffa came from the same gun that was used to kill another man, Albert Lee, who was shot during a robbery nine years earlier. That case was never solved. She's happy to learn that the lead investigator at the time was Harry Bosch, but when she discovers that the murder book about the case is missing, she suspects he took it with him when he retired. It turns out he didn't; someone else in the department must have. He agrees to help Ballard, especially since he has plenty of time on his hands. He's become something of a homebody since daughter Maddie moved out and is now sharing an apartment with her boyfriend. He's also still dealing with treatment for his leukemia, so he's not as active as he once was. But he hasn't lost his appetite for seeking the truth.

Bosch finds a connection between the murders of Raffa and Lee. Both men had to borrow money and then were forced to accept the lender as a silent partner in their businesses. Raffa was a gang member who fourteen years earlier needed $25,000 to buy freedom from his gang. At his death, his partner inherited ownership of his auto-repair shop and, more importantly, the valuable land it sat on. Albert Lee's silent partner ended up the beneficiary of a million-dollar life insurance policy he was forced to take out. Suspicion as to the identity of the lender in both cases falls on an unexpected person, Christopher Bonner, a cop who retired two years earlier from the same night-shift job Ballard now has. Their first meeting is a dramatic one.

Connelly often creates a tense cat-and-mouse game between detective and killer that ends in a dramatic final confrontation between the two. This time he does something different. Ballard's very first encounter with Bonner comes when she awakens from a deep sleep to find him on top of her, his weight pinning her arms down so he can stick a gun in her mouth. She manages to use her lower body to knock him forward enough to escape his clutches. When she hears him cock his gun to shoot her, she elbows him in the throat, causing him to gag for breath.

Ballard tries to save Bonner's life. She phones Garrett Single, the EMS paramedic who had earlier treated her for a slight concussion she suffered on another case, and asks him to guide her through the steps of an emergency tracheotomy. Time is running out and Bonner is turning blue from lack of oxygen. Following Single's instructions, she uses a small knife she finds in a bedside table to make a tiny incision in Bonner's throat to open his windpipe. Then she scrambles to find a small plastic tube she can insert in the opening to allow him to breathe. But in an unexpected twist, once Bonner recovers and realizes the game is up, he pulls the tube out and dies before help arrives.

This creates new problems for Ballard. In the current defensive posture of the LAPD, any cop who gets into a scrape like Ballard's faces immediate dismissal. The last thing the department needs at this time is the image problem of having an ex-cop revealed to be a multiple murderer. She manages to keep her job, but then the Midnight Men cause another problem for the department. An article appears in the *L.A. Times* accusing the department of endangering the lives of women by failing to publicize the first two attacks. The department is caught in a damned-if-you-do-and-damned-if-you-don't dilemma. Keeping silent about their investigation gives the police a much better chance of making an arrest, but it also places possible future victims in danger. Ballard is on the hot seat again because many in the department believe she was the one who leaked the story to the reporter.

As he did in his previous novel *Fair Warning*, where Jack McEvoy interviewed a woman who was left a quadriplegic after narrowly escaping death at the hands of a serial killer, Connelly again emphasizes the long-lasting effects of crime, this time on the latest victim of the Midnight Men, a twenty-nine-year-old divorced woman named Cindy Carpenter. In her case, the trauma is more psychological than physical: "The dark side of the moon was where people lived who had been through what Cindy Carpenter had just been through. Where a few dark hours changed everything about every hour that would come after. The place that only the people who had been through it understood. Life was never the same" (64).

For victims of rapists who enter their homes to attack them, the sense of violation extends beyond the damage to their bodies; it's the realization that no place is safe and that they must live in constant fear that until their attackers are caught they might return. Carpenter also has to be convinced that though she was targeted, she did nothing to deserve what happened to her. When Ballard later drives by Carpenter's house one night, she notices that she now sleeps in the guest bedroom and keeps the light on.

Ballard gets a key clue when she learns that the streetlight in front of Carpenter's home had been deliberately disabled. A visit to L.A.'s Bureau of Street Lighting reveals that the same thing happened in the first two attacks as well, which means the women weren't random victims but were targeted. She asks the bureau supervisor there to let her know if another streetlight becomes disabled. A call from him sends her to the address of a woman she suspects is the next target. She convinces the woman to switch identities with her and enters the house to wait for a possible attack.

When the rapists arrive, she's ready for them with a gun and ends up killing both. This time, however, she won't have to face any disciplinary action from the LAPD because she is no longer a member of the department. Disillusionment at what the department has become and disgust at her fellow cops who have lost all interest in doing their job prompted her earlier that day to text her letter of resignation to her commanding officer. She can now argue that she was simply acting in self-defense when the two men broke into a house whose owner had given her permission to be in.

As was the case in *Fair Warning*, the dark web once again plays a key role in the crime by enabling a pair of creepy men to mount a campaign of sexually assaulting and humiliating women. They create a website on the dark web with the slogan "Teach the Bitch a Lesson," where men like Cindy Carpenter's ex-husband can get revenge against the women they feel have wronged them simply by passing on their names and addresses to the Midnight Men. These two rapists enjoy humiliating women so much they charge no fee for their services.

The prevailing darkness in *The Dark Hours* grows even darker after the storming of the U.S. Capitol Building on January 6. Ballard, however, does find a couple of reasons to be hopeful. She is still mourning the loss of Lola, but she has adopted a new rescue dog, a Chihuahua mix named Pinto. There is also the prospect of a continuing romantic relationship with Garrett Single, the EMS guy who treated her for a concussion. And her connection to Bosch grows even stronger. He's become a trusted friend, mentor, and the go-to guy when she needs a crime-solving partner. In return, she watches out for the old guy, whom she jokingly calls "the oldest living detective in L.A," and takes matters into her own hands when he drags his feet about getting the COVID vaccine. She manages to get him out of his house and without warning him ahead of time drives him to Dodger Stadium to get his shot.

She is also offered a new job. When she returns to her apartment after walking her dog one day, the chief of the LAPD is waiting for her so he can return her badge to her. "The department needs to change," he tells her. "To do that, it has to change from within. How can we accomplish that if the good people who can make change choose to leave?" (387). Better yet, she can even choose the position she wants.

There is indeed some light at the end of the tunnel.

3

Standalone Novels, Short Stories, and Journalism

Standalone Novels

Void Moon (2000)

The novel opens with a brief scene set in the Cleopatra Casino in Las Vegas where an unnamed woman and a man named Max are sitting at a table debating about who gets to do an exciting but dangerous thing for the last time. If she isn't the one who does it, she knows she'll miss "the charge it would put in her blood" (4). The man, however, prevails and his parting words sound ominous: "Anything happens," Max said. "I'll see you when I see you" (4).

The novel then jumps ahead six years to Los Angeles where the woman, now identified as Cassie Black, is selling cars at a Porsche dealership. At first, there appears to be nothing unusual about her or her job. It's only when she makes her weekly visit to her parole officer that we begin to get answers about what happened in the six years between Las Vegas and Los Angeles. We learn that she served five years of a seven- to twelve-year sentence for manslaughter at the High Desert Institution for Women. She's been out on parole for ten months, but is getting restless.

But there's still an air of mystery about the woman. Why does she pretend to be a potential buyer of a house for sale just so she can get into the bedroom of the little girl named Jodie Shaw who lives there? Why does she stop each day at a schoolyard to watch a girl wearing a backpack with the *Have A Nice Day* smiley face on it? Who did she kill that got her sent to prison for five years? Whatever happened to Max?

It turns out that selling cars and peeing in a cup once a week for her parole officer don't satisfy an adrenaline junkie like Cassie. She wants back in the game, which for her is located in Las Vegas. She and Max were "hot prowlers" who identified big casino winners and robbed them while they slept. As soon as she connects with her old contact who sets her up in a new caper, she gets that old feeling back, what her partner Max called "outlaw juice," which was "boiling in her blood now, banging through her veins like hot water through frozen winter pipes" (39).

At this point, the novel switches to a heist tale. Cassie heads to Las Vegas and with a passkey she has obtained enters the room of her intended target, Diego Hernandez, to set things up before he returns. When the camera she hid in his room indicates that he has fallen asleep, it's time for her to quietly slip into his room and get to work.

Cassie's contact is a serious believer in astrology who warns her not to be in the room between 3:22 a.m. and 3:38 a.m., the period of a void when the moon is moving from one house to another, because it means bad luck. Cassie intends to follow his advice, but things go wrong and delay her until she's smack in the middle of the void moon. She grabs the cash Hernandez has put in the room's safe, but the cash from the briefcase he always carries isn't there. The case is still handcuffed to his arm while he's sleeping. She manages to carefully cut it off, but then the promised bad luck hits. He starts to wake up. The scene ends with Cassie pointing a gun at the man in the bed.

The narrative then switches to the office of Vincent Grimaldi, head of security at the Cleopatra Casino, who has summoned Jack Karch, his outside security consultant, to help him with a big problem. Hernandez has been found shot to death in his bed and his briefcase is missing. The problem is the two and a half million dollars in cash it contains wasn't his gambling winnings. He was a courier bringing the money from a Florida mob to Grimaldi to be used as a payoff to permit the mob to buy the Cleopatra Casino. If that money can't be retrieved, Grimaldi will pay with his life. It's Karch's job to find the woman caught on a video camera leaving the casino with Hernandez's briefcase. Cassie Black is now the target.

The mystery of what happened to Cassie's boyfriend Max and why she went to prison is cleared up when we learn that Grimaldi and Karch were with him when he died.

He was caught in a sting operation the two men had set up and accidentally fell twenty stories from a window of the penthouse suite to his death. Cassie was arrested and charged with manslaughter because according to Nevada law anyone who takes part in a criminal enterprise is considered responsible for any death that occurs during the commission of the crime.

Jack Karch, the son of a noted Vegas magician, likes to entertain others with his magic tricks. But that's the only thing entertaining about him, for he is a murderous psychopath. Once he identifies Cassie Black as the thief with the missing briefcase, he sets out to find her and the money, leaving behind a bloody trail of bodies in his wake.

One other mystery is cleared up. The six-year-old girl Cassie has been watching is her own daughter, born while she was in prison and given up for adoption three days later. When Karch finds this out, he kidnaps the girl and takes her to the same room in the casino where her father Max fell to his death. If Cassie wants her daughter to live, she must bring him the money. After several more twists and surprises, including Kerch's death from the same window Max went through and the revelation that it wasn't Cassie who killed Hernandez, the novel ends with Cassie on the way back to L.A. with her daughter and a million dollars in cash. There she reunites her daughter with the only parents she has ever known. She'll have to be content with knowing she was the girl's guardian angel who saved her life.

Although Cassie makes a brief cameo appearance four years later in *The Narrows*, *Void Moon* doesn't really qualify as part of the Bosch megaseries. It differs from those novels in several ways: it's set mainly in Las Vegas rather than L.A.; it features a lead character who's a criminal, not a cop; and it's a heart-pounding thriller rather than a mystery or a police procedural. It has a well-executed plot, parcels out key information in tantalizing ways, and is filled with plenty of surprises. What it lacks, however, is the heft and resonance of the Bosch books.

Like most thrillers it relies on plot and plenty of it for its effects. Although the characters play their assigned roles well, they lack depth. Jack Karch is little more than the villain the plot requires. Cassie Black has more substance thanks to the various roles she plays as grieving lover, secret mother, scarred ex-con, and plucky heroine. But it's clear to see why Connelly never returned to her for additional appearances. He found he could do more with the other characters whose auditions in his standalone novels proved to be more promising.

Chasing the Dime (2002)

Chemist Henry Pierce is the thirty-four-year-old creative genius behind Amadeo Technologies, which is engaged in research in the field of molecular computing. (The company is named after Amadeo Avogadro, the Italian chemist who two hundred years ago was the first to identify the difference between molecules and atoms.) Pierce's company is seeking to create a new generation of computer chips made of organic molecules rather than silicon, which could reduce a room-size computer to the size of a dime (hence the title).

The company's lawyer is about to file nine patent applications for what is called the Proteus project, which is developing a delivery system that would allow human cells to help drive a tiny computer implanted in the body. Such a device could, for example, measure insulin levels and manufacture and release the amount needed. Whichever company wins the race to be the first to accomplish this will reap huge financial rewards. Pierce has lined up a meeting within the next few days with a wealthy investor who is expected to contribute twenty million dollars to the project.

But his personal life is far from rosy. His fiancée Nicole James has just quit her job as Amadeo's intelligence officer and, having grown tired of Pierce's obsession with work, also dumps him. As the novel opens, he has just moved into a fancy apartment in Santa Monica. Almost immediately the phone in the apartment begins ringing with calls from several men asking for Lilly.

(Unlike the idea for most of Connelly's novels, this one didn't come from a true-crime case but from his own experience. He and his family had just moved from L.A. to a new home in Tampa, Florida. The phone in his office began ringing with calls for the previous owner of the number, a woman named Tammy, who had gone missing. Unlike the situation in the novel, he never found out what happened to her.)

Pierce begins snooping around and discovers that he has inadvertently been given the same number on his new phone as Lilly's number on a website advertising sexual services. This explains the calls from all those men. You would think that a man so obsessed with work that he spends his days and nights in his lab would simply have his personal assistant get him a new phone number. But Pierce has a secret in his past, which we don't fully learn until later, that not very convincingly prompts him to decide to look for Lilly, who has mysteriously dropped out of sight.

In a premise that might remind readers of an Alfred Hitchcock movie, Pierce's questionable decision not surprisingly leads him into all sorts of trouble. During his search for the missing woman, he breaks into her apartment to search for clues and even steals her mail. He may be a brilliant scientist but he's a pretty dumb investigator, and it doesn't take long before he ends up on the police radar. He's soon being questioned about his activities by a relentless Bosch-like detective named Robert Renner. Pierce is an inept liar who naively considers lying to be nothing but social engineering: "Turn the truth just a little bit and make it work for you," he says (105). Renner easily trips him up on several of the lies he tells as he tries to hide what he's been doing. He's eventually forced to hire a defense attorney named Janis Langwiser, who had previously appeared in *A Darkness More Than Night*.

It isn't only the police who are interested in his activities. William Wentz controls a fourteen-state empire of Internet sleaze, including the website where Lilly advertised her services. He unexpectedly shows up at Pierce's apartment one day with a thug named Six-Eight, who smashes a telephone into his nose and then dangles his body over his twelfth-floor balcony to warn him to stay off the case. He ends up in the hospital with a concussion, two fractured ribs, and facial injuries requiring 160 stitches. He looks like Frankenstein's brother, but he can't tell anyone what happened to him, for if the news gets out, it would likely scuttle the deal he's hoping to secure with a major investor in his company.

Pierce eventually finds Lilly's body stuffed into a freezer in a storage locker that has been rented in his name and removes it so the police can't find it. He now begins to suspect that maybe he's being set up and framed for her murder. His first two guesses about who might be responsible for that turn out to be dead wrong. Who's left? It turns out to be the least likely suspect, Cody Zeller, his best friend from college who designed the security system for his company and has been helping him in his investigation. Zeller confesses he's being paid by the pharmaceutical industry, which considers Pierce's Proteus project to be a threat to their business. He killed Lilly and used her in an elaborate scheme to frame his old friend. It turns out he knew a deep dark secret about Pierce that he could use to get him to investigate Lilly. How did he know this? Pierce confessed it to him back in his college days when he got drunk, though he has no memory of having done that.

Connelly attempted to link *Chasing the Dime* to the Bosch series in ways both hidden—he gives Pierce the name he originally planned to give Bosch—and obvious—like Bosch, Pierce seeks redemption for the death of a family member, his sister who was a victim of the Dollmaker, whom Bosch killed. He also added some references to darkness and tunnels, e.g., "he was the only one he could rely on to find his way out of this dark tunnel" (302), and even to an Hieronymus Bosch painting. But the book remains an outlier rather than a part of the Bosch universe.

Pierce isn't a very interesting or even likable character, the plot is riddled with implausibilities, and the novel lacks the usual momentum of Connelly's other books. The novel did, however, serve one useful purpose. It gave Connelly another break from the series and time to think about what direction he would take Bosch following his decision to have him quit his job with the LAPD at the end of *City of Bones*. His next book would be a welcome return to Bosch.

Short Stories

Connelly jokes that he was pressured into writing his first short story by Otto Penzler, who had often invited him to contribute to one of the many anthologies of crime stories he edited. Connelly promised him if he ever wrote one, he could have it. So when Penzler mentioned that his next project was a collection of stories about baseball, as a longtime fan he couldn't say no. "Two-Bagger" (2001) is far from his best work, but he said it did enkindle in him a new appreciation for short stories and he would go on to write them fairly regularly.

Of the two dozen or so stories he wrote, sixteen feature Harry Bosch. Some were written to fit the theme of a collection, with mixed results. "Blue on Black" (2010), for example, appeared in a collection titled *Hook, Line & Sinister*, where the theme is fishing. So with the help of a GPS device belonging to a fisherman who is the main suspect in the murders of two women, Bosch goes fishing, not for fish but for bodies. But all he does is sit on the boat while divers search underwater for the location where the killer has anchored seven bodies he can visit whenever he's out fishing. "One-Dollar Jackpot" (2007), which appeared in a collection of stories about poker, is much better and shows Bosch at his cleverest. He is able to confirm his suspicions about a murder suspect, a professional poker player, by challenging him to a game of liar's poker, which provides him with the physical evidence he needs to convict the man.

Among the best stories are those that focus more on character than plot, many of which also qualify as valid entries in the Bosch universe. Some fill in details about Bosch's experiences in Vietnam and about his early days in the LAPD. "Christmas Even" (2004), the first of the Bosch stories, includes a flashback to a Christmas Eve when the nineteen-year-old Bosch was recuperating on a hospital ship in the South China Sea from a knife wound he suffered in a tunnel in Vietnam. The memory was triggered after he came across an old alto saxophone in a pawnshop while investigating a Christmas Eve burglary there. On the instrument he sees the inscription, "Custom made for Quentin McKinzie," a saxophone player Bosch first heard play during his visit to the hospital ship he was on in 1969. The story ends with Bosch tracking McKinzie down to the nursing home where he currently resides to return his saxophone to him.

"Angle of Investigation" (2005) begins in 1992 on Bosch's second day on the job as a patrol officer. He and his partner are called to the home of a woman where a foul odor leads them to the bathroom where they find the decomposing bodies of the woman and her dog in the tub. The smell brings back unpleasant memories to Bosch of the same smell of death he encountered every day during his stint in the Vietnam tunnels where the enemy buried their dead. The case was turned over to a pair of homicide detectives but was never solved until Bosch, now working thirty-three years later on the Open-Unsolved Unit, chooses that case to re-open. He has little to go on aside from a palm print left on the bathroom wall that after all these years leads him to the killer.

Connelly himself edited a collection of stories about cops in 2008 titled *The Blue Religion: New Stories about Cops, Criminals and the Chase*. In his introduction he noted that based upon his experience, most cops believe they are part of a misunderstood breed. "How are we to weigh the burden of the badge if we do not carry the badge?" (viii), he asked himself. He hoped the stories in the collection would help readers understand not only what it's like to unmask a killer but also what some of the emotional costs of doing the job are. The story he wrote for the collection does both of those things.

"Father's Day" opens with the death of a fifteen-month-old severely handicapped child who was left in a parked car on a day when the temperature hit the mid–90s. Bosch is called to examine the body, which is one of the most difficult tasks cops have to deal with. "Bosch had worked thousands of cases, but nothing ever touched him like the sight of a young child's lifeless body" (348). Remembering that it was Father's Day only adds to his emotional burden by reminding him of his own failings as a father since he and his ten-year-old daughter Maddie had only spent one Father's Day together. In the end, however, he at least gets the satisfaction of proving there's more to this case than first meets the eye.

Several stories were inspired by something mentioned in one of his novels. "Cielo Azul" (2005) is an expansion of an incident that's briefly mentioned in *A Darkness More Than Night*. Bosch travels to San Quentin to speak with a serial killer a week before his execution. He hopes the man will finally tell him the name of a fifteen-year-old Mexican girl he murdered years earlier. That was the first case Bosch and FBI profiler Terry McCaleb worked together and ten years later both are still haunted by the death of the girl, whose identity was never learned and whose body was never claimed. Bosch nicknamed the girl Cielo Azul, which was the name McCaleb just gave to his newborn daughter. Also notable about this story is that it's the first time Connelly employed Bosch as a first-person narrator. He enjoyed the experience enough that he used it again in the next Bosch novel he wrote, *Lost Light*.

Some stories read like capsulized versions of a Bosch novel where he must solve a crime within the length of a short story using the same qualities of observation and determination found in the novels. In "Suicide Run," he's called out to the apartment of a young actress who, given the empty bottle of Percodan and the suicide note on a table next to her bed, apparently died by her own hand. But Bosch never takes things at face value, and notes other details that tell a different story. With the help of Kiz Rider, a former partner, he compiles a list of similar suicides and finds the link that leads him to the killer.

In "Switchblade" (2014), Bosch is working in the Open-Unsolved Unit. The woman in charge of sorting through requests about cold cases informs Bosch that she just received an anonymous phone message—"Patrick Sewall killed that boy"—and the boy's name, "Billy." Bosch first has to figure out which case the message refers to, which turns out to be the unsolved stabbing death two decades earlier of a twenty-year-old man. The victim was found naked and the multiple switchblade wounds he suffered suggested he was killed in a rage. The latest DNA technology helps Bosch connect that killing with another committed by Patrick Sewall, who is about to be paroled from San Quentin. Bosch's search for the person responsible for the anonymous phone call and the reason behind it leads to a very satisfying surprise ending.

"A Fine Mist of Blood" (2012) finds Bosch and partner Jerry Edgar seeking to determine if a female stockbroker who was a witness to two murders is, in fact, a hit woman who killed both men. The story ends with a suspenseful standoff with the killer. Fans of the *Bosch* TV series will especially enjoy the audio version of the story, which features the voices of Titus Welliver and Jamie Hector in their familiar roles as Harry Bosch and Jerry Edgar.

Two stories pay tribute to a pair of Connelly's (and Bosch's) favorite artists. In "Nighthawks" (2016), which appeared in a collection inspired by the paintings of Edward Hopper, Bosch is now working as a private eye. He has been hired by a famed Hollywood producer to track down his missing daughter, whose photograph of her in a Chicago bookstore he has just seen. Bosch heads to Chicago and quickly locates the woman, whom he follows each day as she visits Hopper's famous *Nighthawks* painting at the Chicago Institute of Art during her lunch break. The two end up talking, though much of their conversation takes place off the page. Bosch returns to L.A. to report to his client that the woman is not his missing daughter and gives him a sample of her hair he can test to prove it. The hair, we learn, actually belongs to his own daughter, Maddie. Why he does this now makes clear what was talked about in the portion of the conversation we didn't hear.

The story is notable for the connection Bosch himself has to the painting, a framed print of which, a gift from Eleanor Wish in *The Black Echo*, hangs on his wall. Like the young woman, he too identifies with the loner in the painting sitting by himself, ignoring the only other patrons, a couple at the other end of the bar. As he thinks about the painting once again at the end of the story, the same words come to mind that do every time he looks at the print of it on his wall: "*I am that man*" (90).

Although Harry Bosch doesn't appear in "The Third Panel" (2018), a painting by his namesake does. Connelly pays tribute to Hieronymus Bosch by using the third panel of his most famous work, *The Garden of Earthly Delights*, which portrays Judgment Day when evildoers are punished for their sins in gruesome ways. The serial killer in *A Darkness More Than Night* left behind details from the same painting at the scene of his murders in an effort to link Bosch to the killings as it is known that a print of *The Garden of Earthly Delights* hangs on his wall. In this story the killers also leave behind references to the Bosch painting, though they have a much grander purpose in mind for their murders.

Though Connelly's novels are often dark and serious, he reveals a much more playful side in "The Crooked Man" (2014), which appeared in the collection *In the Company of Sherlock Holmes*. Bosch is summoned to the mansion of a man who has been found dead on the floor of his library. The deputy coroner, appropriately named Art Doyle, is so good at interpreting the physical nuances of murder that he has earned the nickname of Sherlock, which he has fun with. He invites Bosch to take a closer look at the body by saying, "Come in to our little circle here. The game is afoot" (5). The Holmesian banter continues when Bosch points out that most homicides in the home are the result of domestic disputes. "Elementary," Doyle replies. "Don't start with that shit," Bosch fires back (11).

Like Holmes, Art Doyle also enjoys showing off his skill in reaching conclusions based simply on his close observations. After observing the sixty-year-old Bosch struggling to stand up from a crouch, he immediately diagnoses a case of Benign Paroxysmal Positional Vertigo (BPPV) and advises him to see his doctor about it. He also deduces that Bosch left a woman behind in his bed before reporting to the murder scene. How does he know that? When Bosch bent down, Doyle noticed he was wearing mismatched socks and concluded he dressed in the dark so as not to disturb a sleeping partner.

In several of the stories Bosch is partnered up with people he's worked with before. In "Red Eye" (2014), however, he's briefly partnered with a stranger, a Boston private eye named Patrick Kenzie. The story, co-authored with Dennis Lehane, gives readers of both writers' books a chance to see their two detectives interact. Bosch has taken a red-eye flight to Boston to try to get a sample of DNA from a man suspected of sexually assaulting and murdering a fourteen-year-old. While there he encounters Patrick Kenzie when both end up surveilling the same suspect's house, and together they save a young girl's life.

The story contains some entertaining banter between the two and also allows us to see each one through the other's eyes. Even though he has known Bosch for a very short time, Kenzie's sharp eye nails his character:

> Patrick got a whiff of something sad coming off the LA cop. Not the kind of sad that came from bad news yesterday but from bad news most days. Still, his eyes weren't dead; they pulsed instead with appetite—maybe even addiction—for the hunt. This wasn't a house cat who checked out, who kept his head down, took his paycheck, and counted the days till his twenty. This was a cop who kicked in doors if he had to, whether he knew what was on the other side or not, and had stayed on after twenty [22].

The remaining stories are a mixed bag: a pair of Mickey Haller tales—"The Perfect Triangle" (2010) and "Burnt Matches" (2016); a ghost story, "The Safe Man" (2005), published anonymously in a collection that challenged readers to guess which of the dozen authors listed on the book wrote which story; "Mulholland Dive" (2007), a crime story with an ironic noir twist at the end; and "Shortcut" (2009), included in a collection of short horror stories for kids. This one is about the fear experienced by a young boy in thinking about the prospect of going through a dark tunnel under a railroad embankment, thoughts of which Connelly says gave him nightmares when he was a young boy. Despite its brevity (only five paragraphs long), the story will likely have the same effect on the kids who read it.

Journalism

Crime Beat (2004)

Crime Beat: A Decade of Covering Cops and Killers is a collection of twenty-two articles Connelly wrote between 1984 and 1992 that appeared

3. Standalone Novels, Short Stories, and Journalism 171

in the three newspapers he worked for during his journalism career. The selections will certainly be of interest to fans of true-crime stories, but they are also helpful in understanding Connelly's crime fiction. Reading through these stories, one can see how the reportorial skills Connelly learned in crafting them influenced how he would later write his novels.

The book begins with "Lauderdale Homicide," which Connelly said in the book's introduction was the single story that influenced his writing more than any other. Appearing in the *South Florida Sun-Sentinel* in 1987, it chronicles the week Connelly spent closely following a Fort Lauderdale homicide squad during its investigation into a trio of murders. It was here where he first witnessed the day-to-day work of the homicide detectives, especially Detective George Hurt. Hurt's dedication to the job and description of it—"I could say that old saying about it being a dirty job but somebody has to do it, but I don't look at it that way. I see it as being a dirty job but somebody has to know how to do it. We know how. We do good work here" (36)—were early inspirations for the character of Harry Bosch.

He also wrote about murderers. In 1984, he published a trio of stories about the nationwide search for Douglas Wilder, a serial killer who fled Florida after killing a pair of Miami models. Posing as a professional photographer and talent scout gave him easy access to young, attractive women, eleven of whom he murdered. He was eventually killed when he accidentally shot himself in a struggle with a police officer in New Hampshire. A 1991 *Los Angeles Times* story featured a killer named Jonathan Lundh, who was arrested for the murder of a woman in a parking garage in Los Angeles nine years after her death. A con man who claimed to have studied law at Harvard (there is no evidence that he was ever a student there), he served as his own attorney. He was eventually convicted and given a life sentence.

Connelly includes an update to the original story by adding that after his conviction, Lundh phoned him frequently from prison to protest his innocence: "I remember hanging up the phone each time and feeling lucky that we were separated not only by the phone line but by the concrete and steel of the jail as well. No person I have ever spoken to in my life was creepier than Jonathan Lundh" (13).

The selections also illustrate Connelly's skill in weaving together the who-what-where-when-and-why details of a crime into compelling reading that is much more than a simple factual account of that crime. "Billy the Burglar," a 1987 story from the *South Florida Sun-Sentinel*, tells the tale of twenty-four-year-old Billy Schroeder, who began sampling drugs when he was eleven, the same year he was caught committing his first burglary. Over the next decade he became a crack addict and a busy burglar who in one year broke into at least 350 homes and stole an estimated $2 million worth of property.

The story illustrates the importance of colorful quotes and telling details, both of which he also brought to the writing of his fiction. Billy was no master criminal. His method was simple: "I would drive down a street and decide, eenie, meenie, minie, moe, that's the house I'm going to do" (323). One time he noticed a lighted Christmas tree in the window of a house as he was driving by and broke in through the front window to steal all the presents under the tree. He had to go back three more times to get them all.

The story also reminds us that every crime has a victim. As one local cop put it: "I like Billy Schroeder.... But I have no sympathy for him. I have sympathy for the people he stole from. They have to put up with the feelings of intrusion and their losses for the rest of their lives. They worked all their lives so they can have some of these possessions, and somebody breaks in and it's all gone" (328).

Some stories are of interest because of their connection to the novels. "Who Shot Vic Weiss?," about a man who was found shot to death in the trunk of his Rolls-Royce, was used for the main plot of *Trunk Music*. "Ambush Shooting," about a murder in the hills above Studio City at the intersection of Montcalm Avenue and Woodrow Wilson Drive near the home owned by famed artist David Hockney, first brought Connelly to the hillside site on Woodrow Wilson Drive where he decided to locate Bosch's house.

The voice we hear in all the stories—authoritative, direct, unfussy—laid the foundation for the narrative voice of the Bosch novels. This beginning of "The Mail-Order Murders," for example, could easily pass for the opening of a Harry Bosch novel: "It would have been comical if it hadn't been so deadly, if lives hadn't been mercilessly ended or, at the very least, haunted by terror. They were called the gang that couldn't shoot straight, yet they were a gang that had so many shots, they were bound to hit their targets sometimes, and people were bound to die" (213).

"Tarzana Man Held in Murder of His Missing Father" highlights the fact that despite their best efforts, the police are often frustrated in their search for justice. A young man has murdered his father. A fingerprint left on a parking-lot ticket at the airport leads detectives to a man who admits he helped his friend kill his father. The police have no choice but to grant him immunity for his testimony against his friend. The problem is the son has vanished and they have no idea where he is. Stories where the crime remains unsolved serve to remind us of an important difference between Connelly's fiction and the crimes he wrote about in the newspaper. In real life, the bad guys often get away with murder.

4

Movies, Television, and Podcasts

Movies

Blood Work (2002)

The first of Connelly's novels to be filmed, *Blood Work* is more a Clint Eastwood movie than a faithful adaptation of a Michael Connelly book. A seventy-two-year-old actor famous for playing a detective hero named Dirty Harry Callahan thirty years earlier clearly differentiates his Terry McCaleb from the forty-six-year-old McCaleb of the novel. In addition, the novel's McCaleb receives his heart transplant after his own is weakened by a virus caused by the stress of his job as an FBI profiler tracking down serial killers. Eastwood's character is felled by a heart attack while chasing down a suspect, whom in typical Dirty Harry fashion he still manages to blast away with his trusty .44 Magnum Smith & Wesson revolver.

Much of the film's interest comes from Eastwood playing off that Dirty Harry image as he portrays an aging hero who proves he's still got it, even though he is often shown checking his heart and maybe even wondering if he can still be a Dirty Harry with a woman's heart now beating in his chest.

The script by Brian Helgeland sticks pretty close to the novel for the first half of the movie, and even retains many of the book's best lines. But things go haywire at the end. In the novel, readers are likely to become suspicious about the character of Buddy Lockridge (Jeff Daniels), McCaleb's marina neighbor and driver. He always seems a bit too nosy about what McCaleb is trying to do. Of course he's much too obvious a suspect to turn out to be the killer in a Connelly novel. Not so in Eastwood's film, where to no one's surprise he's revealed to be the villain. As the novel slowly lumbers towards its inevitable conclusion, Eastwood reverts to his famous film persona and guns begin blasting in an all-too-familiar Dirty Harry way. There are too many gratuitous gunfights and far too many shots of Eastwood brandishing his huge pistol for the camera.

The film received some acclaim for Eastwood's portrayal of an aging detective hero. As A.O. Scott put it in his *New York Times* review, "There is something comforting in seeing this old warhorse trot gamely out of the gate for yet another run on familiar turf." But other critics were less kind. In a review for the BBC, Nev Pierce deemed it "a bloody mess" with an "atrocious script" and an execution that "beggars belief."

Connelly's judgment was mixed: "It wasn't a great movie; it certainly wasn't a bad movie. It was somewhere in the middle ... an okay movie" (McDonald). He enjoyed his experience with Clint Eastwood, whose Dirty Harry was one of the detectives named Harry (the other was Harry Caul, played by Gene Hackman in Francis Ford Coppola's *The Conversation*) that influenced his own Harry Bosch. Seeing Eastwood play one of his characters on the big screen was a special thrill.

Even before the film was released, Connelly gave it a plug in *Angels Flight* where Bosch spots an ad for it, which he mentions was based on a true story about an FBI agent he knows (76). Two pages later, another character says she saw Terry McCaleb on TV and remarks that to her he didn't look anything like Clint Eastwood (78). And in *The Narrows*, Clint Eastwood even pays his respects to McCaleb, the man he played in the film, by showing up at his funeral.

The Lincoln Lawyer (2011)

Connelly was much happier with the film version of *The Lincoln Lawyer* (directed by Brad Furman; screenplay by John Romano). Unlike *Blood Work*, where he had little to do with the movie, this time he had a choice over who would get to make the film. He also got to read a few scripts over the years—fourteen in all—and meet with Matthew McConaughey to talk about the character of Mickey Haller before filming began. McConaughey told Connelly he looked forward to playing a character he described as someone "who could dance between the raindrops without getting wet" (Priddle).

The result is a faithful adaptation of the novel that rises above the standard legal thriller thanks to outstanding performances, especially McConaughey's, whose previous four films seem to have destined him to a career of nothing but romantic comedies. In *The Lincoln Lawyer*, his good looks and charm are on full display, but he also reveals a steely resolve beneath Mickey Haller's smooth-operator image. He captures his skills, both in court and in knowing how to play the game, always with an eye on the dollar.

The film is also energized by fine performances by Ryan Phillippe as Haller's client Louis Roulet, William H. Macy as his private investigator Frank Levin, and Marisa Tomei as his ex-wife and often prosecutorial antagonist in court Maggie McPherson. The scenes between McConaughey and Tomei effectively capture the warm personal relationship that remains despite their divorce and legal differences.

As it so often happens in Hollywood productions, the movie has a more upbeat ending than the novel it's based on. Haller is back to work and pleased to learn that Jesus Martinez, the innocent man who has been languishing in prison because he advised him to accept a deal and plead guilty despite his pleas that he was innocent, has finally been freed. The novel's conclusion is much darker. After Haller is shot by his client's mother, who is revealed as the killer of his private investigator, he spends five months in the hospital recovering from three surgeries he had to undergo. His law license was suspended for three months and medical and legal expenses ate up the six-figure fee he earned for defending Roulet. More importantly, he is shamed, not comforted, by Martinez's release from prison. He now knows that the person he pressured into pleading guilty in order to avoid the death penalty was really the innocent client he needed to be concerned about. And though Martinez is now a free man, he has contracted AIDS in prison, where he never should have been in the first place.

Television

Bosch (2015–2021)

Connelly was understandably thrilled when Paramount Studios optioned the rights to his first three Harry Bosch novels because the money he received allowed him to quit his journalism job and become a full-time writer. Although there were at least six different scripts written over the years (two of them by Connelly), no film was ever made, mainly because a 110-page screenplay wasn't long enough to do justice to the character of Harry Bosch. Each script ended up focusing on plot rather than character, so each one if filmed would have been a run-of-the-mill cop movie.

Paramount owned the rights to Harry Bosch, but Connelly learned that after fifteen years he could buy back his character. He was eventually required to pay Paramount three million dollars to reimburse the studio for all the expenses it incurred in trying to get a film made, but he now could look for a new deal. Rather than pursuing another movie deal, he began looking at television. Thanks to groundbreaking season-long hit shows like *The Sopranos* and *The Wire*, the TV landscape had changed dramatically. What particularly interested Connelly was how viewing a multiple-episode streaming show where one could choose to move through the story at one's own pace was similar to the experience of reading a novel.

At this point, Amazon Studios entered the picture. It had begun streaming an original comedy series and was now looking for its first dramatic one. Having sold millions of Bosch novels, Amazon approached Connelly about a Bosch streaming series. Connelly decided to go with Amazon for several reasons. The creative team he would work with had a history of producing the kind of season-long storytelling he felt was the best way to present his character. He also wanted a deal where he wouldn't just sell the rights to his character unless he was part of the package. Instead of asking for script approval, he wanted to be involved in the script-writing process itself as one of the eight writers who worked on the series. It also occurred to him that a successful series would likely bring him more readers and "the idea of having one-hour commercials just one click away from my books made me think, 'Where do I sign?'" (Lowman).

Connelly teamed up with Swedish producer Henrik Bastin and Eric Overmyer, a veteran of shows like *The Wire, Law & Order,* and *Homicide: Life on the Street*. He and Overmyer wrote the one-hour pilot, which was shot in November 2013. Amazon put it up for viewing along with a few other shows in early 2014 and asked its subscribers to vote on which ones they wanted to see more of. It wasn't long before Amazon ordered a 10-episode series of the show. The pilot was rewritten and *Bosch* began streaming its first season of ten episodes on February 1, 2015.

The first piece of business—finding the right actor to play Harry Bosch—was crucial. The team had six weeks to cast someone who could project Bosch's inner world, who could portray a character with baggage without ever having to say, "I have internal baggage." But time was running out. Connelly had originally suggested Titus Welliver after seeing him in an episode of a TV show called *Touch* with Kiefer Sutherland, where he played a guy with PTSD, but he was listed as currently working on a film in Hong Kong and therefore unavailable. However, as the casting sessions were winding down, Welliver returned to L.A. and agreed to come in for an audition. Though suffering from jet-lag, he nailed the audition. All those in the room unanimously agreed they had found their Harry Bosch and he was hired before he left the parking lot.

Based on his extensive TV experience, Overmyer knew that changes had to be made when it came to translating the Bosch novels to TV. For one thing, Titus Welliver couldn't be in every scene, so the roles of Bosch's partner Jerry Edgar, his boss Grace Billets, and Deputy Chief Irvin Irving were expanded, and their private lives would play a larger role. Adjustments to the character of Bosch also had to be made. In the novels, he was a Vietnam vet who was now in his late sixties. Titus Welliver's Bosch would be a forty-year-old veteran of the Army Special Forces in Desert Storm and the war in Afghanistan and the father of a fourteen-year-old daughter when the series begins.

Though Welliver doesn't look the way Connelly pictures him in his mind (he has no mustache), the actor had what Connelly was hoping for—a quiet intensity that perfectly captured Bosch's drive and relentlessness. He *is* Harry Bosch, which is reinforced by the fact that he's now the voice on the audiobook versions of the novels. The other actors were equally well cast. Lance Reddick and Jamie Hector, with whom Overmyer had previously worked on *The Wire*, played Chief of Police Irvin Irving and Bosch's partner Jerry Edgar respectively. Others included Amy Aquino as Lt. Grace Billets, Bosch's supervisor; Mimi Rogers as attorney Honey Chandler; and Madison Lintz as Bosch's daughter Maddie. One of the treats of the series is watching Maddie grow from an awkward fourteen-year-old girl into a confident, twenty-one-year-old woman over the course of seven seasons. The quiet moments between her and her father reveal a softer side of Bosch, a loving father deeply concerned about his daughter's safety and well-being in a world he knows can be a dangerous place.

Each season, Connelly would select three of his novels to serve as the main narrative, and then prepare a sixty-page summary of what the season would look like. Part of the fun for him was the opportunity to reimagine books he had already written. Then he and the other seven writers would meet for several hours each day to outline the ten episodes, then go off on their own to write their assigned episodes. He himself wrote or co-wrote several episodes including the final episode of most seasons.

Connelly insisted on the same kind of accuracy he strove for in his novels and the production department obliged. According to his contract, every scene had to be filmed in L.A., and most of the show is filmed on location. Well-known landmarks like Angels Flight and famous eateries like Musso and Frank's restaurant are featured, but so, too, are back alleys and places few people other than cops get to see, like the city's underground tunnels. Some scenes were actually shot in the real LAPD Homicide Station, where the cops in the background look like real cops because many of them were.

When a real location couldn't be used, like the Bone Lab at the Los Angeles Sheriff's Department, an exact duplicate was built. And to ensure that all the details of policing were accurately portrayed, the series employed as technical consultants the three LAPD cops that were Connelly's advisors for his novels. Also worthy of mention is the overall look of the production. Many scenes are set at night and the frequent use of drone shots from the air captures both the familiar neon glow of the city along with many unfamiliar but no less intriguing parts of the city.

Although Connelly has often said he has no intention of ending the Bosch books, he agreed that the TV series needed some sort of conclusion. In the final episode, co-written by Connelly and Overmyer, Bosch sabotages a joint operation between the LAPD and the FBI that was aimed at ensuring the re-appointment of Chief Irving for another term because it would have involved allowing the man responsible for the death of a ten-year-old-girl to go free. His actions cost him his job and he turns in his badge.

"Who are you if you don't have the badge?" Irving asks. "I'm going to find out," replies Bosch. He takes the first step by applying for his private-eye license and Maddie announces she wants to help in whatever he decides to do. As the episode ends, we hear two appropriate songs—Bosch's favorite jazz recording of Frank Morgan's "Lullaby" followed by Creedence Clearwater Revival's "Long as I Can See the Light"—which remind us that he will keep moving forward.

The series ends one chapter of Bosch's life, but a new one is scheduled to begin in a spin-off series being produced by the same creative team behind *Bosch*. Titled *Bosch: Legacy*, it will feature Bosch, now a private detective, daughter Maddie, and attorney Honey Chandler. Episodes are due to begin streaming in 2022 on Amazon's ad-supported platform IMDb TV. A new series featuring Mickey Haller is also scheduled to debut in 2022 on Netflix.

Bosch wasn't Connelly's first foray into television. In 2000, he was one of the creators and writers of *Level 9*, a science-fiction series about a secret government agency whose job is fighting cybercrimes. The series, which appeared on the UPN network, lasted for only nine episodes. He also made several appearances on another TV series called *Castle*, which ran for eight seasons beginning in 2009. Richard Castle, portrayed by Nathan Fillion, is a best-selling crime novelist who assists the NYPD with some of their cases. Connelly plays himself in a regular poker group with some of his writer friends—Stephen J. Cannell, James Patterson, and Dennis Lehane. In an episode that aired in 2011, a new player joins the game and is the first to offer Castle his suggestion as to which character he should make the murderer in his new book. "How many books have you written?" asks Connelly. The answer is one. "You know what I did after I wrote my first novel?" Connelly says. "I shut up and wrote twenty-three more."

Podcasts

Connelly was inspired to create his first podcast by the same impulse that prompted him to write another novel about Jack McEvoy in *Fair Warning*. He wanted to provide an update on the profession of journalism and to spotlight places where it is still being practiced. The podcast allowed him to revisit his own past as a reporter and to tell a true crime story once again as a way of reminding his listeners of the crucial importance of the truth: "It's not a political story at all, it's a murder story, but it's about truth, it came out of something in me saying, let's tell a true story, and to me it's a true story about heroes, and some of the heroes are the type that are being slighted now by our politicians, by our politician in chief at the moment" (Hughes).

Murder Book Podcast Season One: The Tell-Tale Bullet, which debuted on January 28, 2019, and ran for fourteen episodes, chronicles a murder case from the time it happened on the streets of L.A. in 1987 until the killer was brought to justice. This crime didn't make any headlines; it was just another fatal shooting in a city that averaged more than two murders a day. What makes it noteworthy is the amount of time it would take to finally get justice—thirty-two years. The judge in the trial called it the most tortured history of any case he had ever worked in his life. The story isn't a whodunit—the main suspect is identified within a few days—but a deep dive into the justice system that details how justice is often frustratingly delayed. But thanks to the relentless efforts of many people, the killer is finally brought to trial and the case can be closed.

It begins with the shooting death of twenty-one-year-old Jade Clark, who was gunned down during an attempted hijacking of his car late one night in 1987. The lead investigator of the incident was Rick Jackson, one of the homicide detectives with whom Connelly has been consulting for many years. There was an eyewitness to the crime (a passenger in Clark's car), a bullet with some human flesh on it that apparently passed though the shooter's arm when Clark managed to fire his gun at him before dying, and an anonymous tip that led to the arrest of a suspected gang member named Pierre Romaine.

Years later, more sophisticated tests of the DNA on that bullet confirmed that it belonged to Romaine. But what followed was a lengthy series of frustrations in trying to get Romaine convicted. It would take thirty years before the trial actually began and another two years of legal wrangling before he was finally sentenced. Like a good crime novel, the podcast takes the listener on a journey with many unexpected twists and turns, including how a murder suspect like Pierre Romaine could end up working as a police officer for the Department of Defense.

Listeners to the podcast don't need to know anything about Connelly's novels to fully enjoy the story, which is fleshed out with interviews of many of the principal characters, wiretaps of Philip Romaine's phone conversations, and extensive audio tapes of the trial, which the judge allowed Connelly to record. We are also reminded of the human tragedy of the case in remarks made by Jade Clark's mother, who expresses the pain of losing a son she loved and then having to wait for over three decades to get justice.

But for readers of the Bosch books there are special treats. We learn how Connelly conducts research for his novels by listening in on his conversations with the three detectives who worked on the case—Rick Jackson, Tim Marcia, and Mitzi Roberts—who have been his longtime technical advisors. We also get to hear his discussions about court procedure with Dan Daly, an attorney friend who advises him on the Mickey Haller novels. Connelly also explains a key difference between the podcast and his fiction. In his novels, Harry Bosch sometimes feels he must step over the line in pursuit of the truth, but in real life, as the podcast makes clear, these detectives always played by the rules.

The subject of Connelly's second podcast, *The Women Who Stopped Sam Little* (2020), is also a man who got away with murder for four decades before being convicted of killing three women in Los Angeles in 2014. The difference between the two cases is that Pierre Romaine never killed again and in fact became a police officer. Sam Little, the man in the second case, admitted to killing a total of ninety-three women before he was finally caught and convicted, making him America's most prolific killer in history.

Little has garnered plenty of attention since his history as a serial killer became known. What makes the podcast noteworthy is that the homicide detective who finally managed to arrest him was Mitzi Roberts, Connelly's model for Renée Ballard. In 2012, Roberts was assigned the cold case of the murders of two women in Los Angeles in 1989. Both were strangled and naked from the waist down when they were found. Advances in testing revealed that DNA found on both women belonged to a drifter with an extensive criminal record named Sam Little. In 1984, he had been acquitted of murdering a woman in Florida and later accepted a plea deal of two and a half years in a case in San Diego where he was stopped by the police in the act of strangling a woman. Roberts's job was to prepare a case that would lead to Little's arrest and conviction in the 1989 murders, which finally occurred in 2014.

The podcast highlights the combined efforts of three women—Mitzi Roberts; Beth Silverman, the prosecutor of the case; and Jillian Lauren, a journalist writing a book on it—whose dedication went beyond ensuring that Little was locked up for the rest of his life (he died in prison in 2020). They also became victim advocates who sought to provide closure to the families of the dead women by working to confirm Little's guilt in as many of the ninety-three murders he confessed to following his conviction as they could. (To date, fifty of those killings have been confirmed.)

Among the important questions the podcast asks is how could Sam Little get away with killing so many women for so long. One reason is that he chose his victims carefully. Most were vulnerable women living on the fringe of society, drug addicts and prostitutes who went willingly with him to have the sex he agreed to pay for. He then strangled them during or right after sex when they were most vulnerable.

But it's also clear that these women were considered "throwaway victims" who didn't matter much. Few police departments had someone like Harry Bosch with an everybody-counts-or-nobody-counts mission on their staff to investigate these murders. Also, for most of the years of Little's killings there were few female cops who might have taken a stronger interest in the murders. When Mitzi Roberts was asked how many female names of investigators she came across when she reviewed cases around the country with similar killings, she could name only one. It took the joint efforts of the women featured in the podcast to finally identify Little and put an end to his record-breaking string of murders.

Connelly's first two podcasts dealt with under-the-radar crimes.

By contrast, his third, *The Wonderland Murders & the Secret History of Hollywood (2021)*, features one of L.A.'s most notorious, the murders of three men and a woman who were brutally bludgeoned to death with hammers in a house on Wonderland Avenue in 1981. The case immediately gained notoriety for two reasons: the murders, as shocking as the Manson murders twelve years earlier, were committed in Laurel Canyon, a peaceful neighborhood which in the mid-'60s and '70s was home to members of the Byrds; the Mamas and the Papas; Crosby, Stills & Nash; and singers Joni Mitchell, Carole King, and Linda Ronstadt, among many others who helped create the folk-rock, peace-and-love music of the period; and it involved a pair of minor celebrities—John Holmes, the most famous porn star of all time, and Scott Thorson, at the time the companion of Liberace. (In a 2012 movie based on his book, *Behind the Candelabra: My Life with Liberace*, Thorson was played by Matt Damon.)

Connelly was drawn to the story for several reasons. It was his friend Rick Jackson who arrested Scott Thorson on a robbery charge in 1988 when he first admitted he knew who gave the order for the Wonderland killings. He himself also later lived in a house in Laurel Canyon not far from where the murders took place. And it was the fortieth anniversary of the violent murders.

Connelly's previous podcasts, which he has called "how-do-we-get-em" stories (Murphy), focused closely on both the homicide detectives who investigated the case and those who worked with them to achieve a conviction. There is little that is new to report about the Wonderland murders, which have been the subject of a 2003 movie (*Wonderland*); a book in 2018 by the two lead detectives, Tom Lange and Bob Souza (*Malice in Wonderland: The Inside Story of the Police Investigation of the Laurel Canyon Murders*); and numerous articles and TV shows over the years.

Consequently, Connelly is forced to shift his focus to the personalities of several of the notable participants. He conducted interviews with several key figures—the cop who was the first on the scene of the murders, the two lead homicide detectives on the case, and especially Scott Thorson, who spoke with him many times over the course of a year. He also was able to draw upon a 150-page transcript of an interview with John Holmes that had not been available before.

This is no whodunit. Suspicion immediately fell on Eddie Nash, owner of several L.A. nightclubs (one of his financial investors was Liberace), which were fronts for his lucrative drug business. The murder victims, with the help of John Holmes, had broken into Nash's home and stole drugs, money, and jewelry. Two days later, Nash ordered their

4. Movies, Television, and Podcasts

deaths as revenge and a warning to others that he wasn't to be messed with. Scott Thorson would later testify that he happened to be in Nash's home to buy drugs when he heard him give the orders for the murders. Nash was twice charged with the killings but the first trial ended with a hung jury—it was later confirmed that Nash had bribed an eighteen-year-old female juror to vote not guilty. He was found not guilty in a second trial. No one has ever been convicted of the murders.

But the real star of the podcast is Scott Thorson, the only one of the leading figures still alive. He's a great storyteller but, as Connelly reminds us, an unreliable one, given to embellishing and/or totally fabricating the so-called truths he claims to know about the case. That may be true, but he's certainly entertaining to listen to.

5

Artistry: Turning Fact into Fiction

If you want to have a successful series, you can't spend several years writing each novel. You need a much faster pace. You don't have to be as productive as Georges Simenon, creator of the acclaimed Inspector Maigret series, who wrote 192 novels under his own name and as many as 200 more under several pseudonyms. He accomplished this by several times a year hanging a "Do Not Disturb" sign on his office door and locking himself in for eight to eleven days, no more, before emerging with a completed novel. In terms of speed, Michael Connelly is no Simenon but he has successfully kept a series alive and well for three decades.

Connelly maintains he wouldn't have become a crime novelist if he hadn't first been a reporter on the crime beat. "I could not write about my fictional detective Harry Bosch without having written about the real detectives first. I could not create my killers without having talked to a few of the real ones first" (*Crime* 13). He might also have added that he wouldn't have been able to write his novels the way he did without having learned the craft of writing at a newspaper.

It takes plenty of discipline to average more than one novel a year for thirty years as Connelly has done, but that is the first thing a reporter learns. There is no such thing as writer's block in the newsroom. He also learned how to write fast in order to meet a daily deadline. "I was writing multiple stories a day, and after the pressure of that, writing fiction with one deadline a year is kind of a breeze" (Lester). However, one should never make the mistake of equating speedy writing with inferior writing. "Writing is all about finding momentum and keeping it" (Charney), Connelly says, and he believes that by writing fast, he creates more momentum. The novels he wrote the fastest, he says, "have been my best—because I caught an unstoppable momentum in the writing" (Connelly "By").

Like many writers, Connelly follows a few rituals. Before beginning a novel, Elmore Leonard would regularly page through a copy of *For Whom the Bell Tolls* to remind himself how Hemingway, his favorite writer, set his scenes, used dialogue, and made the words he chose count. For Connelly, it's Chapter 13 of Raymond Chandler's *The Little Sister.* "I am a student of Chapter 13," he says. "I read it before I start every book I write. It's a pep talk from the master. It reminds me of the higher game that is afoot" ("Little"). He also begins each day by playing Frank Morgan's "Lullaby," Bosch's favorite song, and he listens to instrumental jazz while writing to get him in the proper mood and to cut down on the outside noise. What he hears on any given day is what Bosch is listening to at that time.

He ordinarily begins before the sun comes up and writes in a room with blackout shades so he can focus entirely on the screen of his laptop. With each book, he starts out slowly, writing for only a couple of hours as he gradually feels his way into the story. He likens this to having to do a lot of paddling before you can ride the wave. Once the story gets going, he will sometimes write for as many as fourteen hours a day.

He never outlines his novels in advance, citing the advice from Hemingway that "if you outline your books, you'll know where you're going and so will your reader" (Grossman). Besides, he says, "I wouldn't want to start each day by looking away from my screen at a piece of paper that tells me what I'm going to do that day" (Willets). What happens as he creates his story is, like a jazz artist's performance, the result of improvisation. He feels confident that he will find his way to the end, which to him "is like the light at the end of a tunnel" ("Bloody").

Connelly freely confesses he's no creative genius. "I am a journalist by heart and so rather than sit in a room and try to make it up, I go out like a reporter to get the real stuff. That is where inspiration lies for me" (Burke). He compares what he does to a fisherman who throws out a nice spread of net. "I then pull up all kinds of stuff—anecdotes, clever pieces of dialogue, sometimes whole book stories—and my skill is that I know how to pick and choose what's come up in the net, slap on a layer of fiction, and then cobble it all together into a story" (Burke).

Connelly doesn't believe in waiting around for inspiration; instead, he puts himself in a position to be inspired, and what inspires him are the tales his police and lawyer friends tell him. He doesn't have a long-range plan for his novels. He mulls over several possibilities, some for years, until he selects the one he wants to write. Only when he has a clear idea how that novel will begin and end, what he calls the A and Z of the story, does he actually begin writing. And he doesn't skip any of the letters between A and Z. His novels, which average in the neighborhood of four hundred pages, are filled with enough action, characters, plots and subplots to give his readers full value for their money.

Some writers are skilled at creating great openings; others are masters of the surprise ending. But what trips up many is losing their way midway through the book. For Connelly, a good day isn't measured by the number of words or pages he writes, it's how much he advances his story each day. "An advance in the story can be anything," he says, "a paragraph, one line of story or a piece of dialogue. As long as I've moved the story along, I've had a good day. If I have a couple of hundred good days, I'll have a book" (Fishman).

Though he may not be, as he admits, a creative genius when it comes to the stories he tells, Connelly is undoubtedly one in the construction of his plots. Having abandoned his original plan to become a builder of houses like his father, he has instead become a master builder of fiendishly clever and suspenseful plots, filled with unexpected twists, turns, and surprises. While on occasion he needs to resort to convenient coincidences and last-minute rescues to make his plot work, what is surprising is that this happens so rarely in the three dozen novels he has written.

There are writers who love the sound of words and labor to make their sentences sing. Connelly, on the other hand, is interested in the individual sentence to the degree that it connects the one before with the one after, always in the service of moving the story forward. That doesn't mean he doesn't pay attention to his prose. Nor does it mean he doesn't appreciate writers like Raymond Chandler and James Lee Burke who are justly celebrated for their exquisite use of language. But he deliberately avoids ornate language, the kind that makes the reader want to stop and savor the choice of words or elegant phrasing. He doesn't want anything to inhibit the forward momentum he is working to create.

His prose style is essentially the one he learned as a reporter—clear, direct sentences with few literary flourishes. It's important to note that writing simple sentences can also be an art, as Ernest Hemingway, another ex-reporter, so effectively demonstrated in his fiction. Dashiell Hammett, another master of the simple style, once described clarity as "the first and greatest of literary virtues. The needlessly involved sentence, the clouded image, are not literary. They are anti-literary." He went on to argue that "simplicity and clarity are not to be got from the man in the street. They are the most elusive and difficult of literary accomplishments, and a high degree of skill is necessary to any writer who would win them. They are the most important qualities in securing the maximum desired effect on the reader" (Johnson 54).

5. Artistry: Turning Fact into Fiction   187

The final step in Connelly's process is perhaps the most important. "Re-writing is king," he insists. "Whether you make it or don't make it is in the re-write" (Fishman). He begins by reading and revising the previous day's work, which provides the impetus for that day's writing. His first draft often runs to 120,000 words, but as he re-writes he eventually whittles it down to 100,000 by the third and final draft. The finished version ends up shorter, tighter, and has even greater momentum.

Although moving from journalism to novel writing gave Connelly the freedom to make up whatever he wanted, he instead opts for accuracy, especially in his portrayal of police procedures. In the early years of the crime narrative, there was little effort at realism. In two of the earliest classics, Poe's "The Murders in the Rue Morgue" and Doyle's "The Speckled Band," the killers turn out to be an orangutan and a poisonous snake respectively. Dashiell Hammett and Raymond Chandler brought a heightened sense of realism to the genre, both in the portrayal of the crimes—Chandler praised Hammett for giving murder "back to the kind of people that commit it for reasons, not just to provide a corpse; and with the means at hand, not with hand-wrought duelling pistols, curare, and tropical fish" ("Simple" 989)—and in the character of the private detectives who solved them. These tough, gritty novels lacked realism in only one area: the fictional private eyes bore little similarity to real ones. In the real world, it is the police who solve most crimes and they do it by using resources unavailable to amateur sleuths and private eyes.

The crime novel took a giant step toward realism with the emergence of the police procedural, first popularized by Georges Simenon in his Inspector Jules Maigret series, which debuted in 1931. But it was *Dragnet* that was the first to make a concerted effort to emphasize the realism of police work. Created by Jack Webb, who also played the leading role of LAPD Sergeant Joe Friday, the series (which was produced with the cooperation of the LAPD) debuted on radio in 1949 and two years later moved to TV, where it ran until 1957.

Each televised episode opened with the no-nonsense voice of Joe Friday announcing, "This is the city. Los Angeles, California," followed by a brief introduction where he would mention the date, the crime, the weather, and the names of his partner and commanding officer. Then his badge No. 714 would appear on the screen while an authoritative voice promised the viewer, "The story you are about to see is true. The names have been changed to protect the innocent." The crime in each episode would be solved before the end of the half hour, followed by the results of the trial of the accused.

Dragnet was a major influence on Ed McBain, who in 1956 launched a groundbreaking series of police novels about a squad of detectives assigned to the 87th Precinct in Isola, a fictional stand-in for New York City. He emphasized the authenticity in his portrayal of police work by including a headnote in each novel that read: "The city in these pages is imaginary. The people, the places are all fictitious. Only the police routine is based on established investigatory techniques." In *Cop Hater* (1956), the first 87th Precinct book, he even included in the text several documents pertaining to the case: an application for a gun license; the coroner's reports on the results of an autopsy on a murder victim and on the bullet recovered from the murder scene; and the official record of another character's conviction on a drug charge.

Joseph Wambaugh, who spent fourteen years on the LAPD, brought an insider's knowledge of the police to a series of bestselling novels about cops that began with *The New Centurions* in 1971. His novels largely focus on patrol officers rather than homicide detectives, so little attention is paid to investigative procedures. Instead, he was more interested in the raunchy off-duty behavior of his cops. His novels are notable for their dark humor, which helped his cops maintain their sanity in the face of the disturbing things they routinely encountered on the job.

But no one has achieved greater realism in the portrayal of police and authentic investigative procedures than Connelly. In order to get the details right, he relies on a trio of homicide detectives—Rick Jackson, Tim Marcia, and Mitzi Roberts—whom he has known for years. He regularly meets with them over meals, not for a formal interview but simply to listen to the stories they tell. Whenever a question about police procedure comes up while he's writing, he simply calls or texts one of them to get an answer.

His goal remains the same as it was when he was a reporter checking and double checking the accuracy of what he wrote. "I wanted to write stories that made people say, 'Wow, that's how it must really be.' But what I was aiming for was only the veneer of accuracy. I didn't want it to be completely accurate because I knew that would be boring. It's important to get the procedure right, but you have to be aware of the drama of the piece, the character, the momentum of the story" (Willits). In the rare instances when he takes a shortcut, as he does in *The Night Fire* when, for dramatic purposes, he shortens the process of obtaining a court-approved wiretap, he acknowledges that fact in an Author's Note at the end of the novel.

Accuracy plays a vital role in Connelly's novels because he wanted Bosch to be the only thing in them that wasn't real. "The best way to sell a made-up character," he insists, "is to plant his feet into the real earth" (Walker).

6

The Portrait of L.A. and the LAPD

The City of Los Angeles

Setting often plays a prominent role in a crime series and several writers have taken ownership of the cities they write about. Think Boston and you think of Robert B. Parker. Chicago? Sara Paretsky; Edinburgh? Ian Rankin; Venice? Donna Leon. And the list goes on. But when you think of L.A., there's a pause. The City of Angels is also the City of Sleuths. Raymond Chandler, Ross Macdonald, Joseph Wambaugh, Walter Mosley, James Ellroy, and many others have claimed L.A. as their own in their crime novels.

One reason for this is the sheer size of the city—extending over some 4000 square miles, L.A. County is larger than the combined area of Delaware and Rhode Island. Its population of ten million is the largest of any county in the U.S. There's plenty of L.A. to go around. But the writer who can rightfully claim the biggest chunk of it is Michael Connelly, who over the course of thirty-six novels has painted a large scale, richly detailed portrait of a city that is constantly changing.

It was the L.A. novels of Chandler, Macdonald and Wambaugh that first inspired Connelly to want to be a crime writer and eventually drew him to the city at the age of thirty. "People pack their hopes and dreams in a suitcase," he once said, "because wherever they're coming from, it's not working. I'm one of those people. I wrote a couple of novels in Florida and knew they weren't good enough to be seen or sent out. I knew it wasn't happening for me back home, so I decided to change my life and move three thousand miles" (Pembrey).

L.A. for Connelly is more than just the background setting in his novels; it is one of his main interests. It is also his muse. There is no better illustration of this than the fact that on his very first day in the city, he read a story in that day's newspaper about a tunnel robbery under a bank that inspired the plot of his first Bosch novel, *The Black Echo*. The city and its diverse neighborhoods have continued to inspire his work ever since.

"Los Angeles is a wonderful place to live," Connelly says, but then adds it might even be "a better place to write about" (*Blue*). He believes that writers who set their crime novels in L.A. have an unfair advantage over those who set their novels elsewhere. "I'm lucky I write about Los Angeles," he says. "It is 100 different cities in one and I can explore a new place each time" (Stewart). "Los Angeles puts a lot of paint on your palette," he notes, and he uses all of it to paint to the four corners of his large canvas (Clute).

Fans of Arthur Conan Doyle can take a Sherlock Holmes walking tour of London. Fans of Ian Rankin's John Rebus can do the same thing in Edinburgh. But there is no Harry Bosch walking tour. Angelenos seldom walk. The city is too big and too spread out. Connelly instead follows the example set by Raymond Chandler in *The Little Sister* of always describing in detail the route Bosch drives from one place in the city to another. One could in fact do a Harry Bosch virtual riding tour of the city by using Google Maps to travel along with him.

The reader could also do a dining tour of the restaurants where Bosch eats, for they are all real places. Like Bosch, you could grab a donut for breakfast at Bob's Coffee and Donuts or a plate of pancakes at Du-par's. For lunch you might stop by for a burger at an In-N-Out. You could sit down at dinner time to enjoy a steak at Pacific Dining Car or seafood at The Water Grill. One of Bosch's favorite meals is the chicken pot pie at the famous Musso and Frank Grill (established in 1918), where writers like F. Scott Fitzgerald and William Faulkner often dined.

Connelly has described his novels as "love letters to Los Angeles" (*Blue*) and perhaps the best introduction to what the city means to him and to Bosch can be found in a limited-edition DVD that was given free to purchasers of *The Narrows* in 2004. *Blue Neon Night: Michael Connelly's Los Angeles* contains a generous selection of passages about L.A. taken from fourteen of Connelly's novels read by actor William Petersen over scenes of the locations that inspired the words being spoken.

It also includes clips of Connelly talking about what the city means to him. He takes us to the opening of the tunnel where the robbers entered on their way to rob the bank in *The Black Echo*; the turbulent waters of the L.A. River rushing through the concrete walls in *The Narrows*; and Woodrow Wilson Drive, where Bosch lives in his cantilevered house overlooking the city. An added bonus is a number of close-up details from Hieronymus Bosch's *The Garden of Earthly Delights*, which

6. The Portrait of L.A. and the LAPD

helps to understand the vision of the world that influenced Connelly in the writing of his novels.

A goodly portion of the portrait Connelly paints of L.A. is a dark one, but it has to be for it reflects the views of a character who spends most of his time seeing the worst side of the city. Connelly uses Bosch's comments to reveal as much about his character as they do about the city where he was born and raised. He also wants the novels to mirror the dark world portrayed in Hieronymus Bosch's paintings. L.A. is unquestionably a place of great beauty and diversity—ocean, mountains, deserts and valleys—but, as Connelly notes, "it is damaged by man and nature. Smog, over-development, crime, earthquakes, wildfires. It seems to have it all but it can't seem to keep it all. In many ways it has taken the serpent's apple. It's a place of angels and demons and users and predators. One of those angels is Harry Bosch" (Filippi).

"I live in a place where the randomness of crime and chaos is always near and poison literally hangs in the air" (*Narrows* 36), Bosch says and finds evidence all around him to support that claim. Graphic photographs he examines of a fifteen-year-old girl who had just been brutally raped "were a depressing testament to all that was wrong with the city.... Sometimes Bosch thought of his city as some kind of vast drain that pulled all bad things toward a spot where they swirled around in a deep concentration. It was a place where it seemed the good people were often outnumbered by the bad. The creeps and schemers, the rapists and killers" (*Trunk* 354).

Bosch acknowledges the enduring power of the Hollywood myth that continues to draw countless young people westward in search of fame and fortune in the movies, but he's seen enough of the painful reality to warn us that Hollywood was always best viewed at night: "It could only hold its mystique in darkness. In sunlight the curtain comes up and the intrigue is gone, replaced by a sense of hidden danger. It was a place of takers and users, of broken sidewalks and dreams. You build a city in the desert, water it with false hopes and false idols, and eventually this is what happens. The desert reclaims it, turns it arid, leaves it barren. Human tumbleweeds drift across its streets, predators hide in the rocks" (*Lost* 114).

The picture, however, isn't always so dark. Bosch is always looking for some light at the end of the tunnel, as can be seen in passages like these: "Los Angeles is a place that operates on hope and there is still something pure about that. It helps one see through the dirty air" (*Narrows* 36); "Los Angeles had changed in the last few years, but then there was nothing new about that. It was always changing and that was why he loved it" (*Concrete* 247).

Connelly gives the reader a more expansive view of the city by bringing Bosch to locations that provide some historical background and social significance. One of Bosch's favorite buildings is the Bradbury, "the dusty jewel of downtown" (*Angels* 90). What impresses Bosch most about the building is that it was designed in 1892 by a $5-a-week draftsman named George Wyman, who never designed another building of any significance. "The idea of a man leaving his mark with the one shot he's given appealed to him.... He believed in the one shot. He didn't know if he'd had his yet ... but he had the feeling that it was still out there waiting for him" (*Angels* 91).

Directly across the street is another favorite sight—a five-story mural on a brick wall of actor Anthony Quinn. Known as "The Pope of Broadway," Quinn is depicted with his arms outstretched like a Christ-like figure watching over all the homeless in the area as he performs a traditional dance from the 1964 film *Zorba the Greek.* In the parking lot beneath the painting Bosch notices a pair of homeless men sleeping under blankets of newspaper. Like the Bradbury and Angels Flight, the mural is one of the many little things that make Bosch like downtown so much: "Little pieces of grace were everywhere if you looked" (*Angels* 105).

Connelly uses his crime scenes as another way of filling out his portrait of the city and some of its people. In *The Scarecrow*, Jack McEvoy visits one of the most crime-infested areas of the city when he pays a visit to a huge public-housing complex in Watts called Rodia Gardens, named after the creator of one of the wonders of the city, the Watts Towers. "There wasn't anything wonderful about Rodia Gardens," McEvoy says. "It was the kind of place where poverty, drugs and crime had cycled for decades. Multiple generations of families living there and unable to get out and break free. Many of them had grown up having never been to the beach or on an airplane or even to a movie in a theater" (*Scarecrow* 35).

Echo Park is one of L.A.'s oldest neighborhoods. Located under the glow of lights from Dodger Stadium, it was at one time home to the city's immigrant underclass, a place where one could read signs in five or more languages on the storefronts. Now a gentrified neighborhood of artists, writers, and musicians, it was once the only place in the city "where at night the air could be split by the sound of gang gunfire, the cheers for a home-run ball, and the baying of the hillside coyotes—all in the same hour" (*Echo* 57).

Nearby Chavez Ravine is where Dodger Stadium was built in 1962. It was once home to poor Mexican immigrants who lived in crowded shacks among the hills. After World War II, federal money became available to provide housing for its poor residents. Everyone was moved out with the promise that low-income housing would be built on the site, which would be called Elysian Park Heights. Houses, churches and schools were razed. But then the city changed its mind and instead built a new baseball stadium to entice the Brooklyn Dodgers to move to L.A. That's why so many of those immigrant families and their descendants refuse to set foot in Dodger Stadium.

Connelly's novels are filled with snapshots like these that give them such a vivid and meaningful sense of place. No matter where you look on his broad canvas, like in the paintings of Hieronymus Bosch, you will find rich details to savor.

The LAPD

Connelly's portrait of the LAPD, and especially the work of its homicide detectives, is as detailed, authentic, and important to the novels as is his picture of L.A. While one might read a single novel about someone sitting at a desk all day long trying to write a novel, or a tax attorney poring over numbers and researching tax loopholes every day, no one would want to read dozens of novels about either of these professions. But the work of a homicide detective is different.

Genius detectives like Sherlock Holmes seldom describe in detail the process of thinking that allows them to solve the crimes they investigate. The procedure private detectives employ is often a variation of Sam Spade's trusty method of heaving "a wild and unpredictable monkey-wrench into the machinery" (*Maltese* 86). But the day-to-day nature of a police detective's job is far more complex and a mystery to most readers. Connelly's novels offer the most detailed description of that work in all of crime fiction.

Connelly's never been a cop, so what qualifies him as an expert on the subject? Primarily, it was the fourteen years he spent in police stations and at crime scenes while working as a reporter. This gave him intimate access to the way homicide detectives actually do their job. In his novels, Connelly combines his behind-the-scenes knowledge with a reporter's distance from his subjects, which allows him to paint a more objective picture that honors the hard work cops do but doesn't ignore the negative side of what some of them do.

Connelly begins by detailing basic police procedure, much of which isn't especially exciting. At the crime scene cops scour for clues that might help them determine how the victim was killed and where the murder took place, where the body was found or somewhere else. Then they need to head back to the station to do the often-tedious paperwork. They start by preparing the murder book, a case file that is a complete paper trail of the investigation from the time of the murder to the arrest of a suspect.

Sometimes they might even have to sort through boxes of 3 × 5 index cards patrol cops have filled out with information about suspicious persons they might have questioned in the area. Outside the station, much of their time is devoted to attending autopsies, interviewing everyone who might have witnessed the crime, and viewing and re-viewing hours of surveillance video of the crime scene looking for any detail that might provide a clue.

Having spent three decades chronicling Bosch's work as a cop, Connelly is also able to describe the many changes in the way cops do their job. In the early days of his career, if Bosch wanted to take a picture at the crime scene, he had to remember to bring a Polaroid camera with him. And film. If he needed to make a phone call while out of the station, he had to find a public phone booth and hope he had enough quarters in his pocket. Major advancements in DNA technology and new computerized databases have had a profound effect on how cases are now solved. "Science has seemingly replaced shoe leather," Connelly notes. "Investigators are more likely to solve a case with a walk to the forensics lab than down the mean streets where a murder has occurred." ("Art"). But those mean streets still exist and Harry Bosch, whose watchword is "time to get off your ass and knock on doors" (*Closers* 359), will continue to venture out despite the dangers.

Connelly adds some color to his description by including a generous sampling of authentic (or at least authentic sounding) cop language. Since most cops keep their guns in a closet while off duty, "going to the closet" is slang for a cop killing himself. Making a miscue that taints a case with constitutional or procedural error is called "leaving hair on the cake." When cops have to undergo therapy sessions that are held at a building on Hill Street near Chinatown, they refer to it as "going to Chinatown" and the cop who is going there as suffering from a case of the "Hill Street Blues." "Freeway therapy" refers to a cop's posting so far away from his home that it requires a two-hour commute both ways which is designed to convince that cop it's time to retire. At least one example of cop lingo in the books didn't come from police usage. "High jingo," Bosch's term for political interference in an investigation, comes from a song with that title performed by jazz artist Art Pepper.

Amateur sleuths and private detectives don't have to contend with bosses constantly looking over their shoulders, but a homicide detective is a member of an organization that is often one of the biggest obstacles in the performance of his job. Connelly describes Bosch's workplace as a "bureaucratic labyrinth that hindered rather than eased the job of the cop on the street. It was eight floors with fiefdoms on every hallway on every floor. Each was jealously guarded by commanders and deputy chiefs and assistant chiefs. And each group had its suspicions about the others. Each was a society within the great society" (*Ice* 74).

One of the biggest problems is the department's desire to protect itself from negative publicity. Bosch hates to hear the words "it's for the good of the department," for what that often means is that the department is looking to bend the truth to fit the picture it wants to present to the public and avoid any embarrassment it might suffer. Bosch denigrates the team that investigates officer-involved shootings as the "pencil squad" because to get the right story to the public "often meant using the pencil and eraser, never ink, never a tape recorder" (*City* 250).

Connelly is no apologist for the LAPD. He doesn't shy away from describing the many problems that have besieged the department over the years. Events like the Rodney King beating and the O.J. Simpson trial and frequent complaints about corruption, violent policing methods, lack of accountability, and civil rights infractions have led many to accuse the LAPD of being a fascist and paramilitary organization. Bosch is also critical of the behavior of some of his fellow cops, whom he dismisses as lazy clock watchers who are going through the motions until they can get their pensions. Many of the bad guys he exposes are cops, some of them even his bosses, who have gone over to the dark side. There is no doubt that many positive changes have been made over the years (e.g., banning the chokehold), but many problems still remain and to deny them would undermine the realism of the portrait Connelly is painting.

In the end, the negativity in Connelly's portrait serves to highlight the dedication and hard work of the good cops like Bosch and Ballard who, Connelly says, are engaged in "one of the last noble causes. Just because of the danger of what they do. And I'm not talking about the danger from bullets, I'm talking about going into human darkness as a matter of course, every day.... And that darkness, some of it's going to get in you. And you've got to figure out how to do that, how to live with that, how to keep yourself safe from that" (Anglen).

What Raymond Chandler once said of Philip Marlowe—"If there were enough like him, I think the world would be a very safe place to live in, and yet not too dull to be worth living in" ("Simple" 992)—applies equally to Harry Bosch, Renée Ballard, and all those other dedicated detectives for whom the job is a sacred calling, not just a career.

Conclusion: Connelly's Recipe for Success

Calling a crime series "formula fiction" is far from a compliment. It's a derogatory term that suggests the writer is simply cranking out books in assembly-line fashion that repeat one another to a large degree. However, all series writers must repeat certain familiar features to ensure that each book rightfully fits into an ongoing series. What sets a successful series formula apart from formula fiction is the skill in which the ingredients are used. In Connelly's case, it is perhaps more accurate to call what he uses a recipe rather than a formula, for like a master chef he knows how to skillfully blend his ingredients each time into a tasty meal that is both nutritious and fully satisfying.

What makes his novels so enjoyable to read yet at the same time have important things to say about good and evil, about being human, about the role of the police in our society, and so much more? Perhaps the best answer comes from Connelly himself who in a talk before an audience in Holland (the birthplace of Hieronymus Bosch) explained what he aims to do in his novels by employing the metaphor of a car, so appropriate for someone writing about Los Angeles.

> You have the plot and that's the car, that's the machinery.... The car has got to be really nicely painted, it's got to look good, it's got to have a big engine, it's got to have a loud thrumming sound coming from its exhaust pipes. It's got to really be a cool car. But that car will go nowhere without a driver and your character is the driver and so therefore he is the most important part of the whole thing.
>
> What happens when you open a book is that the door of that car swings open and that driver says to you, "Do you want a ride?" And we all know, we are taught at a very early age, don't go with strangers. This driver has to be someone you somehow trust. You have to trust the driver enough to get in the car with him, close the door, and it takes off.
>
> And of course he's got be a good driver and he's got to be heavy on the gas because you want that thing to move. He's got to know all the curves

and have you bouncing around in your seat and when you see up there he's going to turn left he suddenly turns right. And the next time he puts on his left turn blinker and you say, "Oh now we're turning left," and he turns right again. He's got to keep you in suspense [The John].

Connelly here isolates the two most important reasons for his success. The first is the story. It has to grab your attention from the start, move along at a fast clip, keep you off balance, and provide some unexpected turns before you arrive safe and sound at your destination. But as he reminds us, it is the driver that makes the car move, that propels the action. And the driver must be someone whose company we enjoy.

Bosch isn't always the most likable guy in the world, but the reader can still relate to him. We admire survivors and Bosch has had to overcome an extremely difficult past: a mother murdered when he was eleven; raised in juvenile facilities and foster homes; traumatized during wartime military service; narrowly escaped death numerous times on his job. We also admire him for the way he does a dangerous and demanding job. We see how much he cares about the victims of crime and how hard he works to ensure he finds their killers, thus giving them justice. He's the kind of detective, Connelly says, "whom readers would want on the case if it was ever them or a loved one lying on the stainless-steel table in the morgue" ("Hieronymus" 55).

"I think we are looking to connect with someone whose job is one we have no earthly idea what it's like to do," Connelly says. "Ninety-nine percent of us do not solve murders for a living, but we know it's a high stakes avocation with amazing stressors" (Davis). Although few of us may be homicide detectives, many of Bosch's experiences mirror our own. Like him, many of us are familiar with workplace bureaucracy. Also, Bosch often has to make difficult moral choices, as we all do, and we can ask ourselves what we might do in a similar situation. And because he's human, like us he sometimes makes mistakes.

There are two other important reasons for his success, and they too can be described using his car metaphor. One is that while the reader is enjoying the ride, he or she can look out the window at the passing scene. Ride with Connelly long enough and you will get a detailed picture of L.A. in all its variety and diversity. You will drive by mansions in Beverly Hills and homeless encampments under freeway underpasses. You'll see the bright lights of the city from the top of Mulholland Drive and the dark alleys in the poorest sections of the city.

And while you are looking out the window at the passing sights, the car radio switches back and forth from a jazz station—where you can listen to the soulful music that is so important to Bosch—to an all-news station where you will hear what's going on in the city and the nation that day. From the beginning Connelly wanted his novels to be enjoyable to read, but he also aimed at being more than an entertainer. In his view, contemporary crime novels are "much more immediate in terms of their reflection of society than any other form of fiction" (MacDonald) and he wanted his novels to say something about the world we live in: "To me social commentary is a very important part of the process. To me the crime novel is simply a framework for that social commentary. I think it is what gives every work undertaken the chance of jumping from something that is simply entertainment to something that can also be seen as art" (Davies 163).

When asked why crime is so fascinating, Connelly replied, "I don't know if it's we find crime so fascinating. I think we find the pursuit of the bad people fascinating. We want to know (A) could we solve something like this? And (B) we want to ride with someone who's working against the odds and on a noble pursuit. I mean, there's nothing more important than finding the person who took another life" (Simon).

It is the artful combination of these four ingredients that has made Connelly's books proven crowd-pleasers that have also earned widespread critical acclaim. They have won virtually every award in the genre—the Edgar, Shamus, Nero Wolfe, Anthony, Macavity, Italy's Premio Bancarella, France's Grand Prix de Littérature Policière, and the Diamond Dagger, the British Crime Writers' highest honor for sustained excellence in crime fiction. He has been called everything from "the Tom Brady of Procedurals" (Hetzel) to "today's Dostoyevsky of crime literature" ("Review"), and is frequently compared to his literary idol Raymond Chandler. "If Chandler has any direct literary descendent, then, any fit wearer of his illustrious crown," Dennis Lehane argued, "it can only be Michael Connelly." Jeff Ayers agreed, calling him "the Raymond Chandler of this generation" whose readers "will be studying his writing methods decades from now."

His novels have also been recognized for their success in blurring the line between the high entertainment of the crime genre and serious literature. Jonathan Yardley, for one, praised Connelly for writing "grown-up novels that—along with work by the likes of Scott Turow, Elmore Leonard and John Grisham—remind us that the place to look for serious American fiction is not in the schools of creative writing but out there in the real world" (Yardley). And John Wilson agreed: "Many current crime novelists regard themselves not simply as storytellers but as historians of the present, telling us what is 'happening' with an immediacy and an imaginative depth that 'the news' can't match. Michael Connelly has been doing that for a long time, even before it became fashionable, and there is no one who does it better."

Bibliography

The following is not a complete bibliography of Michael Connelly's work. It includes the editions of the novels used in the preparation of this book as well as information about his other work. Readers interested in more information are directed to his website (michaelconnelly.com), a treasure trove of information that is regularly updated. It contains exhaustive information about all of his work, plus multiple videos, a complete bibliography of his short fiction, and a listing of nearly 200 print, audio, and video interviews.

Primary Sources

Novels

Angels Flight. New York: Little, Brown, 1999.
The Black Box. New York: Little, Brown, 2012.
The Black Echo. New York: Warner Books, 2002.
The Black Ice. New York: Grand Central, 2013.
Blood Work. New York: Little, Brown, 1998.
The Brass Verdict. New York: Little, Brown, 2008.
The Burning Room. New York: Little, Brown, 2014.
Chasing the Dime. New York: Little, Brown, 2002.
City of Bones. New York: Little, Brown, 2002.
The Closers. New York: Little, Brown, 2005.
The Concrete Blonde. New York: St. Martin's Paperbacks, 1995.
The Crossing. New York: Little, Brown, 2015.
The Dark Hours. New York: Little, Brown, 2021.
Dark Sacred Night. New York: Little, Brown, 2018.
A Darkness More Than Night. New York: Little, Brown, 2001.
The Drop. New York: Little, Brown, 2011.
Echo Park. New York: Little, Brown, 2006.
Fair Warning. New York: Little, Brown, 2020.
The Fifth Witness. New York: Little, Brown, 2011.
The Gods of Guilt. New York: Little, Brown, 2013.
The Last Coyote. New York: St. Martin's Paperbacks, 1996.
The Late Show. New York: Little, Brown, 2017.
The Law of Innocence. New York: Little, Brown, 2020.
The Lincoln Lawyer. New York: Little, Brown, 2005.
Lost Light. New York: Little, Brown, 2003.
The Narrows. New York: Little, Brown, 2004.
The Night Fire. New York: Little, Brown, 2019.
Nine Dragons. New York: Little, Brown, 2009.
The Overlook. New York: Little, Brown, 2007.
The Poet. New York: Little, Brown, 1996.
The Reversal. New York: Little, Brown, 2010.
The Scarecrow. New York: Little, Brown, 2009.

Trunk Music. New York: St. Martin's Paperbacks, 1998.
Two Kinds of Truth. New York: Little, Brown, 2017.
Void Moon. New York: Little, Brown, 2000.
The Wrong Side of Goodbye. New York: Little, Brown, 2016.

Short Stories

"Angle of Investigation." In *Angle of Investigation: Three Harry Bosch Stories.* E-book ed. New York: Little, Brown. 2011. Kindle.
"Blue on Black." In *Hook, Line & Sinister: Mysteries to Reel You In.* Ed. T. Jefferson Parker. Woodstock, VT: The Countryman Press, 2010.
"Burnt Matches." In *The Highway Kind: Tales of Fast Cars, Desperate Drivers, and Dark Roads.* Ed. Patrick Millikan. New York: Mulholland, 2016.
"Christmas Even." In *Angle of Investigation: Three Harry Bosch Stories.* E-book ed. New York: Little, Brown. 2011. Kindle.
"Cielo Azul." In *Suicide Run: Three Harry Bosch Stories.* E-book ed. New York: Little, Brown, 2011. Kindle.
"The Crooked Man." In *In the Company of Sherlock Holmes.* Eds. Laurie R. King and Leslie S. Klinger. New York: Pegasus Books, 2014: 1–14.
"Father's Day." In *The Blue Religion: New Stories about Cops, Criminals and the Chase.* Ed. Michael Connelly. New York: Little Brown, 2008: 348–66.
"A Fine Mist of Blood." In *Mystery Writers of America Presents Violence.* Ed. Lee Child. New York: Mulholland, 2012.
"The Guardian." In *Tampa Bay Noir.* Ed. Collette Bancroft. New York: Akashic Books, 2020.
"Mulholland Dive." In *Mulholland Dive: Three Stories.* E-book ed. New York: Little, Brown, 2012. Kindle.
"Nighthawks." In *Sunlight or in Shadow: Stories Inspired by the Paintings of Edward Hopper.* Ed. Lawrence Block. NewYork: Pegasus, 2016: 81–90.
"One-Dollar Jackpot." In *Suicide Run: Three Harry Bosch Stories.* E-book ed. New York: Little, Brown, 2011. Kindle.
"The Perfect Triangle." In *The Dark End of the Street.* Ed. Jonathan Santlofer. New York: Bloomsbury, 2010.
"Red Eye." In *FaceOff.* Ed. David Baldacci. New York: Simon & Schuster, 2014: 4–29.
"The Safe Man." In *The Secret Society of Demolition Writers.* Ed. Marc Parent. New York: Random House, 2005.
"Shortcut." In *Half-Minute Horrors.* Ed. Susan Rich. New York: Harper, 2009.
"Suicide Run." In *Suicide Run: Three Harry Bosch Stories.* E-book ed. New York: Little, Brown, 2011. Kindle.
"Switchblade." E-book ed. New York: Little, Brown, 2014. Kindle.
"The Third Panel." In *Alive in Shape and Color: 17 Paintings by Great Artists and the Stories They Inspired.* Ed. Lawrence Block. New York: Pegasus, 2017: 49–58.
"Two-Bagger." In *Mulholland Dive: Three Stories.* E-book ed. New York: Little, Brown, 2012. Kindle.

Nonfiction

"Betting on Bosch." In *Hollywood vs. The Author.* Ed. Stephen Jay Schwartz. Los Angeles: Barnacle Books, 2018.
"By The Book." *The New York Times Book Review.* 12 Dec. 2013. Web. 12 Jan. 2021.
"Characterization." In *Writing Mysteries: A Handbook by the Mystery Writers of America.* 2nd ed. Ed. Sue Grafton. Cincinnati: Writer's Digest Book, 2002: 57–64.
Crime Time. A Decade of Covering Cops and Killers. New York: Little, Brown, 2006.
"Hieronymus Bosch." In *The Lineup: The World's Greatest Crime Writers Tell the Inside Story of Their Greatest Detectives.* Ed. Otto Penzler. New York: Little, Brown, 2009: 47–59.
"Introduction." *The Blue Religion: New Stories about Cops, Criminals and the Chase.* Ed. Michael Connelly. New York: Little, Brown, 2008: vii–viii.
"The Little Sister by Raymond Chandler." In *Books to Die For: The World's Greatest Mystery Writers on the World's Greatest Mystery Novel.* Eds. John Connolly and Declan Burke. New York: Emily Bestler Books, 2012: 129–132.
"Once Upon a Midnight Dreary." In

the Shadow of the Master, Ed. Michael Connelly, New York: HarperCollins, 2009.

Podcasts

Murder Book Podcast Season One: The Tell-Tale Bullet, murderbookpodcast.com, 2019.
Murder Book Podcast Season Two: The Women Who Stopped Sam Little, murderbookpodcast.com, 2020.
The Wonderland Murders & the Secret History of Hollywood, Audible.com, 2021.

DVD

Blue Neon Night: Michael Connelly's Los Angeles. Produced and directed by Terrill Lee Lankford. Incline Entertainment Production, 2004.

Secondary Sources

Anderson, Jean, Carolina Miranda, and Barbara Pezzotti, eds. *Serial Crime Fiction: Dying for More*. New York: Palgrave Macmillan, 2015.
Anderson, Patrick. "Michael Connelly's 'The Black Box.'" *The Washington Post*. 25 Nov. 2012. Web. 8 June 2021.
_____. *The Triumph of the Thriller: How Cops, Crooks, and Cannibals Captured Popular Fiction*. New York: Random House, 2007.
Ayers, Jeff. "In the 'Lab' with Michael Connelly." *The Writer*. 122:10 October 2009: 20–23.
Bertens, Hans, and Theo D'haen, Eds. *Contemporary American Crime Fiction*. New York: Palgrave, 2001: 105–112.
Birnbaum, Robert. "Interview with Michael Connelly." *The Narrative Thread*. 13 May 2002. Web. 9 April 2021.
"Bloody Scotland presents Michael Connelly and Ian Rankin." *Bloody Scotland*. 6 Nov. 2020. *YouTube*.
Brooks, Darren. "Detective Harry Bosch." In *Detective*. Ed. Barry Forshaw. Chicago: Intellect, 2016: 56–66.
Burke, Alafair. "A Journalist at Heart." *Los Angeles Review of Books*. 28 Aug. 2017. Web. 12 Feb. 2021.

Chandler, Raymond. "Introduction to 'The Simple Art of Murder.'" In *Raymond Chandler: Later Novels and Other Writings*. New York: The Library of America, 1995: 1016–1019.
_____. "The Simple Art of Murder." In *Raymond Chandler: Later Novels and Other Writings*. New York: The Library of America, 1995: 977–992.
Charney, Noah. "How I Write: Michael Connelly." *The Daily Beast*. 8 Jan. 2014. Web. 3 July 2021.
Clute, Shannon, and Richard Edwards. "Michael Connelly Revealed." *Behind the Black Mask*. 14 Oct. 2008. Web. 12 Nov. 2021.
Connolly, John. "*The Black Echo* by Michael Connelly." In *Books to Die For: The World's Greatest Mystery Writers on the World's Greatest Mystery Novels*. Eds. John Connolly and Declan Burke. New York: Emily Bestler Books/Atria, 2016.
Corbett, David. "Michael Connelly: Every Story Matters." *Writer's Digest*. October 2017. Web. 27 Sept. 2021.
Davies, Christopher J. "Michael Connelly Interview: 9/11, *City of Bones* and *Lost Light*." *The Human: Journal of Literature and Culture*, Issue 5. June 2015: 160–174.
Feldman, Lucy. "Michael Connelly Chooses 'The Long Goodbye' for WSJ Book Club." *Wall Street Journal*. 8 Jan. 2016. Web. 16 March 2021.
Filippi, Jacques. "A Tunnel of Hope Through the Dark." *The House of Crime and Mystery*. April 2011. Web. 5 March 2021.
Fishman, Roland. "Michael Connelly Interview—How Harry Bosch Inspired the Making of Carter." *The Writer's Studio*. 2015. Web. 1 Aug. 2021.
Flood, Alison. "'I don't like Jack Reacher that much': Lee Child and fellow crime writers on their creations." *The Irish Times*. 30 June 2020. Web. 23 Nov. 2021.
Grossman, Andrea. "Michael Connelly with Paul Bishop." *Writers Bloc*. 19 April 2001. Web. 6 May 2021.
Hammett, Dashiell. *The Maltese Falcon*. New York: Vintage Crime, 1992.
Heilpern, John. "Writer Michael Connelly's Brush With Crime." *Vanity Fair*. 5 Feb. 2015. Web. 4 May 2021.

Hughes, Declan. "Michael Connelly: From Bosch and Ballard to real-life detectives." *The Irish Times.* 27 Oct. 2018. Web. 2 Aug. 2021.

James, P.D. *Talking About Detective Fiction.* New York: Knopf, 2009.

The John Adams Institute. "Michael Connelly on Lost Light." *YouTube.* 8 Aug 2017.

Johnson, Diane. *Dashiell Hammett: A Life.* New York: Fawcett Columbine, 1987.

Karim, Ali. "Not One To Be Overlooked." *The Rap Sheet.* 11 July 2007. Web. 13 May 2021.

Kellogg, Carolyn. "Michael Connelly on 'The Black Box,' his new Harry Bosch novel." *YouTube.* 26 Nov. 2012.

Lehane, Dennis. "The Lost Coyote: Michael Connelly's Bosch Novels." *Il Corriere della Sera,* 2009. Available on Connelly website.

Lester, Amelia. "The fatherly advice that changed author Michael Connelly's life." *The Sydney Morning Herald.* 8 July 2017. Web. 28 July 2021.

Lowman, Rob. "Michael Connelly's L.A. centric book becomes Amazon's first drama series." *Los Angeles Daily News.* 12 Feb. 2015. Web. 12 Oct. 2021.

Lutz, Tom. "There's No Writer's Block in a Newsroom." *Los Angeles Review of Books.* 5 April 2015. Web. 6 May 2021.

Maslin, Janet. "Cold-Case Trial: Two Opposites on Same Side, Facing Down a Killer." *The New York Times,* 6 Oct. 2010. Web. 8 June 2021.

McDermott, Peter. "Crime Master." *The Irish Echo.* 30 Nov. 2011. Web. 15 June 2021.

McDonald, Craig. "Michael Connelly: The Trouble With Harry." *Art in the Blood: Crime Novelists Discuss Their Craft.* E-book ed. Cincinnati: F+W Media, 2011. Kindle.

"Michael Connelly's Five Favorite Crime Novels of All Time." *Novel Suspects.* Web. 6 Feb. 2021.

Murphy, Dwyer. "Michael Connelly on Cold Cases, Police Stories, and his New Podcast." *CrimeReads.* 14 March 2019. Web. 10 Aug. 2021.

Oates, Joyce Carol. "Earthly Delights: Michael Connelly investigates L.A.'s dark heart." *The New Yorker.* 5 Feb. 2001: 88–89.

Ott, Bill. "Nine Dragons. By Michael Connelly." *Booklist.* 15 Sept. 2009. Web. 12 Oct. 2021.

Pembrey, Daniel. "An Interview with Michael Connelly." *DeadGoodBooks.* 4 Nov. 2016. Web. 5 Oct. 2021.

Perri, Camille. "Michael Connelly: Why Everyone Should Read *To Kill a Mockingbird.*" *Esquire.* 6. Nov. 2014. Web. 8 June 2021.

Priddle, Clive. "The Current, Episode 33: Michael Connelly." *YouTube.* 5 Feb. 2021.

Rubinstein, Mark. "Michael Connelly: Is Bosch an Alter Ego?" In *The Storytellers: Straight Talk from the World's Most Acclaimed Suspense & Thriller Authors.* Ashland, OR: Blackstone, 2021.

Schneller, Johanna. "Kobo Writing Life Podcast—Episode 048—Michael Connelly." *KWL Podcast.* 6 Jan. 2016. Web. 7 Sept. 2021.

Silet, Charles L. P. "Angels Flight: Michael Connelly." *Talking Murder: Interviews with 20 Mystery Writers.* Princeton: Ontario Review Press, 1999: 39–57.

Simon, Scott. "Novelist Connelly Revisits His 'Crime Beat' Days." *NPR.* 29 April 2006. Web. 19 Oct. 2021.

Stewart, Cameron. "Formula to a career jackpot." *The Weekend Australian Magazine.* 18 Oct. 2019. Web. 9 Sept. 2021

Sykes, Jerry. "Interview with Michael Connelly." In *Speaking of Murder: Interviews with Masters of Mystery and Suspense.* Vol II. Eds. Ed Gorman and Martin H. Greenberg. New York: Berkley Prime Crime, 1999: 196–201.

Szewczyk, Elaine. "Michael Connelly Can't Stop Chasing Leads." *Publishers Weekly.* 3 Sept. 2021. Web. 30 Nov. 2021.

Taylor, Michael Ray. "Building Momentum: Michael Connelly discusses his popular detective series, his journalism background, and the future of the book." *Chapter 16.* 17 Feb. 2010. Web. 9 May 2021.

Tierney, Bruce. "Final Deadline." *BookPage.* June 2009. Web. 2 Feb. 2021.

Walker, Tim. "The Modern Raymond Chandler on Bosch, 'The Long Goodbye,' and L.A.'s neighborhoods." *Inde-*

pendent. 10 March 2016. Web. 15 July 2021.

Weber, Bruce. "Watching the Detectives." *The New York Times Magazine.* 9 May 2004: 39–41.

Willets, Paul. "Michael Connelly Interview." *Book and Magazine Collector.* Sept. 2004. Web. 28 Mar. 2021.

Witley, Skye. "Nonprofit newsroom dissolves over allegations directed at founder." *Current.* 25 Feb. 2021. Web. 5 Aug. 2021.

Index

Altman, Robert 4, 78
Amazon Studios 16, 176
"Ambush Shooting" 172
Anderson, Patrick 98
Angels Flight 43–48, 60, 133, 174
Angels Flight 43
"Angle of Investigation" 167
Anthony Award 199
Antonioni, Michelangelo 119, 120
Aquino, Amy 177
Archer, Lew 55
The Art of the Cape 8
Ayers, Jeff 199

Ballard, Renée 130–134, 138–143, 143–146, 155–160, 181, 195
Bastin, Henrik 176
Behind the Candelabra: My Life with Liberace 182
The Big Sleep (Chandler) 126
"Billy the Burglar" 171
Black, Cassie 161–163
The Black Box 111–114, 125
The Black Echo 7, 9, 10, 11, 17–20, 21, 42, 169, 190
The Black Ice 8, 20–24, 77
Blake, Robert 66
Block, Lawrence 7
Blood Work 14, 40–43, 48
Blood Work (film) 15, 66, 173–174
Blow-Up (film) 119, 120
Blue Neon Night: Michael Connelly's Los Angeles (DVD) 190
"Blue on Black" 166
The Blue Religion: New Stories about Cops, Criminals and the Chase 167
Bob's Coffee and Donuts 190
Bolger, Ray 91
Bosch (TV series) 127, 131, 133, 168, 175–178

Bosch, Hieronymus 9, 10, 45, 49, 50, 52, 79, 87, 90, 130, 165, 169, 190, 191, 197
Bosch, Maddie 94, 96, 97, 102, 111, 114, 118, 120, 129, 157, 167, 178, 193
Bosch: Legacy (TV series) 178
Bradbury Building 192
Brady, Tom 199
The Brass Verdict 84–88
Bratton, William J. 67
Brooks, Darren 9
Bundy, Ted 66
Burke, James Lee 7, 8, 186
The Burning Room 118–122, 131
"Burnt Matches" 170
The Byrds 182

Callahan, Dirty Harry 10, 173, 174
Cannell, Stephen J. 179
Car (Crews) 4
Castle (TV series) 179
Caul, Harry 10, 120, 174
Chandler, Honey 24, 25, 26, 27, 31, 178
Chandler, Raymond 4, 5, 7, 8, 9, 15, 21, 48, 59, 62, 77, 78, 125, 126, 133, 185, 186, 187, 189, 190, 195, 199
Chasing the Dime 163–166
Chavez Ravine 192
Christie, Agatha 3, 13
"Christmas Even" 59, 129, 166
"Cielo Azul" 52, 62, 167
City of Bones 53–59, 65, 166
Clapton, Eric 104
Clark, Jade 180
Clinton, Pres. Bill 8
The Closers 67–71, 108
Conan Doyle, Arthur 14, 187, 190
The Concrete Blonde 8, 24–28, 31
Connelly, Mary McEvoy 3
Connelly, Michael: awards 7, 106, 198; childhood 3, 4, 10, 170; education 4, 5; family 3; journalism 5, 6, 7, 34, 36, 92, 93,

111, 131, 150, 151, 170–172, 184, 193; marriage 5; move to Florida 3; move to L.A. 7, 189; return to Florida 57, 164; on writing 6, 62, 84, 92, 93, 184–188
Connelly, W. Michael 3
The Conversation (film) 10, 120, 174
Cop Hater (McBain) 188
Coppola, Francis Ford 10, 120, 174
Cornwell, Patricia 82
Covid-19 pandemic 154, 155, 159
Creedence Clearwater Revival 178
Crews, Harry 4, 10
Crime Beat: A Decade of Covering Cops and Killers 170–172
"The Crooked Man" 169
Crosby, Stills & Nash 182
The Crossing 122–125, 136

Daly, Dan 180
Damon, Matt 182
Daniels, Jeff 173
The Dark Hours 155–160
Dark Sacred Night 138–143
darkness 9, 11, 15, 16, 52, 54, 80, 97, 133, 144, 159, 165, 191, 195
A Darkness More Than Night 14, 48–53, 54, 62, 64, 89, 165, 167, 169
Davies, Christopher J. 58
Daytona Beach News-Journal 5
Delta Flight 191 7
deus ex machina 19
Devil in a Blue Dress (Mosley) 15
Devon, PA 3, 10
Diamond Dagger Award 199
Dickens, Charles 81
Dolarhyde, Francis 32
Dostoevsky, Fyodor 199
Dragnet 187
"Dream-Life" (Poe) 34
The Drop 106–111, 114, 129
drug addiction 134, 136, 137, 138
Du-par's 190

Eastwood, Clint 10, 41, 66, 174, 175
Echo Park 77–81
Echo Park 192
Edgar, Jerry 47, 54, 56, 71, 77, 112, 136, 168, 177
Edgar Award 7, 37, 199
Ellroy, James 11, 189
evil 10, 56, 75, 99, 106, 110, 131, 136, 150, 197

Fair Warning 146–151, 158, 159, 179
FairWarning (website) 146, 147
"The Fall of the House of Usher" (Poe) 34

"Father's Day" 167
Faulkner, William 190
The Fifth Witness 102–106, 153
Fillion, Nathan 179
"A Fine Mist of Blood" 168
Fitzgerald, F. Scott 190
Floyd, George 107, 156
Fogerty, John 53
For Whom the Bell Tolls (Hemingway) 185
Franklin, Lonnie David, Jr. 108
Friday, Joe 187
Furman, Brad 174

The Garden of Earthly Delights (H. Bosch) 9, 49, 50, 87, 169, 190
The Gods of Guilt 114–118, 153
The Goodbye Look (Macdonald) 126
Gould, Elliott 78
Grand Prix de Littérature Policière 199
The Grim Sleeper 108
Grisham, John 199

Hackman, Gene 10, 120
Haller, Mickey 15, 24, 72–77, 84–88, 95, 96, 98–106, 114–118, 122–125, 128, 129, 130, 137, 143, 151–155, 170, 174, 175, 178, 180
Hammett, Dashiell 186, 187
Hansen, Terry 42
Hardy Boys 3
Harper Lee Award for Legal Fiction 106
Harris, Thomas 32
Hearst, Patty 11
Helgeland, Brian 173
Hemingway, Ernest 185, 186
Hiaasen, Carl 4
High Tower Apartments 77, 78
Hitchcock, Alfred 164
Hockney, David 172
Hollywood 84, 144, 191
Holmes, John 182
Holmes, Sherlock 14, 190, 193
Homicide (TV series) 176
Hong Kong 94, 95
Hook, Line & Sinister 166
Hope, Bob 129
Hopper, Edward 20, 168
Hurt, George 6, 171

In-N-Out Burger 190
In the Company of Sherlock Holmes 169
The Innocence Project 135
Inspector Maigret 184, 187
The Internet 90, 91, 92, 148, 150, 159, 165

Jackson, Rick 130, 180, 182, 188
James, P.D. 3

Index

jazz 12, 184
journalism 5, 6, 7, 34, 36, 92, 93, 111, 131, 150, 151, 170–172, 184, 193
"Judgement Day" (song) 104
justice system 134, 135, 151, 152, 179

Kelly, Grace 13
Kenzie, Patrick 170
Kerr, Philip 9
Kesey, Ken 4
King, Carole 182
King, Rodney 27, 28, 43, 108, 111, 195

Lange, Tom 182
The Last Coyote 8, 11, 28–32, 37, 39, 48
The Last Judgment (H. Bosch) 49
The Late Show 130–134
"Lauderdale Homicide" 171
Laurel Canyon 182
Lauren, Jillian 181
Law & Order 176
The Law of Innocence 151–155
Lecter, Hannibal 32
legal system 72, 77, 101, 103, 105, 153, 154
Lehane, Dennis 170, 179, 199
Leon, Donna 189
Leonard, Elmore 15, 82, 185, 199
Level 9 (TV series) 178–179
Levin, Myron 146, 147
Liberace 182
light 12, 16, 51, 63, 80, 87, 104, 160, 185, 191
The Lincoln Lawyer 71–77, 78, 84, 86, 87, 106, 115
The Lincoln Lawyer (film) 15, 96, 174–175
Lintz, Madison 177
Little, Sam 180, 181
The Little Sister (Chandler) 185, 190
Lolita (Nabokov) 44
"Long As I Can See the Light" (song) 178
The Long Goodbye (film) 4, 78
The Long Goodbye (novel) 8, 21, 126, 133
Los Angeles 189–193, 198; riots 28, 93, 108, 111, 112
Los Angeles Police Department 27, 28, 45, 67, 107, 142, 156, 158, 159, 178, 188, 193–195
Los Angeles Times 7, 8, 89, 93, 131, 146, 147, 171
Lost Light 59–63, 97, 129, 167
"Lullaby" (song) 178, 185
Lundh, Jonathan 32, 171

Macavity Award 199
MacDonald, John D. 3, 13
Macdonald, Ross 7, 15, 29, 55, 62, 125, 126, 189

Macy, William H. 175
"The Mail-Order Murders" 172
Malice in Wonderland: The Inside Story of the Police Investigation of the Laurel Canyon Murders 182
The Maltese Falcon (Hammett) 20, 76
The Mamas and the Papas 182
Mangold, Tom 10
Manson Murders 182
Marcia, Tim 66, 122, 180, 188
Mariachi Plaza 119
Marlowe, Philip 5, 8, 9, 21, 66, 78, 126, 195
Marvel Cinematic Universe 15
Maslin, Janet 98
McBain, Ed 187
McCaleb, Linda 5, 130
McCaleb, Terry 14, 15, 40–42, 48–53, 64–66, 89, 130, 167, 173, 174
McClure, Robert 7
McConaughey, Matthew 96, 174
McEvoy, Jack 14, 32–37, 48, 50, 88–93, 95, 130, 146–151, 158, 179, 192
McGee, Travis 3, 13
McKinzie, Quentin 59, 129, 166
Mitchell, Joni 182
Morgan, Frank 12, 178, 185
Morrison, Van 53
Mosley, Walter 15, 189
"Mulholland Dive" 170
Munch, Edvard 17
Murder Book: The Tell-Tale Bullet (podcast) 151, 179–180
"The Murders in the Rue Morgue" (Poe) 187
Musso and Frank Grill 190

Nabokov, Vladimir 44
The Narrows 34, 64–67, 81, 89, 163, 174, 190
Nash, Eddie 182, 183
Neeson, Liam 97
Nero Wolfe Award 199
Netflix 16, 178
The New Centurians (Wambaugh) 188
The New York Times 81, 98, 174
Nietzsche, Friedrich 16, 61
The Night Fire 143–146, 188
Nighthawks (Hopper) 20, 168
Nine Dragons 93–98

Oates, Joyce Carol 53
Ogden, David 72
One-Dollar Jackpot 166
Operation Desert Storm 113, 177
Ott, Bill 97
Overlook 81–84, 106, 143
Overmyer, Eric 176, 178

210　Index

Pacific Dining Car 190
Paramount Pictures 8, 175, 176
Paretsky, Sara 189
Parker, Robert B. 189
The Patriot Act 60
Patterson, James 179
Penycate, John 10
Penzler, Otto 166
Pepper, Art 12, 194
"The Perfect Triangle" 170
Petersen, William 190
Peterson, Laci 66
Phillippe, Ryan 175
Pierce, Nez 174
Poe, Edgar Allan 34, 36, 64, 65, 79, 90, 187
The Poet 14, 32–37, 49, 50, 64, 65, 88, 91, 92, 145, 147, 148
Poirot, Hercule 13
Premio Bancarella 199
prescription drug epidemic 136
Pulitzer Prize 7

Quinn, Anthony 192

racism 28, 47, 47, 68, 69, 71, 129
Rankin, Ian 189, 190
Rawlins, Easy 15
Rebus, John 190
Red Dragon (Harris) 32
"Red Eye" 170
Reddick, Lance 177
redemption 12, 54, 57, 65, 108, 109, 121, 134, 165
Reinke, Malinda 7
The Reversal 98–102
Roberts, Mitzi 122, 131, 180, 181, 188
Robicheaux, Dave 7
Rocky Mountain News 32, 93, 146
Rodia Gardens 192
Rogers, Mimi 177
Romaine, Pierre 180
Romano, John 174
Ronstadt, Linda 182

"The Safe Man" 170
St. Thomas Aquinas High School 4
USS *Sanctuary* 127, 129
The Scarecrow 88–93, 145, 192
Scott, A.O. 174
The Scream (Munch) 17
Scudder, Matt 7
September 11, 2001 58, 60, 61
Serial Crime Fiction 14
setting 189–193
sexism 139, 140, 142, 145
Shamus Award 199

"Shortcut" 170
Silverman, Beth 181
Simenon, Georges 184, 187
Simpson, O.J. 36, 43, 45, 66, 195
Smart, Elizabeth 66
social commentary 27, 28, 43, 47, 60, 61, 77, 84, 92, 135, 136, 148, 152, 197, 199
"Somewhere Over the Rainbow" (song) 13
Soprano, Tony 31
The Sopranos 31, 175
Sound of Redemption 12
South Florida Sun-Sentinel 5, 7, 171
Souza, Bob 182
Spade, Sam 20, 76, 193
"The Speckled Band" (Doyle) 187
Spitzer, Philip 7
Springsteen, Bruce 52
The Stone Operation (H. Bosch) 49
"Suicide Run" 168
Sutherland, Kiefer 176
"Switchblade" 168
Symbionese Liberation Army 11

Taken (film) 97
"Tarzana Man Held in Murder of His Missing Father" 172
"The Third Panel" 169
Thompson, Hunter S. 4
Thorson, Scott 182, 183
To Kill a Mockingbird (Lee) 106
Tomei, Marisa 175
Touch 176
Trunk Music 37–39, 48, 60, 82, 83, 172
tunnels 7, 10, 11, 12, 17, 18, 19, 22, 55, 80, 87, 104, 160, 165, 166, 167, 170, 185, 189, 190, 191
The Tunnels of Cu Chi 10
Turow, Scott 82, 199
"Two-Bagger" 166
Two Kinds of Truth 134–138

University of Florida 4
UPN Network 178

Venice Beach 132
Vietnam 4, 10, 11, 18, 19, 20, 21, 23, 55, 59, 126, 129, 166, 167, 177
Vietnam Veterans Memorial 19, 126
Void Moon 134, 161–163
Vonnegut, Kurt, Jr. 4

Walling, Rachel 34, 35, 36, 64, 65, 81, 82, 84, 88, 89, 90, 91, 92, 148, 150, 151
Wambaugh, Joseph 7, 9, 15, 187, 188, 189
The Water Grill 190
Watts Towers 192

Welliver, Titus 16, 168, 176, 177
"Who Shot Vic Weiss?" 172
Wilder, Douglas 171
Wilson, John 199
The Wire (TV series) 176, 177
Wish, Eleanor 18, 19, 20, 38, 39, 44, 47, 94, 95, 169
The Wizard of Oz (film) 91
The Women Who Stopped Sam Little (podcast) 180–181
The Wonderful Wizard of Oz (Baum) 91
Wonderland (film) 182
The Wonderland Murders & the Secret History of Hollywood (podcast) 182–183
Woodrow Wilson Drive 12, 172, 190
The Wrong Side of Goodbye 125–130

Yardley, Jonathan 199

Zorba the Greek (film) 192

www.ingramcontent.com/pod-product-compliance
Lightning Source LLC
Chambersburg PA
CBHW032043300426
44117CB00009B/1174